The book that will settle arguments—and start them!

The Best

ballpark billboard was in Queens, N.Y. An optician suggested people come to him for eye examinations by saying, "DON'T KILL THE UMPIRE, MAYBE IT'S YOUR EYES."

The Worst

football game of the century was the Notre Dame–Army game of 1946. The pre-game publicity raised scalpers' prices to $200 a ticket. The score was 0–0.

The Most Unusual

golf course regulation is at the Hillcrest Country Club in Southern California. Players are required to wear pants. One hot day, Harpo Marx and George Burns took their shirts off. A member complained they were breaking a club rule by golfing shirtless. Marx and Burns then took off their trousers, giving birth to the new rule.

Also Available
from Fawcett Crest:

The Best, Worst and Most Unusual in Sports

Stan and Shirley Fischler

Research Editor: Ira Lacher

FAWCETT CREST • NEW YORK

THE BEST, WORST AND MOST UNUSUAL IN SPORTS

THIS BOOK CONTAINS THE COMPLETE TEXT OF THE ORIGINAL HARDCOVER EDITION.

Published by Fawcett Crest Books, a unit of CBS Publications, the Consumer Publishing Division of CBS Inc., by arrangement with Thomas Y. Crowell Company

ISBN: 0-449-23816-4

Selection of the *Sports Illustrated* Book Club

Printed in the United States of America

10 9 8 7 6 5 4 3 2 1

TO BEN
Who always has been, and always will be,
the best, the most, and just occasionally
runs offside.

We would like to acknowledge the exceptional efforts of our research editor, Ira Lacher, and also to thank Rich Friedman, Alan Mann, Bob Stampleman, Steve Namm, Dick Selby, Joe Resnick, Paul Gardella, Dave Rubenstein, Gus Engelman, Karen Robertson, Robert Klepper, Mike Caruso, Paul Ringe, Bud Rosenthal, Ira Gitler, Dick Epstein, Craig Wolff, and Barry Wilner. Thanks, too, should be proffered to the numerous libraries, librarians, sport association experts and inveterate trivia nuts who helped in the research!

Contents

Photographs follow page 128.

Baseball

Best Hitting Team. The New York Giants, 1930. Playing at the horseshoe-shaped Polo Grounds in Harlem, the club, managed by John McGraw, hit for a collective average of .319. Those who made this mark possible included first baseman Bill Terry, whose .401 average led the Giants; third baseman Fred Lindstrom, second on the pride of Manhattan; and Mel Ott, who not only batted .349 but hit 25 home runs.

Both Terry and Ott later became lionized, to a degree, as Giants managers. Prior to Leo Durocher, Terry did as much as any Giant to fan the flames of the then perennial Giants-Dodgers feud with his deathless line in 1937: "The Dodgers? Are they still in the National League?"

Beloved for his soft nature and unique kick before swinging for the right-field stands, Ott could never be accused of antagonizing the Brooklyn foe with his rhetoric.

The Giants' pitching in 1930 was less awesome than the hitting. McGraw's pitchers finished with a collective earned run average of 4.60, fifth best in the National League.

(Note: The best hitting team of the nineteenth century was the 1887 Detroit National League club, which finished first and hit for a collective average of .347.)

Best Trick Play—That Failed. "The Safety Ball," used by the Baltimore Orioles in 1890. This was a pluralized version of the hidden-ball trick. In this case the Orioles outfielders would plant a few baseballs in strategic locations near their positions. The theory was that when a ball was hit in their vicinity, they occasionally might be able to utilize one of the "safety" balls in order to hold the batter to a single; even if the ball happened to fly over the outfielder's head.

The ploy that failed occurred when an opponent hit a sharp drive to left-center field. Pursuing the legitimate ball, the left fielder suddenly came upon a "safety" ball, picked it up and hurled the sphere to second base, thereby holding the amazed batter to a single.

Unfortunately for the Orioles, the industrious center fielder had tenaciously pursued the correct baseball, finally trapped it, and heaved the ball back to the infield. At first thinking he was suffering from double vision, the umpire suddenly realized a ruse was afoot and charged Baltimore with a forfeit defeat.

Best Team (Twentieth Century). Chicago Cubs, 1906. Hollywood, the Bronx Chamber of Commerce, and Joe DiMaggio would have you believe it was any one of a dozen New York Yankees teams, especially the 1927 edition of "Murderers' Row." But the 1906 Cubs, with an unchallengeable record of 116 wins and only 36 losses, top the Bronx Bombers anytime. In winning the National League pennant, the Cubs finished 20 games ahead of the second-place New York Giants, a club with a respectable 96 victories.

No doubt, the 1906 Cubs lacked a good press agent of Yankees vintage. The Chicago team had innumerable stars, including Joe Tinker, Johnny Evers, and Frank Chance, who could execute double plays in their sleep. Leading an impressive corps of Cubs pitchers was Mordecai "Three-Finger" Brown, who produced a league-leading 1.04 earned run average. The collective earned run average of the Chicago pitching staff was an arrestingly low 1.76. The Cubs also led the league in hitting with a .262 team average. They scored 704 runs, tops in that department. The only smudge on their otherwise unblemished 1906 record was an upset defeat at the hands of the Chicago White Sox in the World Series.

Best Start for a Pitcher. Rube Marquard, New York Giants, 1912. With an opening win over Brooklyn (18–3), Marquard became the most feared pitcher in baseball. By July 4, 1912, he had totaled a 19–0 record, the longest winning streak in a single season.

One reason for Marquard's success was the awesome hitting displayed by his teammates. During the nineteen-game streak the Giants outscored their opponents, 129–49, averaging almost seven runs per game. Marquard's streak included only one shutout and it wasn't until his thirteenth win that he had to struggle, his team ahead only by one run.

His most dramatic victory was the nineteenth, a 2–1 triumph over Brooklyn. His pitching opponent was Napoleon Rucker, who allowed four Giants hits. One of New York's runs came as a result of a dropped pop-up by Bert Tooley, Brooklyn's shortstop. Brooklyn threatened in the ninth inning with the winning runners on base and one out, but Marquard struck out heavy-hitting Zach Wheat and ended the game with a fly ball out. Rube's luck ran out on July 9 at Wrigley Field in Chicago. The Chicago Cubs routed Marquard and the Giants, 7–2. From then on Rube faltered and ran up a dismal 7–11 won-lost mark for the rest of the season.

Best Pitching Performance in a World Series. Christy Mathewson of the New York Giants shut out the A's three times in the 1905 World Series.

The Philadelphia Athletics went into the 1905 World Series after surviving a late season slump that threatened to knock them out of the top spot in the American

League which they had occupied since August. In addition, the A's had lost their ace starter, Rube Waddell (26–11, 287 strikeouts), in an off-the-field accident. If this wasn't bad enough, they faced a New York Giants team that cruised to the National League pennant with a 105–48 record, capturing the flag by nine games. In this fall classic, the A's would have to face the great Christy Mathewson, who was in the midst of a brilliant seventeen-year career in which he gained 373 victories, placing him third on the all-time wins list, to go along with a career earned run average of 2.13. For the 1905 season, Mathewson had a record of 33–12, with a 2.03 ERA, which was good enough to make him the second best pitcher on the staff that year to "Iron Man" Joe McGinnity (35–8, 1.61 ERA). So the A's had little reason for confidence as they entered the Series, but it's doubtful that any of Connie Mack's men suspected that they would make such an undistinguished trip into the record books.

Although McGinnity had a statistical edge for the season, it was Mathewson who was named to start game one. If this caused any relief on the part of the A's, it was short-lived. Matty dispensed of the A's on four hits, shutting them out, 3–0. In the second game, Philadelphia, relieved temporarily of Mathewson's tantalizing fade-aways, tied the Series by shutting out the Giants and McGinnity. But then bad luck struck the A's in the form of a rainstorm which pushed the Series back one day and allowed Mathewson to return for game three. The result was another four-hit shutout. After watching McGinnity get revenge by blanking the A's in the fourth game, Mathewson took the mound for the clincher. Despite eighteen previous innings of experience, the A's still could not solve Matty, and the result was a 2–0 victory and a world championship for the Giants in five games, each a shutout.

Mathewson's three Series shutouts in themselves were an incredible achievement that has never been duplicated; in fact, Christy's four lifetime World Series shutouts also is a record. But consider this: in 27 innings, he allowed just 15 hits, walked one, struck out 16. Mathewson was so overpowering that not one Athletic runner reached third. And this was against a club that had led the American League in hitting and runs scored, and was second in home runs.

The Philadelphia A's must have had many winter dreams of Christy Mathewson's fadeaway, but they probably couldn't hit it then either.

Best Strikeout Performance in a Single Game. Steve Carlton, St. Louis Cardinals vs. New York Mets, September 1969, Busch Stadium. Carlton's problem was that he was facing "the Amazin' Mets" during the year they surmounted a nine-and-one-half-game deficit in late August to win the National League's East Division crown by eight games. "It was the best stuff I ever had," said Carlton of his effort that night, and the records substantiate his claim. He struck out nineteen batters, a record, yet the Mets won the game, 4–3, on two home runs by Ron Swoboda. Carlton struck out the side in four out of nine innings and struck out the side in the ninth to set the record. However, Carlton himself allowed that his performance was flawed. "When I had nine strikeouts, I decided to go all the way. But it cost me the game because I started to challenge every batter." It was a two-strike pitch that Swoboda hit for his first home run in the fourth inning, and a 2–2 pitch that Swoboda pulled into the seats in the eighth, giving the Mets a 4–3 lead.

Tom Seaver, while pitching for the Mets before being traded to the Cincinnati Reds in 1977, once struck out nineteen batters—in 1970 against the San Diego Padres—and the last ten in a row.

Best Performance by a Relief Pitcher. Ernie Shore, Boston Red Sox, June 23, 1917. Thanks to teammate Babe Ruth, Shore was able to make a name—albeit small—for himself in baseball history. Ruth had been named starting pitcher for Boston against the Washington Senators, but lasted for only one batter. The Babe, then known for his hurling more than his batting, walked the first batter and then uttered more than a few impudent remarks in the umpire's direction. Before Ruth could wind up for the second batter, the umpire ejected Babe from the game, whereupon Ernie Shore was called in from the bullpen as the unexpected reliever for Ruth.

As Shore tossed his first pitch to catcher Sam Agnew, the runner on first bolted for second. Agnew's peg was fast and accurate and the runner was called out. From there Shore was unbeatable. He pitched to the next twenty-six men, got all of them out, and was credited with the shortest perfect game in baseball history; all because of Babe Ruth's big mouth.

Best Pitcher at Finishing What He Starts. Denton "Cy" Young, who pitched for Cleveland, St. Louis, and Boston in the National League and Cleveland and Boston in the American League, won 511 games, more than anyone in major league baseball history; and Young completed more than anyone. The right-hander started 816 games and finished 750. A surplus of Cy Youngs could have wiped out the relief pitching industry.

Best Home-Run Hitter Before Babe Ruth. Roger Connor, an outfielder–first baseman who spent eighteen years in the National League before the turn of the century, blasted 136 home runs, in addition to 441 doubles and 233 triples, fifth on the all-time list behind notables Ty Cobb, Honus Wagner, and Sam Crawford. He also compiled a lifetime batting average of .317.

Born on July 1, 1880, in Waterbury, Connecticut, Connor played semipro ball up and down New York's Hudson River Valley and started his major league career with the Troy Harverstraws, then of the National League. His first year in the bigs Connor hit .332 with three home runs. Finally, in 1883, the club signed him to a whopping $1,800 contract—which, with bonuses, came to $2,100—this in an era when a steak dinner cost a whole quarter. Connor justified manager John Clapp's faith in him, hitting .357 to lead the club.

Connor played for Troy for eleven years, was released in 1894, and immediately signed with the St. Louis Browns.

One year to the day after joining the Browns, Connor found himself back in New York. He celebrated his return by smacking three singles, two doubles, and a triple, as the Browns rolled, 23–2. Each time up to the plate, the fans gave him a standing ovation.

Roger Connor died in Waterbury on January 4, 1931, forgotten by all, but not before he witnessed a fellow named Ruth perform some Connorian baseball feats.

Best Pitcher Against Babe Ruth. Hubert Shelby "Hub" Pruett, St. Louis Browns. Judging by Ruth's impotence at bat against Pruett, the Babe could have been mistaken for a fourth-string pinch hitter instead of "the Sultan of Swat." By contrast, Pruett's efforts against Ruth would seem to qualify him for the Hall of Fame were it not for his otherwise mediocre won-lost record of 29–48 and 4.63 earned run average.

Against Ruth, Pruett was more like Grover Cleveland Alexander. The first time "Hub" as a Browns rookie pitched against the Babe he struck him out. Any suggestions that the feat was a fluke were soon dispelled. Ruth struck out nineteen out of the next twenty-three times he batted against Pruett.

Best Ball Park Billboard. Dexter Park, Woodhaven, Queens, New York. A Jamaica optician bought billboard space at the home of the semipro baseball team the Bushwicks. DON'T KILL THE UMPIRE, MAYBE IT'S YOUR EYES. The message then suggested that irate fans visit the Jamaica optician for an eye exam.

Best Ball Park Seat for the Price. Ebbets Field, 1944. For 55 cents a customer could obtain a seat in the Ebbets Field bleachers. If the patron arrived early enough he could sit in the bleachers' boxes (still for 55 cents), a location unparalleled considering the price in terms of proximity to athletes. The first row of the upper bleachers overhung center field, within easy conversational distance of the center fielder (useful during batting practice), and provided a panoramic, unobstructed view of the entire bandbox ball park.

Best Foul Ball Hitter. Luke Appling, Chicago White Sox. A member of the Hall of Fame, Appling enjoyed a lifetime .310 batting average with Chicago in the forties, but the record books fail to indicate Appling's unerring proclivity for whacking foul balls, deliberately as well as accidentally.

Once, Appling unleashed a rash of fouls in protest against the New York Yankees' management, which had failed to provide a few passes for Luke's friends when the White Sox visited the Bronx. During batting practice that day, witnesses reported that Appling hit a gross of foul balls into the stands. Since the Yankees paid for the balls, the bill was infinitely higher than it would have been for the free tickets.

Appling occasionally used the foul ball for strategic purposes. Once, when he was facing Yankees pitcher Red Ruffing, Appling took two quick strikes and appeared headed for a quick exit from home plate. Luke was disturbed since the White Sox had two men on base and there were two out.

It was time to slow down Ruffing, so Appling fouled off the next four pitches until Ruffing threw one so wide that Luke didn't bother reaching for it. He then fouled six consecutive pitches until Ruffing hurled two more egregiously bad pitches which Luke ignored. The count now was three and two as Ruffing bore down once more; but so did the king of the fouls. For his *chef d'oeuvre* Appling fouled the next fourteen pitches in a row before Ruffing, frazzled and furious, finally walked Appling to fill the bases.

Impatient, Ruffing grooved a magnificent strike down the middle which the next batter, Mike Kreevich, lined for a bases-clearing double. That catapulted Yankees manager Joe McCarthy out of the dugout to remove his ace. On his way to the showers, Ruffing paused for a few words with Appling at third base: "You did it! You did it with those bleepin' foul balls!"

Best Joke by a Manager. Leo Durocher. Although Leo later changed the venue of this gag from Ebbets Field to the Polo Grounds, the story he told on himself originally had a Brooklyn locale. As Leo told it, the gag went as follows:

"A horse trotted up to me in the dugout and said he wanted to play for the Dodgers. 'Okay,' I said, and went out to the mound to pitch a couple in to him. The horse takes the bat in his teeth and hits two or three into the stands.

"So I says to him, 'Not bad, but can you field?'

"So he trots out to the outfield and I fungo a few, and this nag snares each one cleanly between his teeth.

" 'Pretty good,' I have to admit to him. 'But one more thing. Can you run?'

" 'Run?' the horse whinnies. 'If I could run do you think I would be out here looking for a job?' "

Over the years the punch line was altered to fit the occasion, i.e., "If I could run I'd be at Belmont!"

Still another version had the horse actually belting an inside-the-park blast 500 feet to the foot of the Polo Grounds clubhouse, but being pegged out at home plate. In this gag, Durocher demands. "Why the hell didn't you run faster?" To which the nag snaps: "If I could, I'd win the Derby!"

Best Answer to a Reporter's Question. A product of the New York City sandlots, Billy Loes of the Brooklyn Dodgers made his way to the majors amid much fuss and fanfare, especially in the Manhattan dailies. The lean, lanky Loes was admired for his droll and occasionally bizarre humor. His most widely played retort was delivered during the 1952 World Series when he mistook the velocity of a grounder to the mound and erred on the play. Questioned about the error, Loes replied with a straight face: "I lost it in the sun!"

A lesser but philosophically better line was delivered late in Loes's career. Many observers wondered why a pitcher with so much natural talent could continually fail to win more than fourteen games a season, even though he was backed by a strong club. When a reporter questioned Loes about his perennial failure to reach the twenty-win plateau, Billy mulled over the query for a moment and then rather candidly commented that such a Promethean effort would be damaging to his psyche: "If you win twenty," said Loes, "they want you to do it *every* year."

Best Contractual Squelch.   When Hank Greenberg was general manager of the Cleveland Indians he once received an unsigned contract from one of his players. Greenberg immediately dispatched a telegram to the player: IN YOUR HASTE TO ACCEPT TERMS YOU FORGOT TO SIGN CONTRACT.

A few days later, Greenberg received a return wire from the player: IN YOUR HASTE TO GIVE ME A RAISE YOU PUT IN THE WRONG FIGURE.

Best Hitter.   Ty Cobb, "the Georgia Peach," of the Detroit Tigers. In his twenty-three-year career, Cobb produced 4,192 hits and a lifetime batting average of .367. To put Cobb's achievement in proper perspective, consider that Rogers Hornsby, the remarkable St. Louis Cardinals slugger, enjoyed a lifetime average of .358 over twenty-two years, yet had 1,262 *fewer* hits than Cobb.

Best Clutch Hitter.   Babe Ruth. The heavyweight among the Bronx Bombers, Ruth drove in a run every 3.79 times at bat. His colleague on the New York Yankees, Lou Gehrig, is second with a 4.02 success ratio.

Best Individual Comeback.   John Hiller, Detroit Tigers, 1973. A relief pitcher, Hiller won ten games and saved thirty-eight for the Tigers as the top reliever for the Detroit club. To accomplish this, Hiller first had to overcome the aftereffects of a heart attack.

On the advice of physicians, Hiller missed the entire 1971 season following the attack. Following recuperation, Hiller obtained his doctor's permission to work out during the Tigers' batting practice. The sabbatical had no apparent effect on Hiller's ability to throw a strike, so manager Billy Martin restored him to the active roster in 1972. The rejuvenated pitcher responded with a 2.05 earned run average, the best of his career. A year later he pitched well enough to become the ace of the Tigers' bullpen corps.

Best Ball Park Band. Brooklyn Dodgers Sym-Phony, Ebbets Field, 1938–1958. Occupying Section 8, Row 1, Seats 1 through 7, the Dodgers' Sym-Phony was regarded as the zaniest musical combination ever to have a long run at a major league park.

At their most serious, the Sym-Phony played such immortal tunes as "The Brooklyn Baseball Cantata" and warbled lines including:

"Leave us go root for the Dodgers, Rodgers,
They're the team for me.
Leave us make noise with the boisterous boys
On the BMT."

There were seven members in the Sym-Phony, led by Brother Lou Soriano. They wore frock coats and top hats and directed much of their musicianship toward needling the opposition and the resident umpires. When the National League added a fourth umpire to each umpiring team, it disturbed Soriano. "How the hell," he asked, "can you play 'Four Blind Mice'?"

Brother Lou claimed that the Sym-Phony's finest hour occurred in 1948 when the group was invited to stroll the aisles during the Republican Convention in Philadelphia. "Governor Tom Dewey said we were great," said Soriano, "and when he wins the election we're going to give a concert in the White House. Now that's beautiful because it's a sure thing that Harry Truman can't win. But our bum loses!"

Best Eater (Trencherman). Babe Ruth. On an off-day "the Sultan of Swat" could also have been mistaken for "the Sultan of Suet." Eyewitnesses reported that Ruth could down three thousand calories as quickly as he could swing his 41-ounce bat against a fat pitch.

One such Ruth-watcher, former *Sporting News* publisher J. G. Taylor Spink, recalled a Ruthian culinary round-tripper. "In St. Louis," said Spink, "Babe usually was to be found at Busch's Grove, an eating place in St. Louis County. He frequently would go there for breakfast. It was not unusual for Ruth to eat two fried chickens and wash them down with goblets of beer.

"For dinner the Babe would order a porterhouse steak, a double order of lettuce and Roquefort dressing, a double order of cottage-fried potatoes, a double order of pie à la mode, and a large pot of coffee. When Ruth finally called the waiter and asked for the check there was not enough left on his plates to feed a sparrow!"

Paul Derringer, who pitched for the Cardinals, Reds, and Cubs, described his first meeting with Ruth in the dining car of their Pullman:

"I was eating at a single table and the seat opposite me was the only vacant one in the car. In came Ruth, alone. Seeing the empty chair, he sat at my table. The Babe called over a waiter and ordered a pitcher of ice, a pint of ginger ale, a porterhouse steak garnished with four fried eggs, fried potatoes, and a pot of coffee. He told the waiter to be sure to bring him the pitcher of ice and ginger ale right away.

"A few minutes later the waiter set the pitcher of ice and pint of ginger ale in front of Ruth. The Babe pulled a pint of bourbon out of his hip pocket, poured it over the ice, poured the ginger ale, shook up the mixture—and that was Ruth's breakfast juice.

"Sometime later I happened to meet his roommate and related to him what had happened in the diner that morning. He told me that it was nothing more than a daily habit. Ruth generally drank a quart mixture of bourbon whiskey and ginger ale at breakfast, before attacking a steak, garnished with four or six fried eggs and potatoes on the side!"

Best Pitcher with a Weak Team. Tom Seaver, New York Mets. A mediocre pitcher can win a spate of games if his team scores enough runs for him. But the mark of a superior pitcher is one who wins despite inferior hitting and fielding behind him. Tom Seaver suffered such a fate through many seasons with the Mets. Yet, by the end of his Met career (1967–June 1977), Seaver had amassed 198 wins.

From 1967, when Seaver first broke in with the Mets and won the National League's rookie-of-the-year award, to the beginning of 1977, the Mets had barely won 50 percent of their games. However, in that span, Seaver won nearly 65 percent of his decisions.

Best Baseball Nostalgic. Bob Broeg, St. Louis *Post-Dispatch*. Sports editor of the *Post-Dispatch,* Broeg, although still commenting on the contemporary scene, fills *The Sporting News* with a column almost every week devoted to baseball's past. Usually, it makes delightful reading. A close second is Joe Falls, columnist of the Detroit *Free Press.*

Best Home Run Efficiency. Babe Ruth. *El Bambino* hit a home run every 11.76 times at bat. Hank Aaron, owner of the all-time home-run record, averaged a round-tripper only every 16.23 times at bat. Ralph Kiner is second to Ruth with a homer every 14.11 times at the plate.

Best Disguised Baseball Columnist. The Old Scout, New York *Sun*. For more than a decade, starting in 1935, a brilliantly written column appeared in the *Sun* with no byline other than "The Old Scout." The author was Herb Goren, a Brooklynite, who covered baseball and hockey for the paper. Goren inherited the column from Sam Murphy, the original "Old Scout" who *did* have his byline on the six-day-a-week opus. When sports editor Wilbur Wood decided to make a change, he gave the column to Goren. "Unfortunately," Goren recalled, "he couldn't let me put my byline on a column called 'The Old Scout' for a very good reason—I was only nineteen years old!"

Best Slugger. Babe Ruth. The slugging percentage is thought by baseball statisticians to reflect the true value of a hitter's power. It is obtained by dividing possible total bases into actual total bases. Ruth's lifetime slugging percentage was .690. Ted Williams was second with .634, followed by Lou Gehrig at .632.

Best Allusion to Baseball in a Non-Baseball Movie. *Mogambo* (Metro Goldwyn Mayer), 1953. Grace Kelly, responding to Clark Gable's identification of a group of scurrying animals as "Thomson's gazelles," asks: "Who is this man Thomson that gazelles should be called after him?"

Ava Gardner, in jealous pursuit of Gable's charms, and definitely another kind of lady, answers sardonically: "He's a third baseman for the Giants who hit a home run against the Dodgers once."

According to experts on films, this could be the closest adherence to baseball fact ever achieved in a Hollywood production. "Baseball movies," writes film critic Paul Ringe, "traditionally have been viewed with suspicion by baseball fans. But *Mogambo* did justice to both Bobby Thomson and gazelles."

Best Silent Films about Baseball. *How the Office Boy Saw the Ballgame* (1906) and *Bush Leaguer* (1917).

Best Hitting Team to Finish in the Cellar. Philadelphia Phillies, 1930. Although the second-place New York Giants set a record by hitting for an average of .319, the Philadelphia Phillies did almost as well——.315, belting 1,783 hits, 14 *more* than the Giants. The difference was that the Phillies finished last in the National League because of inferior pitching. Philly pitchers allowed almost seven runs per game.

Best Hit for Fewest Bases. Josh Gibson, Homestead Grays. The legendary black catcher in the Negro National League, Gibson stroked his notorious elongated double-that-should-have-been-a-home-run at Dexter Park in Woodhaven, Queens, New York. Playing for the Grays against the Bushwicks, Gibson stroked a 500-foot drive to dead center field. Dexter Park had no fences at center field, only a ten-foot hill on which D-E-X-T-E-R P-A-R-K was spelled out. The hill was topped by a flat plain on which the ball rolled. A normal runner could have circled the bases twice, with ease, but Gibson, in his late forties, had trouble lumbering to second base. He stopped there, sat down on the bag, and watched as the Bushwicks' center fielder finally retrieved the ball and relayed it to the mound.

Best Baseball Jazz Work. "Van Lingle Mungo" by Dave Frishberg. Originally pressed as a single record by pianist Frishberg, "Van Lingle Mungo" later was incorporated in a long-playing record album by Frishberg called "Oklahoma Toad." The subject of Frishberg's original success, Mungo, pitched for the Brooklyn Dodgers, all of which is incidental to the tune. On the record, pressed by the CTI label in Rockefeller Center, New York, Frishberg, with a sparkling jazz background, reels off a list of old-time ballplayers including "Big" John Mize, Barney McKoskey and, of course, the ever popular Mungo. The words, as written, go as follows:

Hen-ry Ma-je-ski, John-ny Gee, Ed-die Joost,
    John-ny Pes-ky, Thor-ton Lee,
Roy Cam-pa-nel-la, Van Lin-gle Mung-o.
White-y Ku-row-ski, Max La-nier, Ed-die Wait-kus
    and John-ny Van-der-meer,
Dan-ny Gar-del-la, Van Lin-gle Mung-o.
Au-gie Ber-ga-mo, Sig-mund Jack-uck-i, Big John-ny
    Mize and Bar-ney Mc-Cos-key, Hal Tro-sky.
Au-gie Ga-lan and Pin-ky May, Stan Hack and
    French-y Bord'-ga-ray,
Phil Ca-va-ret-ta, George McQuinn, How-ie Pol-lett
    and Ear-ly Wynn,
Bob Es-ta-lel-la, Van Lin-gle Mung-o.
John An-to-nel-li, Fer-ris Fain, Frank-ie Cro-set-ti,
    John-ny Sain,

Har-ry Bre-cheen and Vir-gil Trucks, Frank-ie
  Gus-tine and John-ny Kucks,
  Ed-die Ba-sin-ski, Van Lin-gle Mung-o.

Jazz critic and author Ira Gitler rated Frishberg's opus "one of the best jazz works of the seventies and certainly the best ever done combining jazz and baseball." Gitler, a lifetime Giants fan, added that the fact that Mungo earned his fame as a Dodger did not detract from the record's worth.

The tune, done to a bossa nova beat, also appeared in sheet music (Red Day Music, a division of Daramus, Inc.) when the song was released in 1969. Frishberg, who wrote both the words and music, received raves from all reviewers, although the piece received little promotion.

Best Birthday for a Player. Peewee Reese, Brooklyn Dodgers. For Reese's thirty-sixth birthday, on July 22, 1955, the Dodgers' captain was hailed with a "night" in his honor. He was overwhelmed with gifts, including an automobile (in which his mother, to Peewee's surprise, was sitting), but the *pièce de résistance* came when the houselights dimmed and thirty-three thousand fans lit matches and sang "Happy Birthday" to Reese. The effect of the matches against the black backdrop of the stands was awesome.

Best Way to Foil a Bunt. Bert Haas, a Montreal Royals third baseman, was facing the Jersey City (Little) Giants in 1940 during an International League game. With runners on first and second, a Jersey City batter laid a perfect bunt down the third-base line. At that moment both runners took off, certain that the bunt would remain in fair territory.

Hoping that the bunt would roll foul, Haas suddenly realized that the baseball would hug the foul line on the fair side—unless he did something about it. At that point Haas ran to the ball, leaned over the horsehide, and began huffing and puffing in a desperate attempt to *blow* the ball foul. Finally, the ball, propelled by Haas's oxygen, rolled into foul territory.

The ingenious third baseman then picked up the ball and the umpire immediately ruled it a foul, nullifying the run that had just crossed the plate.

Best Book. *The Summer Game,* Roger Angell. Although Roger Kahn's *The Boys of Summer* gained the most attention, Angell's *The Summer Game,* which had the misfortune of being published in the shadow of the Kahn book, is better written and aptly reflects the genius of Angell's writing in *The New Yorker* magazine.

Best Slugging Team. New York Yankees, 1927. This was the club, managed by Miller Huggins, which added the name "Murderers' Row" to the baseball lexicon. The "murderers" in question included Babe Ruth, Lou Gehrig, Tony Lazzeri, and Bob Meusel, who pounded out a team slugging record of .489! Skeptics who believed that the record was a fluke were proven wrong just three years later when the Yankees' slugging average was .488. Six years later the Bronx Bombers slugged at a .483 clip.

Best Broadcaster. Red Barber, voice of the Cincinnati Reds, Brooklyn Dodgers, and New York Yankees. Barber, a Floridian by birth, emerged as the dean of baseball broadcasters on the basis of his pioneering work in the field as well as the quality of his broadcasts, timbre of his voice, and basic objectivity; not to mention his penchant for innovation.

After working for a Cincinnati radio station, Barber became baseball's first play-by-play broadcaster. When Larry MacPhail, the Reds' general manager who fathered the idea of broadcasting the ball games, moved to Brooklyn where he ran the Dodgers, he took Barber with him.

As the *"Verce* of the Dodgers," Barber became a legend in his time, and so did his original phrases. Red's broadcast booth became known as "the catbird seat." When the Dodgers filled the bases, Red described the situation as

"F.O.B." (Full of Brooklyns). A spectacular play elicited a gushing "Oh! Doctor!" And when manager Leo "the Lip" Durocher became embroiled with umpire George Magurkirth, "the Ole Redhead" described the fracas as "a rhubarb." (Hollywood, seizing on Barber's line, later filmed a Brooklyn baseball movie called *Rhubarb* about a cat who wanted to play for the Dodgers.)

Barber, who was behind the microphone for the 1949 Dodgers-Yankees World Series, was the first to handle a baseball telecast and also introduced the "pregame show" to the air. Red went into the Dodgers' dugout with a microphone before the season opener between the Dodgers and Giants. For the first time, thanks to Barber, listeners actually could hear the ballplayers' own voices.

Before the era when broadcasters traveled with the teams, Barber would re-create the Dodgers' "away" games from telegraph reports which continuously poured into the studio over a teletype machine. Occasionally, the wire would "go out," but Barber never would resort to tactics employed by other broadcasters who would simply waste time by faking action ("Jones has fouled off thirty-seven pitches in a row"). Barber explained: "I assumed my listeners knew that it was a wire re-creation. I even used to have the telegraph machine close at hand, so it could be heard over the microphone. When the wire 'went out' I used to tell my listeners, 'I'm sorry, but the wire has gone out east of Pittsburgh.' "

Barber's influence was felt by all of those with whom he worked. One of the most accomplished—but unheralded—broadcasters was Connie Desmond, who was Barber's Brooklyn sidekick for several years. Red later groomed Vin Scully, who has since been the voice of the Dodgers in Los Angeles and one of the best contemporary broadcasters.

———

Worst Presidential Greeting. Herbert Hoover, Philadelphia, October 6, 1931. One of baseball's most venerable traditions has been the appearance of the president of the United States at opening day of the season and, frequently, at a World Series game. During the 1931 World Series between the Philadelphia Athletics and St. Louis Cardinals, President Herbert Hoover showed up for the third game. Hoover, a Republican, had been elected president in 1929, and was the man generally held responsible for the Great Depression which had blanketed the nation. Nevertheless, it had been traditional for audiences, no matter how unhappy, to greet the presidential party with reverence and applause at sporting events such as the World Series.

When Hoover arrived there was a perfunctory pattering of palms behind the dugouts, whereupon Hoover waved his hat and smiled. But as the president approached his official box, someone booed. Then came another hoot and another. Joe Williams, who covered the World Series for the New York *World-Telegram,* recalled how quickly the decibel count multiplied. "Soon," said Williams, "it seemed that almost everyone in the park was booing."

Prohibition was still in vogue and the crowd, *en masse,* seemed to realize that Hoover had lined up on the side of the drys, supporting the Prohibition law. Suddenly, the boos changed to a deafening chant: "We want beer. We want beer!"

As soon as the first inning was underway the crowd's attention was distracted from the Hoovers to the Cardinals and Athletics. However, at the end of the eighth inning a voice boomed over the ball park loudspeaker. "Silence. Silence, please." Hoover and his party were ready to leave the game. The public address announcer pleaded for courtesy and asked everyone in the stadium to remain seated.

The plea was ignored. Hoover, holding his wife by the arm, walked past the Athletics' dugout amid a cacophony of boos, followed by an equally deafening chant: "We want beer! We want beer!"

Hoover later explained that he walked out before the game's end because he had received two telegrams; one told of the death of a personal friend and the other revealed that the United States had gone off the gold standard. "Under the circumstances," said Hoover, "I decided I had no business watching a ball game." Despite the hostile reaction at the World Series game, Hoover continued to attend baseball games at various stadia in later years.

Worst Attendance (National League). September 27, 1881, Troy, New York. A game between the Chicago White Stockings and the host team from Troy drew an audience of twelve cozy fans to the rain-swept field. The White Stockings, who had the pennant clinched, were playing their final game of the season and boasted such stars as Cap Anson, who hit .399 that year, and outfielder Mike "King" Kelly, who batted .323 and, like Anson, was later elected to the Hall of Fame. Despite the rain, umpires ordered the game played since there were, in fact, a dozen paying customers on hand and it was the last game of the regular schedule.

Worst Complete Game by a Pitcher. Harley "Doc" Parker, who played for both the Chicago Cubs and Cincinnati Reds, between 1893 and 1901, plumbed his pitching depths in 1901. The unfortunate hurler was allowed to remain on the mound for nine full innings during which he allowed 26 hits and 21 runs. Not surprisingly, Parker lost the game and hastened the use of relief pitchers.

Worst Loss for a Pitcher. Harvey Haddix, Pittsburgh Pirates, 1959, County Stadium, Milwaukee. Pitching against the Milwaukee Braves, Haddix pitched 12 innings of perfect ball and retired thirty-six consecutive Braves batters. Yet, after 12 innings, the Pirates and Braves were locked in a scoreless tie. In the bottom of the thirteenth inning Felix Mantilla of the Braves, a .215 hitter, led off with a ground ball to Pirates third baseman Don Hoak, who threw the ball away for an error. Eddie Mathews sacrificed Mantilla to second and then Henry Aaron was purposely walked. He was followed by long-hitting Joe Adcock, who delivered a home run to right-center.

Curiously, Adcock passed Aaron on the basepaths in the ensuing celebration and a dispute arose over the final score. It finally was declared a 1–0 game; the toughest loss of Harvey Haddix's career.

Worst Fielded Game. Detroit Tigers vs. Chicago White Sox, May 6, 1903. The American League rivals managed to commit a total of eighteen errors—the record for a nine-inning game—with Chicago charged with twelve errors and Detroit with six.

Worst Hitting Team to Win a Pennant. Chicago White Sox, 1906. Affectionately known as "the Hitless Wonders," the first-place White Sox put together a modest .228 team average, the worst in the entire league. Their best hitter, who would have had trouble cracking other lineups, was second baseman Frank Isbell, who hit .279. Despite their power shortage, the White Sox finished three games ahead of the New York Highlanders (later to be known as the Yankees). By contrast, the Highlanders had a team average of .299, an astonishing 71 points higher than the champions.

Pitching was the White Sox's forte. They proved the point in the World Series, defeating the Chicago Cubs, four games to two. The Cubs, who had a team hitting average of .262 during the regular National League season, were limited by White Sox pitching to a .196 average at bat. However, "the Hitless Wonders," world champions in 1906, were true to form in the championship. Over six games, their average was .197.

Worst Home Run Hitter. Floyd Baker, a journeyman who alternately played for the St. Louis Browns, Chicago White Sox, Washington Senators, Boston Red Sox, and Philadelphia Phillies. Never to be confused with "Home Run" Baker, Floyd came to bat for a total of 2,280 times in his major league career during which he hit exactly one home run. Baker retired in 1955 with a lifetime .251 batting average.

Worst Mistake by an Umpire. Bill Klem, a member of baseball's Hall of Fame, liked to boast that he never blew a call. However, one afternoon in 1913 he committed an egregious error during a game between the Pittsburgh Pirates and New York Giants. The hotly contested match produced a series of flare-ups which jangled Klem's nerves.

When the Pirates began needling him, Klem strode to the Pittsburgh bench and snapped: "If I hear anything else out of you guys I'll clear this bench! Not one more word!" For the moment, at least, the Pirates clammed up. Manager Fred Clarke then sent a young pinch hitter to the plate. Klem, who had never seen the kid before, asked the lad his name. The kid's reply was inaudible so the umpire shouted: "C'mon, out with it!"

With a straight face, the rookie turned to the esteemed umpire and said: "Boo!"

Livid with rage, Klem ripped off his mask and ordered the young player out of the ball game. Fortunately, manager Clarke, sensing something was amiss, dashed out of the dugout to learn what was the matter. Klem promptly advised Clarke that nobody, especially a smart-guy rookie, was going to say boo to him.

"Sorry, Bill," Clarke replied, "but you'll have to make an exception in this case."

The rookie's name was Everett Booe. He was, in the end, Klem's worst boo-boo.

Worst Pitching Staff. Philadelphia Phillies, 1930. At a time when big-league teams considered it horrendous to allow more than 4.00 earned run averages, the 1930 edition of the Phillies finished the season with an earned run average of 6.71. During the entire season, the Philadelphia pitchers were able to put together only two shutouts.

Worst Performance by a Winning Relief Pitcher. Ed Rommel, Philadelphia Athletics, July 10, 1932. A first-class pitcher for the A's from 1920 through 1932, Rommel appeared in 251 games as a reliever. In his final season with Philadelphia, Rommel appeared in a game which ran through eighteen innings. Rommel's opponents, the Cleveland Indians, were able to connect against him almost every inning, but the A's always rallied to save Rommel for still another inning. In the eighteenth inning, Rommel finally stopped the Indians without a run, enabling Philadelphia to win the match, 18–17. During his career, Rommel won a total of 171 games, all for the Athletics.

Worst Beaning.   Carl Mays, New York Yankees, August 16, 1920. On a gray, misty afternoon at New York's Polo Grounds, the second-place New York Yankees were playing the league-leading Cleveland Indians. In the fifth inning Mays hit Cleveland shortstop Ray Chapman in the head with a pitch. Chapman was rushed to St. Lawrence Hospital where emergency brain surgery was performed. However, the twenty-nine-year-old Chapman died the following morning.

Ironically, the adversity did produce sweet results for the pennant-bound Indians. They needed a replacement at shortstop for the ill-fated Chapman and bought minor-leaguer Joe Sewell from the Southern League. Despite the pressure, Sewell batted .329 from the time of his arrival until Cleveland won the pennant. Then, with Sewell a regular shortstop, the Indians defeated the Brooklyn Dodgers to win the World Series. Sewell went on to enjoy nine .300 seasons with Cleveland and set records for not striking out. He now is a member of baseball's Hall of Fame.

Worst Team.   Cleveland (National League), 1899. Unlike the oft-ridiculed 1962 New York Mets, who finished 60½ games out of first place, the Cleveland club was conspicuously worse. They won only 20 while losing 134 for a .130 percentage, and finished 84 games behind first place. The Clevelanders scored only 529 runs during the entire season while 1,252 were scored against them.

Worst Salary Raise.   Hugh Duffy, Boston, National League club, 1895. A member of the Hall of Fame, Duffy set the all-time batting mark of .438 in 1894 but was refused, at first, a raise by the Boston club's management. Duffy continued to argue his case until the start of the 1895 campaign, when he finally scored a Pyrrhic victory— a $12.50 a month salary increase. However, an amendment to the agreement provided that Duffy also was compelled to become team captain. A clause in the captain's section of his contract stipulated that Duffy, as captain, was responsible for all lost equipment. By the season's end, the club had lost so much equipment that his increased liabilities far outweighed his boost in salary.

Worst Performance Winning a Batting Championship. Carl Yastrzemski, Boston Red Sox, 1968. When the Red Sox won the American League pennant in 1967, Yastrzemski batted .326 and led the league in home runs with 44 and runs batted in with 121. A year after winning the "Triple Crown," Carl repeated as the American League's best hitter. However, in that year of the pitcher, his top average was only .301.

Worst Team to Win a Pennant. New York Mets, 1973. When the National and American leagues agreed to split divisions (four in all) for the 1969 season, purists argued that a team with a .500 record could conceivably win a pennant; especially in view of the best-of-five series which would decide the league championships. In 1973 the Cincinnati Reds had little trouble winning the Western Division championship in the National League (99 wins, 63 losses). But the Eastern Division race was extraordinarily close; the Pittsburgh Pirates, New York Mets, and St. Louis Cardinals matched each other's records and the regular season ended with a three-way tie for first place.

However, the Mets were required to play a doubleheader with the Chicago Cubs on the day following the end of the regular schedule because the two games had originally been postponed earlier in the schedule. If the Mets could win one of the two games they would win the championship. If they lost both ends of the doubleheader, Pittsburgh and St. Louis would have to hold a playoff.

On a gloomy, drizzly day in Chicago, the Mets won the first game of the doubleheader and entered the championship series with a conspicuously mediocre record of 82 wins and 79 losses. Militantly unimpressed with the favored Reds, the Mets conquered Cincinnati on the arms of pitchers Tom Seaver and Jon Matlack. Carrying their extraordinary luck to the World Series, the Mets took the Oakland Athletics to seven games before losing the final match. Never in baseball history has a team with so little gone so far.

Worst Winning Margin in a Pennant Race. Detroit Tigers, 1908. Managed by Hughie Jennings, the Tigers finished only half a game ahead of the Cleveland Indians. Detroit finished with a record of 90 wins and 63 losses. Cleveland was 90–64. The Tigers had played one less match because of a rain-out that never was ordered replayed; thus, they won the pennant by a half a game.

Worst Strikeout Batter. Bobby Bonds, 1970. Although Babe Ruth, Duke Snider, and Mickey Mantle struck out with a flourish, nobody could match the frequency of Bonds during the 1970 season when he batted .302 for the San Francisco Giants. Despite his 26 home runs and 78 runs batted in, Bonds struck out 189 times.

Worst Most Valuable Player. Bob Elliot, Boston Braves, 1947. Never to be confused with Joe DiMaggio, Willie Mays, or Roberto Clemente, Elliot hit .317 for a third-place Braves team. Everything, it seems, Elliot did that year was the right move, in terms of his career before and after. He hit 22 home runs and drove in 113 runs, but never again in his twenty-one-year career did he come close to matching his MVP effort of 1947.

Worst Rookie of the Year. Don Schwall, Boston Red Sox, 1961. A pitcher who compiled a 15–7 record and 3.22 earned run average, Schwall dropped to a 9–15 level a year later and a 4.95 earned run average. He soon was shipped to the Pittsburgh Pirates.

Worst Mistake on the Basepaths. Brooklyn Dodgers, 1926. The Dodgers, alias "Dem Brooklyn Bums," earned a reputation as baseball's "Daffiness Boys" because of an assortment of amusing blunders. The *faux pas* that symbolized the Dodgers' daffiness developed after they had loaded the bases with one out against the Boston Braves. Hank DeBerry was on third base, Dazzy Vance on second, and Chick Fewster on first. The batter was Babe Herman, a potent but occasionally laughable hitter.

Herman stroked the first pitch toward the right field fence. Without question, it would be an extra-base drive. As the ball bounced off the right field wall, DeBerry easily trotted home from third while Vance and Fewster sprinted toward the plate and Herman raced for first. What seemed like a rudimentary run situation suddenly became a comedy of basepath errors when Vance became fearful that he would not reach home plate in time. (Dazzy was unaware that the ball was still bouncing around the outfield.)

Ultracautious, Vance jammed on his brakes after rounding third and decided to return to the base rather than dash for home plate. Meanwhile, Fewster, normally an efficient baserunner, believed that he could reach third base on the long hit. After rounding second, Fewster put his head down for an energetic dash to third, culminating with a vigorous slide.

Unlike Fewster, who took one brief look at the ball and ran like hell, Herman somehow had become mesmerized by his effort. As he rounded second, Herman's eyes remained riveted to the ball and he neglected to notice the traffic jam developing at third base. What followed was a scene straight out of a Three Stooges' slapstick comedy. Three players from the same team slid head-first into the same base.

Seconds later, the ball was pegged to third where the Braves' third baseman, Eddie Taylor, tagged all three converging Dodgers. They then looked to the umpire for
34

his decision. Vance, because he arrived there first, was awarded the base, but Herman and Fewster were called out. To further the Brooklyn tragicomedy, DeBerry's run did not count.

Among the more perplexed onlookers was a rookie on the Dodgers' bench who turned to manager "Uncle" Wilbert Robinson and inquired: "Mister Robinson, what kind of baseball is that?"

"Leave them alone," Uncle Wilbert replied, "that's the first time they've been together all season!"

However, the perfect squelch was inadvertently provided by a taxi driver and his customer after the fare had left the ball park just moments before the third-base incident had taken place.

As soon as the passenger closed the cab door, the taxi driver asked the fan how the game was going. "Pretty good," the fellow replied. "The Dodgers have three men on base."

"Oh, yeah," replied the cabbie, *which base?*"

Worst Scapegoat. Fred "Bonehead" Merkle, New York Giants, 1908. Although his supposed feat of refusing to touch second base and nullifying a winning run for the Giants against the Chicago Cubs is baseball legend, thus branding him with the nickname "Bonehead," eyewitnesses who were at the Polo Grounds that late September afternoon attest that Merkle was a victim, not a perpetrator.

Fred Snodgrass, then a rookie catcher with the Giants, was Merkle's teammate that fateful day, and gave this account:

Fred Merkle had joined the Giants in the fall of 1907, at the age of eighteen, before I joined the following spring. So in 1908, when I met him, and when the so-called Merkle 'bonehead' occurred, he was a kid only nineteen years old. As a result of what happened, he took more abuse and vituperation than any other nineteen-year-old I've ever heard of.

"The famous game in which it all happened took place in New York in late September of 1908. The Giants were

35

playing the Chicago Cubs and we were both about tied for the league lead, with only a week or two of the season remaining. Merkle was playing first base for us. I think that Fred Tenney, the regular first baseman, was injured or something, and that this was the very first game Merkle had been put in the starting lineup all season.

"Christie Mathewson was pitching for us, against Jack Pfiester for the Clubs. The game went down to the last half of the ninth inning, with the score tied, 1–1. And then, in the last of the ninth, with two out and Moose McCormick on first, Merkle hit a long single to right and McCormick went to third.

"Men were on first and third, with two out. The next man up was Al Bridwell, our shortstop. Al hit a line single into center field. McCormick, of course, scored easily from third—he could have walked in—with what appeared to be the winning run.

"Merkle started for a second base, naturally. But the minute he saw the ball was a safe hit, rolling toward the fence out in right-center, with McCormick across the plate and the game presumably over and won, he turned and lit out for the clubhouse, exactly as he had been doing all season long. And that was Merkle's downfall. Because technically the rules of baseball are that to formally complete the play he had to touch second base, since Bridwell now occupied first.

"As soon as McCormick crossed the plate, everyone thought the game was over. Everyone except Johnny Evers, anyway. . . . Evers began to call to the Cubs' center fielder, Artie Hofman, to go and get the ball. Hofman hadn't even chased it, because the game was over, as far as he was concerned. But Evers made so much noise about getting the ball and throwing it in to second base, that Hofman finally retrieved it and threw it in.

". . . Finally, Hank O'Day, who was the senior umpire, ruled that Merkle was indeed out, the third out, and therefore McCormick's run didn't count and that the game had ended in a 1–1 tie.

". . . It is very unfair to put all the blame on Merkle for our losing the pennant in 1908. [Manager John]

McGraw never did, and neither did the rest of us. It was mostly the newspapers. They were the ones who invented the term 'bonehead'."

Most Unusual Player. Pete Gray, St. Louis Browns, 1945. The only one-armed player in big-league history, Gray (real name: Peter Wyshner) played center field for the Browns during World War II. Previously, he had been a star with semipro teams in the New York area. As a batter, Gray would take a normal swing; except that out of necessity, he held the bat in one hand. In the outfield, Gray handled fly balls by catching them in his long, thin, unpadded glove. Then, in an intricate maneuver, he would slip the glove under his armpit, roll the ball across his chest to his throwing arm, and peg the ball to the infield. On grounders to the outfield, Gray would trap the ball with his glove, then push the ball in front of him, slip off the mitt, and toss the ball back to the infield. Despite the novelty of a one-armed player, Gray's appearance in the Browns' lineup was no gimmick. He hit .218 and was an adequate fielder. After the 1945 season, Gray returned to the minors.

(The Browns also were responsible for another unusual player, Eddie Gaedel, a midget who was hired by club president Bill Veeck. Gaedel had one at-bat, on August 19, 1951, in the second game of a doubleheader, was walked, and never played again.)

Most Unusual Regular. Herman A. "Germany" Schaefer. A player who came into his own at the turn of the century, Schaefer variously was employed by the Chicago Cubs, Detroit Tigers, Washington Senators, New York Yankees, Cleveland Indians, and Newark of the Federal League. He was creative enough to be considered flaky by his more conservative teammates and opponents. Once, while Schaefer was playing for Washington against the Chicago White Sox in 1911, the game was tied with the Senators batting in the ninth inning. Schaefer was on first while a speedy baserunner named Clyde Milan occupied third for Washington. On the first pitch to the next hitter, Schaefer sprinted for second base. His theory was that the catcher would attempt to throw him out at second and, in so doing, Milan would dash home safely from third. However, the White Sox catcher didn't fall for the bait. When Schaefer realized that his ruse wasn't working, he wheeled in his tracks and headed back to first. Surely, he thought, the catcher would try to nail him at first. But, alas, still no throw! Meanwhile, the umpires puzzled over what to do about a player who stole first base. After careful consideration the umpires decided that since no one ever had done it before—and there was nothing in the rule book to cover it—Schaefer was safe.

Once the dispute was settled, the White Sox pitcher cranked his arm for another pitch and Schaefer took off for second again. This time the catcher made the peg, but "Germany" evaded the tag and the run scored.

Schaefer's antics were not always as productive. Another time he attempted to score from second on a short outfield fly. Upon his slide into home plate, "Germany" was signaled out by the umpire. "I beat the throw," shouted Schaefer, "and knocked the ball out of the catcher's mitt."

The umpire stared back at Schaefer: "The hell you did." Then he pointed to the ball, snug in the mitt. "But," pleaded Schaefer, "he missed the tag. He never touched me."

"He got you, all right," the umpire insisted.

Finally, Schaefer turned to the grandstand. "Ladies and gentlemen," he begged. "Does anyone have any more excuses? I'm plumb out of them myself!"

Most Unusual No-Hitter. Chicago Cubs vs. Cincinnati Reds, 1917. Although the teams in question were less than spectacular, the Cubs and Reds boasted a pair of superb pitchers: Jim Vaughn for Chicago and Fred Toney for Cincinnati. Vaughn in fact produced three consecutive twenty-game seasons while Toney, in 1917, was to score 24 victories. When the pair faced each other at Wrigley Field in Chicago, they attained the ultimate pitching accomplishment: after nine innings of regulation play neither pitcher had surrendered a single hit; the only double no-hitter in baseball history. The overpowering Vaughn struck out ten, limiting his opponents to first base. Toney, by contrast, struck out three but permitted only one Chicago batter to reach second. The deadlock finally was broken in the top of the tenth inning when Cincinnati shortstop Larry Kopf delivered a clean single. Kopf reached third on a dropped fly ball and scored on Jim Thorpe's infield hit. The final score was Reds 1, Cubs 0.

Most Unusual Steal of Home.   Fred Clarke, Pittsburgh Pirates, 1906. Player-manager of the Pirates, Clarke stole a total of eighteen bases during the 1906 season. His zaniest experience occurred during a game with the Chicago Cubs. Pittsburgh had bases loaded with Clarke edging his way off third. The count on the batter was three and one. When the pitch arrived, to everyone's amazement, the umpire said nothing. Clarke assumed that if it had been a strike, the umpire would have suitably bellowed, *"Strike two!"* With that in mind, Clarke assumed that no announcement meant that it was ball four, thus forcing in a run. So, Clarke trotted nonchalantly home while the batter dropped his bat and ambled toward first. Meanwhile, the Cubs' catcher simply returned the ball to his pitcher.

Just then the umpire shouted: *"Strike two!"* And Clarke crossed the plate unimpeded. As incredulous players turned to home, the red-faced umpire explained: "I got a frog in my throat—I couldn't say a word." The batter returned to the plate, but Clarke's run was allowed to stand. Since there is no other way of scoring it, Clarke was credited with a stolen base.

Most Unusual Criticism of an Umpire.   In 1886, an irate baseball fan, enraged over inferior officiating, composed the following poem:

> Mother, may I slug the umpire,
> May I slug him right away?

So he cannot be here, mother,
When the clubs begin to play?
Let me clasp his throat, dear mother,
In a dear, delightful grip,
With one hand and with the other
Bat him several in the lip.
Let me climb his frame, dear mother,
While the happy people shout,
I'll not kill him, dearest mother,
I will only knock him out.
Let me mop the ground up, mother,
With his person, dearest, do,
If the ground can stand it, mother,
I don't see why you can't, too.

Most Unusual Batting Average Change. Chicago White Sox, 1940. The entire nine-man roster of the White Sox started and finished a game with precisely the same average before and after a match with the Cleveland Indians. Pitching for the Indians was Bob "Rapid Robert" Feller, who hurled a no-hitter. Since the event took place on opening day, 1940, the White Sox opened the game with averages of .000 and finished with exactly the same mark. It was the only occasion in major league baseball history in which a club succumbed to a no-hitter without suffering any loss in their batting averages.

Most Unusual Home Run. George Cutshaw, Brooklyn Dodgers, 1913, at Ebbets Field. The Phillies and Dodgers were tied in an extra-inning game when Cutshaw came up to bat for Brooklyn in the last of the eleventh. Feared for his home-run-hitting ability, Cutshaw stroked the second pitch down the first-base line. It appeared that, with a little luck, he could stretch a single into a double. Meanwhile, Philadelphia's right fielder desperately pursued the ball which was heading for the Bedford Avenue (right field) wall. At the very least, he would play the rebound off the wall and relay the ball back to the infield.

However, the ball was cooperating only with the Dodgers. It struck the embankment that abutted the fence, but never ricocheted back to the right fielder. Instead, it climbed the wall and actually flew over the right field fence and on to Bedford Avenue. In those days, any ball that sailed over the fence—in any manner between the foul lines—was considered a home run. As a result, Cutshaw gained fame as the only ground-ball-hitting home run swinger in baseball history.

Most Unusual Sore Arm Treatment. Guy Bush, Chicago Cubs. A major leaguer in the twenties and early thirties, Bush suffered a sore arm one afternoon before an important game. The Cubs' trainer, Andy Lotshaw, fancied himself an amateur psychiatrist and concluded that Bush's ailment was more psychosomatic than real. However, to placate the "injured" pitcher, Lotshaw produced a bottle that, he insisted, contained a secret potion guaranteed to cure the sore arm. The trainer then rubbed it vigorously from Bush's shoulder blade to his hand and then sent him out to pitch. Remarkably, Bush won the game and Lotshaw immediately was lionized by the pitcher.

When Bush received his next pitching assignment, he demanded more of the "secret" potion rubdown. Lotshaw obliged and, rejuvenated, Bush went on pitching for the Cubs until 1934 when he was traded. However, it wasn't until Bush ultimately retired that Lotshaw revealed the ingredients of his "cure." For the first treatment he reached into his bag for some liniment, but discovered that none was left. Instead, he opened the first full bottle he could find and swabbed the dark brown, sparkly liquid on Bush's arm. The miracle cure was Coca-Cola.

Most Unusual Managerial Birthday Present. When "Jolly" Charlie Grimm managed the Milwaukee Brewers, then of the American Association, he was approached by his boss, Bill Veeck, who realized that Grimm's birthday would arrive soon. Veeck wondered what his manager would like for his birthday.

"A good left-handed pitcher," smiled Grimm, expecting nothing more than a short beer in return.

But Milwaukee long had a practice of honoring its baseball manager's or coach's birthday with a lavish on-the-diamond fete prior to the game. Grimm was toasted with such a celebration at the pitcher's mound.

A huge cake was wheeled on to the field whereupon manager Grimm was presented with a $1,000 savings bond, compliments of the Brewers. When Charlie took the giant knife in hand to cut the cake he discovered that his wish had been granted. Hidden inside the cake was one Julie Acosta, a left-handed pitcher whom Veeck had secretly purchased from Norfolk for his manager's birthday.

"I had called the Norfolk owner," said Veeck, "and said I'd give him $7,500 for Acosta and another $5,000, providing nobody knew he had been bought. Wild horses couldn't have torn the secret out of him."

Grimm was suitably astonished and delighted with Veeck's thoughtfulness. "Well, Charlie," said Veeck, "it *is* the birthday present you wanted—a left-handed pitcher."

The grateful manager then started his new acquisition in the second game of that afternoon's doubleheader. Although he lost the game in thirteen innings, Acosta struck out seventeen batters and later proved to be a major factor in the Brewers' American Association pennant drive.

Most Unusual Publisher. J. G. Taylor Spink. One of the most unpredictable men in baseball was *The Sporting News* publisher J. G. Taylor Spink, who reigned as king of baseball journalism through most of the first half of the century. Spink was both amusing and terrifying. He had a habit of waking his correspondents—working newspapermen in the big cities—at all hours of the night. Some loathed him for that, but others loved him. President Franklin Delano Roosevelt wrote Spink a fan letter during World War II. The high commands of the Army, Navy, and Air Force saluted him for getting 400,000 copies of *The Sporting News* to servicemen every week during the war. At a testimonial dinner for Spink in 1960, the Athletic Goods Manufacturers' Association honored

Spink with a Revere bowl as "America's Foremost Sports Publisher."

Colleagues remember Spink for his eccentricities. He was obsessive about punctuality and hard work. Once a member of the staff was two hours late at the office, whereupon Spink demanded an explanation. "I was kept awake all night by a toothache," said the writer, holding his jaw. To which Spink snapped: "If you couldn't sleep, there was no reason for you to be late this morning."

According to Gerald Holland of *Sports Illustrated,* Spink probably fired most of the correspondents who worked for him. In most cases, however, the staff members returned. "When Spink's temper cooled," said Holland, "Spink usually told them a humorous story, by way of indirect apology, and frequently gave them a raise or a gift to assure them that all was forgiven."

When Spink died in 1962, one of the first to arrive at the publisher's funeral was Dan Daniel, the New York correspondent for *The Sporting News.* When someone asked Daniel why he had arrived so early, the reporter replied: "If I hadn't, Spink would have fired me for the forty-first time."

Before the invention of radar, Spink had a knack of detecting his distant correspondents and cartoonists (such as award-winning Willard Mullin of the New York *World-Telegram*) wherever they might be hiding. "Spink," said Mullin, "could get you on the pipe *from* any place, *to* any place, at *any* time."

Once, Mullin was invited by a friend to play golf on a course that he had never seen before. "All was well," Mullin recalled, "until, as we were putting on the sixth green, a messenger came galloping from the clubhouse, tongue hanging out, with the message from Garcia [Spink]. I don't know how the hell he found me but it was him!"

On another occasion, Spink pulled the telephone off his office wall during negotiations to move the Braves from Boston to Milwaukee. The publisher had been calling Lou Perini, one of the principals in the deal, night and day in an attempt to get the scoop. He eventually got the scoop, at the expense of his phone and the wall. After several dozen calls, he phoned Perini one morning and said: "Hello, Lou. This is Taylor."

There then was a pregnant pause.

"Whaddya mean, Taylor who? TAYLOR SPINK."

Then, another pause to consider the question from the other end. "*SPINK*—S-P-I-N-K, you sonofabitch."

At which point the phone was ripped off the wall.

Carl Benkert, former executive for the baseball bat company Hillerich and Bradsby, attended the Kentucky Derby with Spink. "Throughout the preliminary races," said Benkert, "Spink checked the racing form and yelled at people countless times, asking opinions about which horse would win. He even went to the window to buy his own tickets."

Finally, the race began and several companions wondered which horse the publisher eventually selected. When Middleground crossed the finish line first, Spink leaped for joy. "I had him! I had him! I had $100 on his nose!"

The publisher's companions were suitably impressed until Spink's wife, Blanche, turned to her husband and then her friends. "I have news for you. He also had $100 on each of the other thirteen horses in the race!"

Spink either didn't remember or didn't see every one of his correspondents. During a trip to New York in the forties he was heading for Ebbets Field in Brooklyn when he noticed that the taxi driver's license read Thomas Holmes. Spink was curious. "Are you Tommy Holmes, the baseball writer? The one who works for the Brooklyn *Eagle?*"

The cabby's voice turned somewhat surly. "I am not," he replied to Spink. "But some crazy sonofabitch out in St. Louis thinks I am and keeps telephoning at three o'clock in the morning!"

Red Barber, the beloved radio announcer, found a soft spot in the publisher's heart when he visited Spink's office and noticed an out-of-print book on the shelf. Spink gave it to Barber and the broadcaster immediately offered to pay for the prize antique. Spink refused. "What could I do for you?" asked Barber.

A smile crossed Spink's face. "Be my friend," he said.

Most Unusual Alibi by a Ballplayer Caught after Curfew.
Boots Poffenberger, Brooklyn Dodgers. Notorious for his
carousing, Poffenberger played for Brooklyn when Leo
Durocher was manager. Durocher was well aware of
Poffenberger's habits when he obtained him for the
Dodgers, but the manager believed a pep talk could do
the trick. "You're starting out fresh with me," said
Durocher, "so let's forget all the stories I've heard about
you."

All was well with Poffenberger and Durocher until the
Dodgers checked into Philadelphia for a series with the
Phillies. Durocher herded his men into the headquarters,
the Bellevue-Stratford Hotel, and soon discovered that
Poffenberger had reverted to form.

"If you've ever been to the Bellevue-Stratford Hotel,"
said Durocher, "you know that they had a cluster of
clocks above the cashier's desk; a big one with the local
time and smaller ones giving the times in various cities
around the world.

"The first night in Philadelphia, half an hour past midnight, Dodger president Larry MacPhail and I were sitting
in the lobby and somebody almost stepped on my shoe. I
looked up. My new man, Poffenberger.

"In the morning I tapped Mr. Poffenberger's shoulder
and asked him what time he'd come in. 'Eleven o'clock,'
he said.

" 'You're a goddam liar,' I said. 'I was sitting right there
in the lobby and it was twelve-thirty by the clock on the
wall.'

" 'Well,' he said, 'it depends which clock you were
looking at. One of them clocks there said eleven and *that*
was the clock *I* was going by!' "

Most Unusual Victory for a Pitcher. Nick Altrock,
Chicago White Sox, 1906. Without throwing a single
pitch, Altrock was credited with a victory. It happened
after he was summoned to the mound in relief during a
game when the White Sox were in the top of the ninth and

trailing by two runs. The opposition had the bases loaded with two out. As Altrock leaned in for the sign, the runners led off. Suddenly, Altrock wheeled and fired the ball to first, picking off the runner and retiring the side. In the bottom of the ninth, the White Sox rallied to win the game. Since Altrock was the last pitcher for Chicago, he was credited with the win under baseball's scoring rules. The victory was but one of twenty Altrock would produce for the pennant-bound "Hitless Wonders."

(Altrock also is the only major league player to have played in parts of five decades; he was a regular from 1898 to 1932!)

Most Unusual Cleveland Game. Cleveland Indians vs. Brooklyn Robins, World Series, 1920. In the fifth game of the World Series, which the Indians won, 8–1, at Cleveland, a pair of extraordinary events took place. In the first inning history was made when Cleveland right fielder Elmer Smith hit a bases-loaded home run over the right field fence; it was the first of its kind in a World Series game. The second unique episode occurred during a Brooklyn rally in the fifth inning with runners on first and second. Clarence Mitchell was the batter when Robins manager Wilbert Robinson signaled for a hit-and-run play; as soon as Mitchell swung, the runners were to take off. Mitchell did as instructed, belting a searing line drive over second base. Indians second baseman Bill Wambsganss was so far from the base that he appeared unable to make a play for the hit. "But," wrote Harry Cross in *The New York Times,* "Wambsganss leaped over toward the cushion and with a mighty jump speared the ball with one hand." Pete Kilduff, the runner on second, was on his way to third and Miller, the runner from first, was almost within reach of second.

The quick-thinking Wambsganss touched second base, retiring Kilduff who had almost reached third base. Meanwhile, Miller, who was trapped between first and second, appeared mummified by the proceedings and remained transfixed in his tracks. Wambsganss trotted over and tagged Miller for the third out. Thus, the first unassisted triple play was accomplished in the World Series. "The crowd," reported Cross, "forgot it was hoarse of voice and close to nervous exhaustion and gave Wamby just as great a reception as it had given Elmer Smith."

If that wasn't unusual enough, there was the added spectacle of Brooklyn pitcher Burleigh Grimes's humiliation. "No pitcher," wrote Cross, "has ever been kept in the box so long after he had started to slip. Uncle Robbie kept him on the mound for three and two-thirds innings and in that time he was badly plastered for nine hits, including two home runs and a triple. With a half a dozen able-bodied pitchers basking in the warm sun, Grimes was kept in the game until he was so badly battered that the game became a joke." When the score was 7–0 Grimes finally was removed.

In an ironic contrast, Cleveland pitcher Jim Bagby was hailed as a hero even though no pitcher was ever before pounded for thirteen hits in a World Series and emerged a hero. "He pitched," wrote Cross, "what was really a bad game of ball, but when it was over he was proud of it."

Most Unusual Peewee Reese Error. In 1940, while a young Brooklyn Dodgers' shortstop, Reese was asked to do a special favor by Mrs. Dearie Mulvey, one of the Dodgers' owners. Mrs. Mulvey had heard about a crippled teen-ager, Dot DeMars, who was an avid Dodgers fan. Mrs. Mulvey invited the girl to be her guest at Ebbets Field, so that she could meet her favorite player, Reese. Although Reese was hospitalized with an ankle injury at the time, he made a special trip to Ebbets Field for the occasion. After autographing a baseball and inscribing one of Dot's casts "Speedy Recovery," Reese returned to the hospital. He was accompanied by a New York *Daily News* photographer, who was driving, and *News* reporter Mary O'Flaherty, who was sitting between the driver and Reese on the right in the "death seat." On the drive back to the hospital, Reese committed an error that nearly cost him his career, if not his life. As the auto sped along Flatbush Avenue toward the crowded shopping center at Fulton Street, the car swerved.

The door suddenly flew open and Reese—in his cast—appeared about to fall out. "I grabbed hold of Peewee," said Mary O'Flaherty, "while he grabbed shut the door. How different the story of baseball might have been had he fallen out into the busy Flatbush Avenue traffic."

Most Unusual Canadian Player. Mike Goliat, Toronto Maple Leafs. Although he was a rugged son of the Pennsylvania coal mining country, Goliat was adopted by Canadians when he came to play for the Toronto Maple Leafs of the International League in 1947. (He played for the pennant-winning Philadelphia Phillies Whiz Kids in 1950, but returned to the Leafs the following year for an eight-season stint.) "Mike," said Toronto *Star* writer George Gamester, "was one of Toronto's most colorful athletes."

Goliat once hit a ball into a distant corner of Maple Leaf Stadium in Toronto, but was thrown out at third base because he nonchalantly stopped to pick up his cap when it flew off his head on the basepath. Once, in a game against the Havana Sugar Kings, Goliat faced pitcher Emelio Cueche. Because Goliat was more than a fair hitter, Cueche decided to throw Mike an intentional base on balls. Mike disapproved, reached across the plate, and smacked one of Cueche's wide pitches over the right field wall for a home run.

Most Unusual Baseball Collision. September 1944, between New York Giants outfielders Bruce Sloan and Steve Filipowicz. Sloan, the right fielder, was about five feet, nine inches, but he weighed in at close to 200 pounds. A high fly went to right-center field and Bruce took off after it like a roly-poly lightning streak.

Unfortunately for Sloan, center fielder Filipowicz (who later played for the football Giants, just to give you an idea of his size and heft) was implacably parked right under the fly, looking much like the Colossus of Rhodes.
48

Sloan and Filipowicz collided with such force that they literally disappeared in a dust cloud, and when the scene cleared, Sloan had to be carried off the field on a stretcher.

Filipowicz? He merely shrugged slightly at all the fuss!

Football

Best All-Around Effort. T. L. Bayne, the football coach at Louisiana State University, in 1893, was preparing his team for a game against Tulane University when he learned that Tulane needed a coach that day. Bayne volunteered to coach the opposition as well as his own club. Prior to the opening kickoff, Bayne was informed that several other chores had to be done but there were no volunteers. As a result, the ubiquitous Bayne built the goalposts, managed ticket sales, and refereed the match. In that era, before the advent of sports agents, Bayne's compensation for his total effort was one green umbrella.

Best Combined Kickoff-Touchdown Virtuoso. Homer Hazel, Rutgers University, 1923. Playing Villanova University, Hazel launched the game with a kickoff high and deep into the enemy end zone. The kick was fumbled by Villanova and Hazel, who ran the 100 in ten seconds flat, sped downfield and fell on the loose ball in the end zone to give Rutgers a touchdown—only eight seconds after Hazel booted the ball.

Best Handicapped Field-Goal Kicker. Tom Dempsey, Los Angeles Rams. Although he has only half a right arm and half a right foot, Dempsey holds the National Football League record for the longest field goal—63 yards, against the Detroit Lions, November 8, 1970—as a member of the New Orleans Saints. Enabling Dempsey to perform is a special kicking shoe, approved by the league.

Best Football Humor from Hollywood. The four Marx Brothers in *Horsefeathers* (1932). In the finale to this spoof on collegiate life, Chico, Harpo, Groucho, and Zeppo run wild on the gridiron, playing for Huxley University against Darwin College. In one sequence, Harpo gets his revenge on two Darwin players. One he brings down with a flying tackle (although the opponent isn't carrying the ball); the other is victimized while Harpo is simultaneously playing and eating a hot dog. A pileup ensues and Harpo loses his hot dog. He emerges to find one of the Darwin players lying dazed and Harpo simultaneously realizes that his roll is without its hot dog. Revealing a mustard pot in his pocket, Harpo smears mustard on the roll, wraps the roll around the foe's index finger and takes an angry bite.

Commenting on the denouement, critic Allen Eyles observed: "It is Harpo's inventiveness that wins the game for Huxley. He spreads banana skins behind him, attaches elastic to the ball, and otherwise makes a great effort until something more vital—a loose dog—takes his attention. Harpo leaps into his chariot with his brothers and races up the field. At the far end he finds time to unload some footballs behind the goal, raising the Huxley score with each of them."

Best Hedge Against a Defeat. From 1950 through 1954, the Brooklyn College football team played some of the worst football ever seen anywhere. Normally, the Brooklyn College band would swing into a chorus of the school's vibrant victory march whenever the BC eleven scored a touchdown. But, in 1951, when Brooklyn's team was at its worst, the college band altered its traditional post-touchdown victory march practice and blared the victory march whenever the BC club *made a first down.* "At that," said Bernard Rappaport, a trombonist in the band, "we rarely were called upon to play."

Best Touchdown Ploy. Phil Summers, Green River (Wyoming) High School. During a game against Evanston (Wyoming) High School, Summers, the Green River quarterback, lined up behind his center. Suddenly, he turned to the referee and asked: "Haven't we got a five-yard penalty on this?" Before the official could reply, Summers took the ball from his center and began stepping off the yardage against Evanston. Except Summers never stopped; until he had reached the end zone—71 yards away. The touchdown scored proved to be the margin of victory as Green River won the game, 20–13. Green River coach Jerry McMillan said that Summers had pestered him for months to try the play. "But I didn't think it would work," added the coach.

Best Effort by a Running Back. Leo Schlick of St. Viator College in Indiana. Quick would be an understatement for Schlick who once scored 100 points—including 12 touchdowns—on an afternoon in 1916.

Best Short Explanation by a Losing Coach. Jack Fouts, Ohio Wesleyan. Following a 72–0 defeat by Bucknell, Fouts was confronted by reporters who demanded an explanation of the rout. "Well," said Fouts, "we just weren't up for this one." End of interview.

Best Newspaper Story. Grantland Rice, New York *Sun,* October 19, 1924. Writing about Notre Dame's backfield of Don Miller, Elmer Layden, Harry Stuldreher, and Jim Crowley, Rice opened his article: "Outlined against a blue-gray October sky, the Four Horsemen rode again."

The piece not only immortalized Rice but did wonders for Miller and company. At a dinner honoring the Horsemen, Miller explained what the story had done for them. "Granny," said Miller to Rice, "Rock [coach Knute

Rockne] put us together in the same backfield, but the day you wrote us up as the Four Horsemen, you conferred on us immortality that gold could never buy. Let's face it—we were good, sure. But we'd have been just as dead two years after graduation as any other backfield if you hadn't painted that tag line on us.

"It's twenty-nine years since we played. Each year we run faster, block better, score more touchdowns than ever! The older we are, the younger we become—in legend. Another thing. In business, that tag line has opened more doors, has meant more to us in associations, warmth, friendship, and revenue than you'll ever know."

Best Pep Talk by a Coach. Bob Zuppke, University of Illinois, 1916. Preparing for a game against the University of Minnesota, Zuppke learned that his club had been rated a 40-point underdog. When the Illinois players gathered in the dressing room for the pregame briefing, Zuppke strode to the front of the clubhouse and confronted his athletes.

A hush fell over the room as Zuppke intoned: "I am Louis XIV and you are my court. After us, the deluge!" At that point the players cheered, although they knew not what. Zuppke continued:

"Today, I want you to have some fun. Get beaten one hundred to nothing, if you want to, but have fun . . . I want to tell you something. I've had this great team scouted. On the first play 'Galloping' Sprafka will take the ball. I want eleven of my men to tackle Sprafka. On the next play big Anderson will take the ball. I want all eleven of you guys to tackle Anderson!"

"But," piped up one of the Illini skeptics, "suppose somebody else takes the ball. What then?"

Zuppke stared down the lone doubter and replied: "Then *I'll* tackle him!"

Illinois won the game, 14–9.

Best Impromptu Poem. Herman Hickman. The former player at Tennessee, and later line coach for Army and head coach at Yale, was one of the most erudite football instructors. En route to Philadelphia for the Army-Navy game in 1946, Hickman was asked by Pete Dolan of the New York *Sun* to predict a winner of the annual classic.

Instead of merely reeling off a score, Hickman broke into a string of verse, delivered, according to his companion, "with meticulous inflection."

Vibrantly, Hickman expounded:

> "Though much is taken, much abides; and though
> We are not that strength which in old days
> Moved earth and heaven, that which we are, we
>   are—
> One equal temper of heroic hearts,
> Made weak by time and fate, but strong in will
> To strive, to seek, to find and not to yield."

Hickman has never been equaled among football players for his ability to quote Tennyson's "Ulysses" verbatim, on the spot.

Best Debater. Fielding "Hurry Up" Yost, University of Michigan coach. Notorious for his inability to hear the other person, Yost is remembered for his ability to sustain marathon arguments without fear of exhaustion.

"Once," recalled Grantland Rice, dean of sports journalists, "I met Yost and another coach [engaged] in a violent debate in the lobby of a New York hotel at around 5:00 P.M. I was going to a football party. When I left for home at about 2:00 A.M. they were still involved in the same wordy argument.

"I asked the other coach why he had hung around for seven hours. 'I was trying to get in a word,' he said. 'Just one word.'

"Yost was the most serious man I ever knew. Another time I was hunting wild turkey and quail with him in the east Tennessee mountains one year, around 1908. We started home after dark. We had to ford a shallow, swift-running river. About halfway across, I slipped on a rock and was dumped in the river. I kept yelling, but he never
54

heard me. He was clear across, driving for home, when he first missed me, still unable to make headway against the rocks or current. Finally, Yost realized I was missing. He returned, picked me up, and went on talking as if nothing had ever happened."

Best Undefeated Streak. Washington University, 1907–1917. Although the 1972 team of the Miami Dolphins has received considerable coverage for their unblemished 17–0 record, the Washington University football team went a full decade without defeat, accumulating 59 victories and four ties in 63 games, beginning in 1907 and ending in 1917.

Best Teetotaling Coach. Howard Jones, University of Southern California. Serious to a fault, the ultracerebral Jones coached football on the West Coast in the early 1900s. He prided himself on the fact that he loathed "Demon Rum" as much as W. C. Fields loved it. Once, a rival coach suggested that, despite Jones's success, he would be a still better coach if he indulged in a nip or two. "I never heard of a drink yet figuring out a play," Jones snapped.

The somewhat perturbed rival warned Jones that two drinks had just inspired him to develop three new plays which he later used successfully. The plays worked, but Jones was militantly unimpressed, and never wavered from his endorsement of nothing more potent than one proof buttermilk.

Best Disciplinarian. Percy Haughton, Harvard. In the pre–Vince Lombardi era, the prime perfectionist was the coach of Harvard, who believed that obedience is no heavy task, especially when a few yards, here or there, were involved. Once, Sam Felton, a Harvard end and left-footed kicker, was instructed by Haughton to deliver a 40-yard kickoff.

Felton moved into position, began his forward thrust, and booted the ball 60 yards, a rather effective and normally commendable kick. However, Haughton promptly gave Felton the hook—he was taken out of the lineup.

When the puzzled Felton asked for an explanation, he got it: "I told you to kick 40 yards," said the furious coach. "The ends can cover at that distance. Forty yards doesn't mean 39 yards or 41 yards. It means 40 yards!"

Best Upset to End a College Football Unbeaten Streak. Army vs. Columbia, 1947. One of the best defensive teams of the post–World War II era, Army had won its first four games of the 1947 season without allowing a single point by the opposition. The Cadets shut out Virginia Tech and Colorado by identical 40–0 scores, then defeated Villanova, 13–0, and played a scoreless tie with Illinois. Their unbeaten streak had been extended to thirty-two games. Army's next opponent would be Columbia, which entered the game with a mediocre, 2–2 record, the last two being losses to Yale and Penn. Prior to the Army-Columbia game, *The New York Times* commented: "There should be plenty of excitement and probably a good deal of scoring with the West Pointers accounting for most of it."

By halftime Army was ahead, 20–7. "The Cadets," the *Times* reporter wrote, "battered Columbia almost at will." The third quarter was scoreless, but Columbia showed signs of a revival. Paced by the passing combination of Eugene Rossides and Bill Swiacki, the Lions roared in the final quarter. Swiacki, who finished the day with eight catches, made a spectacular diving, sliding reception of a Rossides pass to cut the margin to 20–14. A few minutes later Swiacki nabbed a 26-yard pass which moved the ball to Army's three-yard line.

Just two plays were required for the Lions to run the ball over the goal line. The extra point was good and Columbia held fast to upset the Cadets, 21–20, ending Army's unbeaten streak at thirty-two games.

Best Shutout (College). Georgia Tech 222, Cumberland 0, October 7, 1916. Tech scored 63 points in the
56

first quarter, 63 in the second quarter, 54 in the third quarter, and 42 in the final quarter. Cumberland experienced difficulty reaching the line of scrimmage. There were, however, extenuating circumstances. Charles Warwick, a Palm Beach, Florida, attorney who played for Cumberland, once explained the roots of the rout.

"The president of Cumberland had written to Georgia Tech seeking a football game, and Tech replied that if Cumberland wanted to play on October 7, 1916, a check for $3,000 would have to be deposited as forfeit money in case Cumberland did not place a team on the field.

"Well, the check was mailed to Tech, with the understanding that it would be held until October 7. Not much was thought about it until next September when it appeared that, with war clouds gathering, Cumberland might not have a football team.

"One day a group of us senior law students were called over to the law dean's office and told about the agreement with Georgia Tech. A committee was appointed to study the exchange of letters and determine whether $3,000 actually had to be forfeited in case the game was not played.

"We of the committee decided that it was a binding contract. Obviously, the next thing to do was to try to get together a football team. Not necessarily a team for the whole season, but a team to 'place on the field' against Tech in Atlanta. We put lots of faith in that clause 'place on the field.' There was nothing in the contract requiring the team to play.

"We rounded up exactly fifteen players, but the truth is that we didn't practice a single game. We got Ernest McQueen, a Cumberland law student who played at Vanderbilt in 1913, to agree to go along as coach. But he wouldn't wear a uniform. He must have known something!

"George Allen, another Cumberland law student, went along as manager of the team. His job, upon our arrival in Atlanta, was to advise Georgia Tech that Cumberland was placing a team on the field, was carrying out its end of the contract. Also, George, being a persuasive fellow, was to seek out Tech's head coach, John Heisman, explain our situation, and request that the quarters be shortened to ten minutes. Heisman would have none of that. He said they had to be fifteen minutes.

"That afternoon, after Tech had scored 18 touchdowns on us in the first half, the quarters *were* shortened. Tech did use two platoons, something we had never heard of. Later we were told that a steak dinner had been promised to the unit that scored the most points."

Despite the overwhelming defeat, Cumberland's football team celebrated with an impromptu fete on the train home. "There were, after all, no serious injuries," Warwick recalled. "And back in Lebanon we remained heroes of a sort for a long time. After all, we saved the school that $3,000!"

Best Blunder. Roy "Wrong Way" Riegels, Rose Bowl, 1929. A lineman with the University of California, Riegels recovered a Georgia Tech fumble and appeared to be in good position to reach the enemy goal line 30 yards away. But, suddenly, Riegels' radar went awry and he whipped around, heading for his *own* end zone. In the definitive "Wrong Way" excursion (to be matched nine years later by pilot Douglas "Wrong Way" Corrigan, who flew from New York to Ireland, believing that he was flying to California), Riegels sprinted all the way to his own two-yard line before being tackled by a teammate.

Riegels' miscarriage of traffic flow stunned the audience, which included broadcaster Graham McNamee who shouted, as Riegels crossed the 50-yard line: "What's the matter with me? Am I crazy?"

The Chicago Tribune reported the *faux pas* as follows: ". . . there was a hush. Riegels had whipped about-face and was starting his historic dash—69 and a half yards in the wrong direction!

"Riegels is a lineman—a center. And centers aren't supposed to be the fastest of runners. But Riegels was grasping at the stuff of which heroes are made. He sprinted like one possessed. Benny Lom (the teammate who, eventually, caught him) was among the first to see that the bottom had fallen out of the world. He tried to overtake Riegels, shouting frantically the while. But the center outran him until he was just about to cross his own goal line. Then Lom pulled Riegels down with a Herculean tug at the latter's arm. The ball was down six inches from California's goal.

"Riegels moved, a dejected, pitiful figure, to the sidelines after the [Georgia Tech] scoring play. Onlookers thought he had been withdrawn, but it was revealed later that he had wanted to leave the Rose Bowl forthwith.

"But teammates wouldn't have it. Eventually the captain-elect yielded to their entreaties, and when the whistle blew for the start of the second half, California's greatest goat was in there battling for all his life was worth."

The final score was Georgia Tech 8–7 over California.

Today, Riegels, a grandfather of six, runs his own fruit business in Woodland, California. How does he feel about the famed gaffe after all these years?

"Never lost any sleep over it," he laughed. "I just got a bit confused because the teams had just changed ends after the first quarter. I'm not ashamed of the mistake— at least I was trying."

Best Rose Bowl Performance. Michigan vs. Stanford, 1889. Using only eleven players, Michigan won the game, 49–0. Although the game was cut short six minutes, out of mercy to the vanquished, Michigan gained 1,463 yards on 142 plays. Forward passing was not yet in vogue.

Best Collegiate Coach. Amos Alonzo Stagg, University of Chicago. Spanning the nineteenth and twentieth centuries, Stagg began his career in the 1880s and was involuntarily retired by Chicago at the age of seventy in 1933, whereupon Stagg took a job at College of the Pacific. When he was eighty-one years old, Stagg was named "coach of the year." He remained coach at College of the Pacific a total of fourteen years and was retired again.

Employing a bit of reverse nepotism, Stagg found himself still another coaching job, working for his son Amos Alonzo Stagg, Jr., at Susquehanna University. This time the elder Stagg worked for six years as the club's offensive coach.

When the old man's wife took sick, he left his son to be with his ailing wife, but eventually returned to coach again at Stockton (California) College. When Stagg was ninety-eight years young, he retired for the last time as a football coach. He died four years later at the age of one hundred and two.

Stagg's record at Chicago was 254 wins, 104 losses, and 28 ties. He had four unbeaten teams (1899, 1905, 1908, 1913) and twelve of his clubs lost only one game. Apart from his coaching proficiency, Stagg was revered for his unwavering honesty. Once, he was asked to referee a game in which his own team was playing. Another time, Stagg insisted that the game officials call back a Chicago touchdown. He pointed out that one of his players had committed a foul which had gone unnoticed by the referee.

Best Touchdown Run. Wyllys Terry, Yale University, November 5, 1884. At a time when a football field measured 110 yards from goal line to goal line, Yale went on offense against Wesleyan on the Eli goal line. Terry accepted the shift from center at a point five yards deep in his own end zone. The Yale tacklers went to work opening up gaps in the Wesleyan line and Terry zigzagged his way 115 yards for a touchdown.

Best Cold-Weather Game. National Football League Championship, 1965, Green Bay Packers vs. Dallas Cowboys. The thermometer registered −14° at opening kickoff in Green Bay. Trailing, 17–14, with 4:54 remaining, the Packers had the ball on their own 32-yard line, but the cold had become numbing to the players. "It was terrible out there," said Cowboys coach Tom Landry, "terrible for both sides." Green Bay next moved into Dallas territory where Packers quarterback Bart Starr threw two passes for a first down on the Cowboys' 30-yard line with only
60

1:35 remaining. Green Bay kept advancing and, with 30 seconds left, moved to the Dallas one-yard line.

Twice, Green Bay's Donny Anderson slipped on the frozen field and the Packers were compelled to use their two remaining time-outs. Now only 16 seconds remained; time for one more play. Green Bay coach Vince Lombardi rejected the idea of a field goal: "The people in the stands didn't want to sit around in the cold any longer." What followed was one of the most famous quarterback sneaks in football history. Starr took the ball just inside guard Jerry Kramer who was blocking all-pro Jethro Pugh for the winning touchdown. He scored and Green Bay won a record third consecutive NFL championship.

Best Passing Performance in a Single Game. Norm Van Brocklin, Los Angeles Rams, vs. New York Yankees, Yankee Stadium, September 28, 1951. In the early fifties the Rams were suffering a quarterbacking "problem." Their dilemma was which of two outstanding pass throwers they should use—Bob Waterfield or Norm Van Brocklin. Waterfield had been the league's leading passer in 1946 and 1951 while Van Brocklin was the National Football League's best in 1950, 1952, and 1954.

Waterfield, who started in 1951, was injured and unable to play on September 28, for a Friday night game against the Yankees in New York. Van Brocklin stepped in and picked up 554 yards via the airwaves. The Rams gained a total 735 yards of which Van Brocklin's passes for touchdowns spanned 46, 47, 26, and one yard, respectively, to the league's leading receiver, "Crazy Legs" Hirsch. Another one, for 67 yards, was delivered to "Vitamin" T. Smith. Despite the effort it was not Van Brocklin but Waterfield who emerged as the top passer in the league that season; yet Van Brocklin threw the winning touchdown—a 73-yard effort—to Tom Fears in the NFL championship game.

Best Jewish Coach. Sid Gillman, San Diego Chargers, 1960–69. Gillman, one of the greatest coaches in the history of professional football, had the San Diegans in the American Football League championship game five times in their first six years. He also has the second best won-loss record in AFL history, behind only Hank Stram, now coach of the New Orleans Saints.

"Gillman's coaching was important," says the NFL's *Official Encyclopedia of Pro Football*. "He was the only original AFL coach with NFL head-coaching experience —but his organizational genius was even more important. As he had always done, Sid surrounded himself with talented assistants that soon were being sought by rival clubs."

Gillman built a young team around standouts like quarterback John Hadl, tackle Ron Mix, end Lance Alworth, and fullback Keith Lincoln. The Chargers became the best offensive team in the AFL, a league whose trademark was offense.

Gillman already had established his winning credentials after several successful seasons at the University of Miami of Ohio and the University of Cincinnati. From there he went on to coach the Los Angeles Rams, who had actively sought him out in one of the most exhaustive coach hunts in football history. Gillman proved he was able to coach in the pros by guiding the Rams to the NFL's Western Division championship in his first term of office. He stayed with the Rams five years—the team had five head coaches in the eleven years before Gillman—and this too was considered a fair barometer of his ability.

Gillman coached the Chargers until 1969, when ill health forced his retirement. He attempted a comeback a few years later, but again had to resign due to health reasons.

Best Lineman. William Walter "Pudge" Heffelfinger, Yale. At six feet, two inches, 200 pounds, Heffelfinger was regarded as one of the fastest big men ever to play football. Among his numerous nicknames, the most applicable was "One Man Army" because of his ability to break up plays single-handedly. During his four-year collegiate career, Heffelfinger played fifty-two complete

90-minute games of which only two were defeats. Heffelfinger was thrice (1889, 1890, 1891) All-American and has been selected to every all-time, all-star roster, the only man ever so honored.

Best Missed Curfew Squelch. Notre Dame quarterback Jim Crowley. Aware that his team was regulated by a midnight curfew, Crowley nevertheless left his room a few minutes before midnight, heading for the local tavern. As he turned the corner, Crowley came face to face with the University's dean of discipline. Noting that it now was two minutes before midnight, the dean wondered whether the sophomore quarterback realized that he soon was due back in his room. "Not until 12 o'clock," said Crowley.

"Do you think you can make it?" asked the dean.

Crowley thought for a moment and then grinned: "Not against this wind, father!"

Best Dentures. "Biter" Jones, Washington University. Notorious for his undershot jaw, Jones's bite was bigger than his bark, which was rather impressive, too. Jones was a guard under coach Jim Conzelman who seemed more amused than angry over Biter's primitive tactics. In fact, Jones thought nothing of chomping on the enemy. "His unusual jaw," said Conzelman, "gave Jones an advantage once he got hold of someone with his mouth. He bit eleven guards, two centers, and a flanker back, but he only lost 65 yards through penalties."

Jones was voted to the Missouri Valley All-Star Team for three consecutive seasons. "He was," said Conzelman, "one of the finest guards I have ever coached. The only criticism he ever got was when the Sigma Chi fraternity broke his pledge for snapping at a house mother."

Best Squelch by a Referee. Jim Durfee, National Football League referee. During a game involving the Chicago Cardinals, Durfee noticed Cardinals coach Milan Creighton shouting illegal instructions at his players. Durfee called a penalty and began walking off the 10 yards against the Cardinals.

"What's that for, Jim?" Creighton demanded.

"That's for coaching from the sidelines," the referee shouted back.

Creighton raised his decibel count: "You don't know what you're doing and that proves it. The penalty for illegal coaching is 15 yards."

"I *know* it," said Durfee, "but the kind of coaching you do is only worth ten yards."

Best Description of a Pass Receiver. W. C. "Bill" Heinz, New York *Sun*. While covering the Columbia University upset victory over Army in 1948, Heinz marveled at the pass reception of Columbia's Bill Swiacki. "That boy," wrote Heinz, "catches passes the way the rest of us catch colds. He knows where he gets some of them, and others he just picks up in crowds."

Best Example of Honesty. Frank Szymanski, Notre Dame University. Testifying in court, Szymanski was asked several questions about his background by the judge, who sought to establish the witness's credibility.

The dialogue went as follows:

> JUDGE: Are you on the Notre Dame football team?
> SZYMANSKI: Yes, Your Honor.
> JUDGE: What position do you play?
> SZYMANSKI: Center, Your Honor.
> JUDGE: How good a center are you?
> SZYMANSKI: Judge, I'm the best center Notre Dame ever had.

Coach Frank Leahy, who was in the gallery, encountered his center after the trial and berated him for his immodesty. "How could you ever stand up there and make a public statement like that?"

Unruffled, Szymanski replied: "I'll admit, Coach, that it was a bit unusual. But, bear in mind, I *was* under oath!"

Best Rivalry. Ohio State University vs. University of Michigan. The intensity of this rivalry is best depicted by an episode that took place on an island in the South Pacific being contested by the American marines and their Japanese counterparts in World War II.

Japanese intelligence included several soldiers who had studied in the United States prior to the war and were acutely aware of the various football rivalries. In battles, they occasionally attempted to exploit these rivalries, utilizing a curious kind of trickery.

The idea was to employ a ruse that would expose the marines to the Japanese fire. One fully armed enemy soldier came running, on this day, toward the marines' line, shouting: "Don't shoot, I'm from Ohio State!"

A marine promptly shot the Japanese attacker, concluding with the retort: "Too bad, bud, I'm from Michigan!"

Best Bad Block. Ron Drziecki, Marquette. Playing against Cincinnati, Drziecki leveled an opposing lineman with a devastatingly perfect block. When the dust had cleared, Drziecki turned to his quarterback, Shockey, and, with a wide grin, requested his critical opinion of the block. Anticipating a rave review, Drzieski was stunned to the core when Shockey shot back: "It was great . . . but, Ron, you were supposed to carry the ball on that play."

Best Prospective Classical Music Halftime Show. At the request of the bureau of symphony music at the Kremlin, composer Dmitri Shostakovich is writing an opus called "Footballistic Symphony."

Best Presidential Birthday Present. John F. Kennedy, renowned as an enthusiastic football fan, recalled his twenty-first birthday. "It wasn't so significant to me as the day that I became eligible to vote, but, rather, as the day Michigan's great Tom Harmon scored 21 points in the first half of a game against California."

Best Put-down of Collegiate Football. Cornell University President Andrew Dickson White. Before Cornell had become a football power, White received a request from the student body to permit Cornell to play Michigan in Cleveland, Ohio. In rejecting the request, President White said: "I will not permit thirty men to travel 400 miles merely to agitate a bag of wind!"

Best Concise Evaluation of a Tackle. Coach Bob Zuppke, University of Illinois. Having infused his tacklers with the notion that the more violent the collision with the enemy the better, Zuppke was approached by one of his more zealous disciples following an intrasquad scrimmage. The player asked the coach whether he had seen the last tackle executed by the player. "Son," Zuppke replied, "I don't look at tackles, I *listen* to them!"

Best Rushing Team. Buffalo Bills, 1973. Led by running back O. J. Simpson, who gained 2,003 yards, the National Football League Bills totalled 3,088 yards gained.

Best Professional Punter. "Slingin'" Sammy Baugh, Washington Redskins. One of pro football's best quarterbacks, Baugh, ironically, never played on a National Football League championship team. During his sixteen-year NFL career, he delivered 338 punts for an average of 45.1 yards.

Best Field-Goal Blocker. R. C. Owens, Baltimore Colts. Originally a member of the San Francisco Forty-Niners, Owens was a proficient basketball player, specializing in grand leaps. While playing for San Francisco, Owens was urged to act as a "goaltender" for the Forty-Niners by blocking potential field goals; however, the idea never was accepted by the Forty-Niners' high command.

Upon being traded to the Baltimore Colts, Owens was asked by coach Weeb Ewbank whether he would be willing to try goaltending against a field-goal attempt. The grand experiment was tried in a match with the

Washington Redskins. Bob Khayat of Washington made the attempt from the Colts' 40-yard line.

As the football completed its arc and began descending toward the goalposts, Owens sprang skyward, his arms stretching to their limits. He blocked the ball, preventing the field goal in the first such "save" in football history.

Worst "Game of the Century." Notre Dame vs. Army, November 10, 1946. The rivalry between Army and Notre Dame has been one of the most consistently exciting football collisions of the century. During World War II, however, the Fighting Irish hit a dreadful slump, losing to Army, 59–0 and 48–0, respectively, in 1944 and 1945. But Notre Dame strengthened its squad in 1946 and, because of that, the match-up between the colleges that year was billed by promoters as "The Game of the Century." It would be played at cavernous Yankee Stadium, where seats were being scalped as high as $200 per ticket. Allison Danzig of *The New York Times* wrote: "Every element that goes into the mounting of the perfect dramatic offering is found in this showdown between the two top-ranking teams in the country, both unbeaten and dead-even in the wagering."

The Cadets' most potent players were the backfield team of Felix "Doc" Blanchard and Glenn Davis. Notre Dame countered with quarterback Johnny Lujack (hampered by an injured ankle). Professional bettors had listed the game as a "pick-em" contest and most observers believed that Army's "Touchdown Twins" (Davis and Blanchard) and Notre Dame's highly acclaimed offense would produce a high-scoring match.

In what evolved as collegiate football's biggest buildup to a letdown, the teams played to a 0–0 tie. Davis was held to just 30 yards gained in seventeen carries. Blanchard, who had been the terror of the gridiron in other games, managed only 50 yards in eighteen attempts. Danzig commented: "For the first time in three seasons of uninterrupted and overpowering success against 25 opponents, Blanchard and Davis, the celebrated Mister Inside and Mister Outside, found themselves shackled and crushed to earth like ordinary mortals throughout their full 60 minutes of devotion and duty."

Worst Embarrassment for the NFL. Nineteen years before "Broadway" Joe Namath and the New York Jets upset the Baltimore Colts and the NFL's claim to superiority in Super Bowl III, another upstart did the same to the champions of the league which even then considered itself invincible.

This upsetter was the Cleveland Browns, champions of the All-America Football Conference, which had been absorbed by the NFL after four years of not-so-friendly competition. The upsetee was the NFL champion Philadelphia Eagles.

The contest was scheduled for the first Saturday of the 1950 season, one day before the regular league schedule was to begin. It was ballyhooed as "the game of the century," the contest that was to put the new kid on the block in its proper place.

"That game," recalled Paul Brown, founder and coach of the Browns, "wasn't really a sporting proposition for the Eagles. The press and the public said we were going to get whipped, 50–0, and this would take a little doing when we had guys like [QB] Otto Graham, [FB] Marion Motley and [receivers] Dante Lavelli, Mac Speedie and Dub Jones.

"Besides," Brown continued, "this was the highest emotional game I ever coached. We had four years of constant ridicule to get ready!"

However, sentiment and logic still were with the powerful Eagles and their marvelous 5–4 defense. A capacity crowd of more than 71,000 jammed Philadelphia Municipal Stadium to witness the execution.

However, it did not go according to plan. By halftime the Browns led, 14–3; after the third quarter it was 21–3 and the game ended 35–10, Cleveland! The Eagles were unable to stop Graham's passing attack. The great Otto threw three early touchdown passes—a 41-yarder to

Jones, 26 yards to Lavelli, and a 13-yarder to Speedie—literally bombing the Eagles out of their once-secure nest.

"We never met a spot-passing program as they had," marveled Eagles defensive back Russ Craft. "We would be on top of the receivers, but they caught the ball anyway because the pass was so well timed."

To make matters worse for the Eagles and the NFL, the Browns beat Philadelphia in the late-season rematch, 13–7, and went on to win the NFL championship in their first year in the supposedly more powerful league, dumping the vaunted Los Angeles Rams, 30–28!

Worst Passing Coach. Gil Dobie, Cornell University, 1925. An ultraconservative among collegiate coaches, Dobie alternately worked for the University of Washington, Navy, and Cornell. He loathed the forward pass and operated on the theory that football offense consisted of plunges through the center and end runs. Passing on Dobie's teams was *verboten*. One Saturday afternoon in 1925, Dobie's Cornell team faced Dartmouth and was trounced, 62–13. Most of the winner's points were gained via forward passes.

Militantly unimpressed, Dobie insisted after the game: "Well, we won, 13–0."

"What about Dartmouth's 62 points?" asked sportswriter Grantland Rice.

Scowling and utterly serious, Dobie replied: "I don't count those scores made by passing. That isn't football!"

Worst Mauling in the Pits. Jim Tatum, University of North Carolina. Badly bruised during his rookie season, Tatum sought advice from veteran end Erwin Walker. "Well," Walker promised, "I'll tip off the official to watch what's happening to you. Then, you call this guy across from you a name. He's sure to slug you and they'll be penalized 15 yards. You're willing to take just one sock in the nose for the old alma mater, aren't you, Jim?"

Tatum agreed and got down on the line. He snarled at his opposite, calling him a big so-and-so. "Bang,"

Tatum recalled, "the guy let me have it." In a split second Tatum was rendered horizontal. Eventually, he clambered to his feet and asked Walker what had happened.

"We scored on the play," Walker revealed, "and had to decline the penalty."

Worst College Team. St. Paul's Poly (Virginia), 1947–53. During a period of six years, St. Paul's lost forty-one consecutive games. Their most disastrous sequence included a run of contests in which St. Paul's was outscored 890–0.

Worst Injured Player. Jerry Kramer, Green Bay Packers. *Before* he became a professional football player, Kramer already had suffered the following injuries: an ax slipped from his grip and sliced his hand; he was cut on the side of his body by an electric lathe; his fingers were disabled by a shotgun blast; he suffered a chipped vertebra. After reaching the National Football League, Kramer suffered a detached retina, broke an ankle, and, in 1965, underwent surgery for removal of a large growth in the gut. During the operation, holes were discovered in his intestines, the remnants of wood splinters left there after he had been hit by the jagged edge of a plank as a youth.

Worst Paid Attendance for College Game. Pullman, Washington, November 12, 1955, Washington State vs. San Jose State. Total paid attendance: one.

Worst Year for Football. 1905. In that season 33 people died as a result of football injuries and 246 were injured. As a result, the NCAA modified the rules and three years later the death list was lowered to 18 deaths and 154 major injuries.

Worst Day for a Professional Team. September 10, 1967. The Denver Broncos lost to the Oakland Raiders in Oakland, 51–0. Denver's yards gained total was minus five, a professional record.

Worst Tackle. Cotton Bowl, 1954. Tommy Lewis of Alabama, seeing Dick Moegle of Rice race unmolested along the sidelines, leaped off the bench to tackle his opponent. Assuming that Moegle would have scored a touchdown had he not been interfered with by Lewis, the referee picked up the ball and carried it the rest of the way to the goal line. Rice won, 28–6.

Worst Reaction to a Mistake. Denny Clark, University of Michigan, 1905. Attempting to run back a punt against the University of Chicago, Clark was tackled behind the goal line for a safety. As a result, Michigan lost the game, 2–0. One newspaper carried a headline: CLARK 2, MICHIGAN 0. Because of his *faux pas,* Clark was ostracized by classmates and quit college a week after the incident. He retired to the north woods where he spent many years as a recluse.

Worst Upset (College). Rose Bowl, 1934, Columbia University 7, Stanford 0. *The New York Times* offered the following report on the game:

". . . a season marked by many reverses was climaxed by probably the greatest upset of them all.

"Surging through a drizzling, disheartening rain to a one-touchdown lead in the second period, the Lions four times thrust back the furious onslaught of Stanford's backfield of Grayson, Hamilton, Van Dellin, and the rest of the Stanford superbacks in the last-half struggle.

"Sixteen first downs for Stanford, 6 for Columbia; 272 yards gained for Stanford, 114 yards for Columbia; and six scoring chances for the Cardinals, three for the Lions. But that scoreboard read, Columbia 7, Stanford 0 at the finish. . . ."

Worst Shutout (Professional). Washington Redskins, December 8, 1940, Griffith Stadium, Washington, D.C. Chicago Bears 73, Redskins 0. Meeting for the National

Football League championship, both Washington and Chicago appeared to be formidable foes. The Redskins were powered by ace passer "Slingin'" Sammy Baugh. His Chicago counterpart was Sid Luckman, an Old Blue from Columbia University. "The weather was perfect," wrote Arthur Daley in *The New York Times*. "So were the Bears. In the most fearsome display of power ever seen on the gridiron, the Monsters of the Midway won before 36,034 stunned and deriding fans."

Chicago scored before the game was a minute old. At the start of the second half it took the Bears only 54 seconds to score. What surprised the oddsmakers was the fact that only three weeks earlier Washington had beaten Chicago, 7–3. The Bears' coach, this time, used every eligible man on his squad (thirty-three) of which fifteen had a share of the scoring. As added humiliation, Chicago even passed for one point after a touchdown.

Luckman launched the attack with precision passes in the first half. "No field general," wrote Arthur Daley, "ever called plays more artistically or engineered a touchdown parade in more letter-perfect fashion. Redskin fans who had watched their heroes win their first seven games of the league season could not believe their eyes.

"So one-sided was the match that press box critics could not single out any of the Redskins players for praise. There was no Redskin hero outside of coach Ray Flaherty, who had to sit on the bench and absorb it all, too much a beating for so fine a gentleman and coach. At the end the Redskin band played 'Should Auld Acquaintance Be Forgot?' If said acquaintance is the Chicago Bears, it should be forgot immediately."

Worst Team (Professional). Chicago Cardinals, 1942–45. The Cards, later to move to St. Louis, dipped to an infamous depth in the period from 1942 to 1945, setting a National Football League record of twenty-nine consecutive losses. When it came to an unimpressive string of losses for a shorter span, the Brooklyn Dodgers of 1942–43 deserve dubious recognition. They lost six consecutive games by shutouts.

Worst Individual Tragedy. Knute Rockne, coach, Notre Dame, March 31, 1931. One of the most revered and inspirational leaders in sport, Rockne molded Notre Dame into one of the nation's most potent football powers. At the peak of his career, Rockne was killed along with seven others when a Transcontinental & Western airplane crashed in Kansas. Typical of the shocked reactions was that of Boston *Post* sportswriter Bill Cunningham who sat down at his typewriter and banged out the following: "This piece is written by a fellow who couldn't be more dazed if he had been belted between the eyes with a poleaxe . . . Rock dead? He can't be. Guys like him don't die."

Worst Uniforms. Although today's football uniforms are brightly colored—the better to transmit on national color TV—the outfits worn by the Denver Broncos when they first entered the American Football League in 1960 were horrible.

The jerseys were a rusty color and the pants a dirty orange—an odd combination. But the real highlight—or lowlight—of the uniforms, were the socks. Instead of horizontal stripes of a contrasting color, they were *vertical*, and made the players appear to be wearing clown suits.

"They were so comical and disgusting," said one former Bronco, "that several players seriously wanted to go out there and play barefoot."

"They were so hideous," said one observer, "that Bronco head coach Jack Faulkner, on hearing that the team was going to get new uniforms, took all the socks and burned them in a public ceremony."

———

Most Unusual Championship Game. Chicago Bears vs. Portsmouth Spartans, 1932. Although the official NFL championship game series was not begun until the following year, a bizarre contest was played between these two teams for the championship of the National Football League—*indoors!*

The game, a tiebreaker between the two clubs, who had finished the regular season tied for first place, originally had been scheduled for uncovered Wrigley Field, but frightful −30° weather and a howling snowstorm cancelled the traditional plans. The only other place to play in Chicago was Chicago Stadium, an indoor arena, used primarily for horse shows and exhibitions.

The Stadium seemed to be the answer, so both parties agreed to it. The game was played on a field only 80 yards long and ten yards too narrow. To compensate for the intimacy, the players agreed to bring the ball in ten yards from the sidelines and to place the goalposts, which previously had stood on the end line, on the goal line to minimize the danger of running headfirst into the wooden wall which surrounded the playing field!

Both players and fans agreed that the changes opened up the game, making it more exciting, and they soon were adopted permanently. The game itself was a defensive struggle with a highly controversial finish. Chicago scored the only points in the game in the fourth quarter, when, after failing to run the ball in from two yards out, fullback Bronko Nagurski faked into the line, then passed to the immortal Red Grange for a touchdown. Portsmouth players objected, charging that the passer had not been the required five yards behind the line of scrimmage; nevertheless, the touchdown was allowed. The Bears later added a safety and beat the Spartans—later to be moved to Detroit where they would become the Lions—9–0.

Most Unusual Equipment. Chicago Hornets, All-America Conference. During the World War II years, several low-budget professional teams experienced difficulty staying in business because of financial problems. One of them was the Hornets who, after consulting their ledger, decided that they couldn't afford long underwear. To avoid suffering chapped thighs—which the long johns would have prevented—the Hornets decided to apply goose grease to their skin. Bill Granholm, the Hornets' equipment manager, remembered it well: "The entire team tried it, and although no one got chapped thighs, the goose grease did have its drawbacks. The stuff made their hands so slippery the club set a league record for most fumbles in one game."

Most Unusual Bowl Games. The following football contests were played by members of the United States armed forces. Tea Bowl (London, England, 1945); Lily Bowl (Bermuda, 1943–45); Arab Bowl (Oran, Algeria, 1944); Riviera Bowl (Marseilles, France, 1945); Potato Bowl (Ireland, 1944); Spaghetti Bowl (Florence, Italy, 1942).

Most Unusual Scandal. Sing Sing Federal Penitentiary, Ossining, New York, 1934. Football was abolished at Sing Sing after it had enjoyed what amounted to a golden age at the institution north of New York City along the Hudson River. When football was originally introduced at the penitentiary, the prison officials were somewhat skeptical. They felt that the crowds would be a disturbing influence on the prison routine. "There was also something about one of the players who wouldn't quit running in the end zone," said *PM* (newspaper) reporter Tom O'Reilly.

Nevertheless, football was introduced and the players, curiously, were coached by a Fordham University scout named John Law. At first the prisoners' team suffered a string of losses to semipro teams such as the New Rochelle (New York) Bulldogs and Danbury (Connecticut) Trojans. Their most humiliating defeat in their first season was at the hands of the Port Jervis Police. In time, however, the Sing Sing team (often referred to as the Caged Tigers, Black Sheep, and Zebras) became at least the equal of the teams that once had routed them.

By 1934 the Sing Sing football team easily outclassed its opposition. "The team's excellence," said Tom O'Reilly, "made it impossible to bet on mere victory or defeat. Any man wishing to back Sing Sing had to give away 21 points. The prisoners were so powerful on the gridiron that, by the time the annual game with the Port

Jervis Police arrived, coach Law announced that he would not be on hand for the game because of a Fordham scouting assignment. He told his players, confidently, "You know what to do. Go ahead and do it."

Which they did. Members of the starting team held a meeting and picked secret agents to go through the prison quietly betting against Sing Sing's chances of winning by 21 points. "They were so delighted at the idea," said O'Reilly, "that they gave nice odds and didn't even inform the members of the second team, who were among the biggest bettors."

Minutes after the opening kickoff it became apparent that Sing Sing could trounce the Port Jervis eleven at will. By the second quarter the prisoners had built up a 20–0 lead. Then, without any apparent cause, Sing Sing began committing blunder after blunder. Soon, the substitutes, of their own volition, began rushing on to the field only to be waved off by the regulars.

Meanwhile, Law discovered that he would be able to get a fast ride back to the game and rushed back to Sing Sing where he arrived at halftime. The coach's entrance coincided with a heated argument between the first- and second-team players for obvious reasons. Apprised of the situation, Law nevertheless dispatched the first team back on the field for the second half.

"He watched them fumble once," said O'Reilly, "and then sent in the second team."

The second team picked up the same pace that the first team employed early in the game. The final score was 50–0 for Sing Sing. "The repercussions that followed," commented the *PM* sportswriter, "caused trouble for months and finally football [at Sing Sing] was queered forever. It was one of the most outrageous betting coups in gridiron history."

Most Unusual Family Act. Six great-nephews of Edgar Allan Poe played for Princeton University at the same time (1899).

Most Unusual Ticket Scalper. During the meat shortage of 1974, Allan Sachs of a Minnesota meat company offered one hindquarter of beef in exchange for a season ticket for the National Football League's Minnesota Vikings. Sachs got the ticket.

Most Unusual Prospect.   When Franklin Delano Roosevelt was editor of the Harvard *Crimson* newspaper, he once wrote an item requesting tryouts for Harvard's football team. One of the readers wrote back that he would be delighted to try out if he could help Harvard win. The writer was Dr. Lyman Abbott who, at the time, was seventy years old.

Most Unusual Rose Bowl Site.   Durham, North Carolina, 1942. Because of fears that the Japanese, who had attacked Pearl Harbor less than a month earlier, might attack California, the Rose Bowl game of 1942 between Oregon State and Duke University was moved east to Duke's hometown, Durham. It didn't, however, help the home team. Oregon won, 20–16.

Most Unusual Request.   Chicago Bears vs. Washington Redskins, championship game, December 8, 1940. Near the end of the rout—Chicago won, 73–0—the Bears were asked not to kick for any more extra points. It was suggested that they run or pass instead since too many footballs were being lost.

Most Unusual Coach.   Dr. Gustave Weber, president of Susquehanna University. After accepting the resignation of his coaching staff, Dr. Weber took over the coaching job. He gave it up after losing two games in a row.

Most Unusual Touchdown Run.   Snooks Dowd, Lehigh University. Preceding the notorious Roy "Wrong Way" Riegels by several decades, Dowd once inadvertently ran the wrong way with the ball—all the way to his own goal line—crossed the wrong goal line, but then realized his mistake. Retracing his steps, Dowd then galloped back in the right direction eluding enemy tacklers, and scored a touchdown.

Most Unusual Injury. Clarence Herschberger, University of Chicago, 1897. Prior to a game against Wisconsin, Herschberger challenged quarterback Walter Kennedy to an egg-eating contest. Herschberger won the contest, devouring thirteen eggs. The overdose of yolks turned Herschberger's stomach and he was unable to play.

Wisconsin won the game, 23–8. "We were not beaten by eleven Badgers," said Chicago coach Amos Alonzo Stagg, "but by thirteen eggs!"

Most Unusual Off-Season Occupation. Stu Clancy, Yale University. An assistant coach to Herman Hickman during the thirties, Clancy worked as an embalmer for a local funeral parlor in the off-season. Once, when Clancy arrived late for one of Hickman's conferences, the head coach frowned and admonished his assistant thusly: "I might as well inform you that there are only two excuses for anybody being late at one of these meetings. They are sickness and death." Then, Hickman stared down Clancy: "And I mean *private*, not professional, deaths!"

Most Unusual Battle Cry. Bo McMillan, Indiana University, 1943. Scrawled on the blackboard of the Hoosier dressing room, McMillan offered the following bit of inspirational prose: "Not one soul shall cross this line—either vertical, horizontal or transverse."

Most Unusual Army-Navy Game. The Arab Bowl, Oran, North Africa, New Year's Day, 1944. The only touch football bowl game in history featured the Army and Navy All-Stars who were then stationed in North Africa. Army won the game, 10–7, amid bizarre surroundings. During halftime, camel and burro races were held with WACs and Red Cross nurses as jockeys. A beauty contest designed to select a homecoming queen ended in a three-way tie which meant that the 1944 Arab Bowl had three queens. The game itself was dreamed up by *Stars and Stripes* sports editor Jim Harrigan. Navy scored first on a blocked punt and a pass, but Army tied the match when Eddie Herbert intercepted a pass near the end of the second half. Army won the game on a field goal.

Most Unusual Penalty. Ohio State vs. California, 1950 Rose Bowl. With the score tied, 14–14, and less than a minute and a half remaining, Ohio State had fourth down with three yards to go on California's six-yard line. Ohio State's coach, Wes Fesler, called for his kicking unit to go in for a field goal attempt.

As Jim Hague, the kicker, and Dick Widdoes, the holder, began to move into position, they were waved off by the team on the field, claiming they wanted to go all the way for a touchdown. An argument between the kicker and the quarterback ensued until the referee finally called a five-yard penalty against Ohio State for delaying the game. Thus, the ball was moved back to California's 11-yard line. This time Widdoes and Hague were allowed to take their kicking positions, but not before they inquired why they were given such a hard time by their teammates. "We weren't crossing up the coach," they were told, "we just wanted that penalty so that we could get you a better angle for the kick."

The ploy worked. Hague's kick was good and Ohio State won, 17–14.

Most Unusual Tackle. Montana quarterback Harry Adams vs. Washington, 1920. Having injured his ankle, Adams had an option to leave the game, but chose to continue, despite the great pain. On one play, Washington punted and Adams, playing safety, had the ball sail over his head. As he hobbled after it, Washington's defenders got closer and closer. When Adams finally picked up the pigskin he was surrounded and, fearfully, braced himself for the blows.

Just then one of the Washington tacklers, realizing Adams' infirmity, shouted: "Don't hit him; he's hurt!" Instead of smashing Adams to the turf, the Washington tacklers gently lifted Adams up and lowered him to the ground.

Most Unusual Marriage Proposal. Lyle Bennett, Brigham Young University, 1975. At halftime of the game between Utah and Brigham Young, sophomore Bennett proposed to his girl friend, Mary Shurtz, a freshman at Brigham Young, without directly speaking to her. Bennett persuaded the team's cheerleaders to use their large letter cards to spell out the message: MARY SHURTZ, WILL YOU MARRY ME? LOVE, LYLE. Without using so ostentatious a means of communication, Mary agreed.

Basketball

Best Coach, Pro or Amateur. This would have to be Bob Douglas, who coached the New York "Rens" (actually the Harlem Renaissance), a barnstorming black team, in the twenties and thirties. The team had a record of 2,318 won, 381 lost under Douglas, and they regularly trounced the original Celtics and the old Globetrotters.

Best Pro Team. The original Celtics of the post–World War I years were members of the old American Basketball League, and had to be the winningest quintet ever, as they won 90 percent of their games one season. The team was disbanded in 1928, until the modern Boston Celtics were created after the Basketball Association of America and the National Basketball League merged to become the National Basketball Association.

Best Player, Professional. With the likes of Kareem Abdul-Jabbar and "Dr. J" around today, this record may soon be authoritatively disputed, but thus far the greatest professional basketball player is undoubtedly Wilt Chamberlain, merely by the number of records he holds: the only player in NBA history to score 100 points in one game; to reach 3,000 points in a single season (1962); to average 50 points a game for a whole season (1962); most rebounds in one game (55) and in one season (2,149 in 1961); most field goals in a game, in succession, in a season, and highest field-goal percentage. Wilt "the Stilt" was the NBA scoring leader from 1960 through 1966, and retired with 31,419 points in regular season play, for a lifetime average of 30.1 points per game.

We felt this category would be incomplete if we did not cite those individuals most responsible for the innovations in the game—for scoring, for the size revolution, and for defense, rebounding, and jumping.

San Francisco is the birthplace of the man who revolutionized scoring in basketball, and Angelo Enrico ("Hank") Luisetti is the man's name. And to think, Hank made the game change by simply taking one hand off the ball!

That's right, Luisetti is credited with developing the one-handed shot—as a high schooler. Later, he literally put the basketball world into a state of shock by scoring 305 points in eighteen games, and 70 points in one two-game weekend, when he was a freshman at Stanford University.

Until World War II it was generally considered that anyone over about six feet, four or five inches—maybe six feet, six inches at the most—would naturally be too clumsy and uncoordinated to make an effective basketball player, where speed, accuracy, and grace are at a premium. But it only takes one outstanding "exception" to put the lie to a misconceived truism, and George Mikan was such a one. His six feet, ten inches and 250 pounds had an enormous effect on both college and professional roundball. The man who once planned to be a priest was All-American in 1944, 1945, and 1946 for DePaul University, and when he went to the Minneapolis Lakers, basketball came of age—and the world began to believe that "titans" could play the game.

Mikan was the first player ever to reach the 10,000-point mark (finishing his ten-year pro career with 11,764), and he aided the Lakers to six NBA titles in his first seven years with the club.

Just about the time Mikan had retired to coach the Lakers for a year, our third innovator appeared: Bill Russell arrived on the Boston Celtics in 1956–57 to assist in the birth of a Boston dynasty.

Russell brought new focus to the arts of rebounding and jumping. While Mikan had made big men acceptable, Russell proved they could do much more than stand in the pivot and dunk shots. Russell developed and perfected the fast break and became known as "Mr. Defense" due to his bewildering array of defensive moves and shot-blocking techniques.

Russell also became the first black major league coach (actually, he was originally player-coach, and when he retired as a player to devote his time to coaching, there were other blacks in that position), topping off a lifetime career of innovation.

Best College Player.   No, it wasn't Oscar Robertson, "Dr. J," "Pistol" Pete Maravich, nor anyone from a nationally ranked college, but Clarence "Bevo" Francis who holds the following NCAA records: most points in a game—113 in 1954 (he set and broke his own record three times in the same season); most field goals, one game—37 (1954); most free throws made, one game—37 (1954); most games over 50 points, one season—8 (1953–54); most games over 50 points, career—14; highest one-season average (1953–54)—46.5 points per game.

Francis was born in 1932, and migrated from his native Ohio at the behest of his former high school coach, Newt Oliver, who accepted the coaching job at Rio Grande College. Francis scored 58 points in his second game at Rio Grande, and after his record of 113, literally put his small college on the national map. "Bevo" dropped out of college as a junior to sign with the Harlem Globetrotters, but after bouncing around the minor leagues for a number of years, disappeared into obscurity.

Best Passer.   Oscar Robertson holds NBA records for

most assists in a career, 9,887, the highest average of assists per game in a career, 9.5, and best average in assists over a single season (1965), 11.5. Former Boston Celtic star Bob Cousy has to get honorable mention for his record of 28 assists in one game which has stood since 1959 (although it was tied by the relatively unknown Guy Rodgers in March 1963).

Best Rebounder. It can't be much of a surprise that Wilt Chamberlain dominates this category of basketball, holding six out of eight records, including most of a career (23,924) and a season (2,149), and highest for a single game (55 against the Celtics on November 24, 1960).

Best (Most Accurate) Shooter. No one in the NBA, not even Calvin Murphy (58) or Bill Sharman (56), who set consecutive free throw records in that league, can even remotely approach the record of an amateur, Ted St. Martin, of Jacksonville, Florida. St. Martin scored 1,704 consecutive free throws in a shooting exhibition on February 28, 1975, literally demolishing the former record of a piddly 200 consecutive free throws set by . . . guess who? Why, Ted St. Martin in 1972! It's obvious that Mr. St. Martin was incapable of moving with the ball, or surely he'd have been making six figures in the NBA today!

Best of the "Little" Men (Professional). Bob Cousy of the Boston Celtics from 1950 through 1963 was unquestionably the best of the "little" men. Cousy stood a mere six feet, one inch, and spent much of his career staring at the breastbones of his opponents, although he claimed that he preferred to go against larger rivals.

"There was always somebody small for me to guard," said Bob, "and try to score against . . . but I actually preferred to play against somebody a little bigger because I knew I would be quicker and faster. Little men always gave me the most trouble."

Born in New York City of French parents, "Frenchy,"

as he was called in his youth, played city street games until his hands first touched a basketball at the age of thirteen. It was love at first touch, and Cousy won the New York City scoring title as a high school senior.

Holy Cross College in Worcester, Massachusetts, became Bob's college, where, after a slow start, he finished as an All-American and number one scorer in Holy Cross history. Incredibly, however, Cousy was passed over in the NBA draft by Celtics Red Auerbach, and ended up with a peculiar outfit known as "Tri-Cities"—a group of towns in Illinois. Almost immediately Cousy was traded by Tri-Cities to the Chicago Stags, and in turn, the Stags went broke even before training camp.

Ironically, Walter Brown of the Celtics picked Cousy's name out of a hat, when the Stags' players were being redistributed throughout the league, and Bob became a Boston player after all.

Which proved to be fortunate for the Celtics, despite Auerbach's misgivings. "Cooz" was rookie of the year in 1950–51, was named MVP in 1956–57, made All-Star ten out of thirteen seasons, and helped the Celtics win six titles. To this day, he is coholder of the record for assists in one game, with 28.

Along with Cousy, the name of Calvin Murphy must be mentioned, for Murphy is, in basketball terms, literally tiny, at five feet, ten inches (both of his parents were six feet and above, so Calvin's "small" stature was a rude shock!).

Breaking into the pros with the San Diego Rockets in 1970, Murphy arrived with a college (Niagara) average of 33.1 points per game, exceeded only by "Pistol" Pete Maravich, Austin Carr, and Oscar Robertson. In the 1975–76 season with the now Houston Rockets, Murphy broke Bill Sharman's former consecutive free throw record of 56 by two, for 58 in a row.

But the most unusual aspect of Murphy is not simply that he is one of the shortest men in pro basketball today, but that he is unafraid to make the moves of a much larger, taller player. A guard, Calvin seems to take great pleasure in foiling opponents who stand a full foot and a half over him, and he is one of the best jumpers in the sport.

In a nationwide contest for the most productive and consistent players, Murphy was the only guard named, placing him with such giants as Kareem Abdul-Jabbar and Julius Erving, a real "Mutt and Jeff" scene if there ever was one!

Best Shooter from the Floor.   Once again, the NBA is nowhere to be seen, proving the contention that basketball is basically a game played on cement playgrounds, where the world's truly greatest players are never seen or heard of by the general public.

Fred L. Newman of San Jose, California, scored 12,874 baskets out of 13,116 attempts for a .982 accuracy percentage, during a twenty-four-hour period from May 31, 1975, through June 1, 1975.

Best Game by a Guard (Professional).   Pete Maravich, New Orleans Jazz. Maravich went on a tear against the New York Knicks on the evening of February 25, 1977, at the Louisiana Superdome, and scored an incredible 68 points—the most points ever scored by a guard in professional basketball.

Maravich, who played 43 minutes, popped in 26 of 43 field-goal attempts, and sank 16 of 19 from the free throw line. Also, to prove that he was not stingy, Pistol Pete contributed six assists!

Maravich was not to be stopped that night, hitting improbable 25-foot jumpers from impossible angles. As an occasional change of pace, Maravich would drive by a startled Walt Frazier of the Knicks, who, despite his reputation as one of the best defensive players in basketball, was powerless to snuff out the smoking Pistol that night.

Maravich's 68 points eclipsed the 67 which Larry Miller of the Carolina Cougars had popped in on March 19, 1972.

Best Individual Performance in a Game (Outside USA). In a regional boys' tournament in Stockholm, Sweden, Mats Wermelin, age thirteen, scored 272 points. In fact, on February 5, 1974, his team won the game, 272 to 0!

Best Year by a High Schooler. The Arkansas School for the Deaf must have been pleased to have Bennie Fuller among their ranks, for Fuller averaged 44.9 points a game as a junior and 50.9 as a senior from fall 1971 through spring 1973.

Best Single-Game Performance by a High Schooler. In 1963 Alabama's Glen Vocational High School in Birmingham took a fair trouncing from West End High, losing 97–54. What made it all the more painful was that West End player Walter Garrett scored all of the winning 97 points!

Best One-Man Team (High School). St. Peter's High School in Fairmont, West Virginia, played an intramural game on March 16, 1937. It was the seniors against the sophomores, but at 32–32, every one of the seniors except Pat McGee had fouled out!

Not only did McGee shut out the sophs for the remainder of the game, but he gleaned three more points as the seniors won, 35–32.

Best High School Performance in a Losing Effort. This category must go to two separate lads—one for scoring and one for overall effort.

In 1965 Rick Morrill scored 78 points as his team, Pembroke (New Hampshire) Academy, lost the game.

But Larry Breer was with Kipp High School in Kansas when all of his teammates fouled out against Aurora High. It seems that Kipp High had only five boys enrolled, so poor Larry had to go it alone for three minutes. Breer held Aurora scoreless for two minutes and 45 seconds, but the opposition finally circumvented him with 15 seconds remaining, to win, 51–49.

Best All-Star Game. It was January 21, 1954, at New York's Madison Square Garden, before 16,478 eager fans, when the East's coach Joe Lapchick gave the immortal pep talk to players Bob Cousy, Bill Sharman, Harry Gallatin, Neal Johnston, and Ray Felix: "Let's go, fellas."

Lapchick was undoubtedly aware that East was favored, despite the fact that West carried such heavies as George Mikan, Jim Pollard, Bob Davies, and Bobby Wanzer. But at halftime the West was only down by four points, and surprisingly, ahead by two after three quarters.

Probably inspired by Lapchick's immortal words, the East struggled back, to lead by two with only six seconds remaining. The West called time out at this point, to set up George Mikan near the basket. Mikan failed to score, but was fouled by the East's Felix and the regulation game ended in a tie. The East's Cousy caught fire in the overtime, scoring 10 of his team's 14 points, and copped the MVP award after the East defeated the West, 98–93.

Best NBA Playoff Final. It was the end of the 1956–57 season, and the St. Louis Hawks were heavily favored to beat the Celtics in what is probably the most exciting seven-game series in basketball—if cliffhangers are what you like.

The series opened with a Hawks victory, 125–123, in double overtime. The Celtics took game number two by a comfortable 20 points, followed by St. Louis' nail-biting 100–98 win in the third. Boston surprised everyone by taking games four and five (123–118 and 124–109), but lost game six to a Cliff Hagen tip-in with six seconds left, and the series was tied at three games.

It is a miracle that there were no incidents of cardiac arrest recorded during the seventh game—the score was tied twenty-eight times and the lead switched thirty-eight times! The Celtics were leading by six at the three-quarter break, but St. Louis' Bob Pettit began a surge which ended in two free throws that tied the game at 103, and the first overtime began. Then a second overtime when the game was tied at 113. With two seconds left to play, the Celtics were ahead, 125–124, when the player-coach for the Hawks, Alex Hannum, threw a court-long pass. It bounced off the backboard right to Pettit, who had been a paragon of accuracy that night. Astoundingly, Pettit's six-footer touched the rim . . . then dropped off, leaving Boston with the title.

Best Comeback in a Game (Professional). The Milwaukee Bucks were leading the New York Knicks by 18 points on November 18, 1972, with only six minutes left in the game. Suddenly, Earl Monroe scored, then Walt Frazier, and the Knicks racked up a quick nine points in a row, narrowing the gap to 86–77.

The Bucks, normally a highly accurate team, took shots from everywhere, but it was as though someone had sewn webbing over the basket, as they scored only a single point in the six-minute Knick spree.

With only 47 seconds left, the Knicks trailed by only one point when Lucius Allen of Milwaukee was fouled. The mysterious ailment continued, however, as Allen missed both free throws! Frazier took the rebound, passed to Earl ("the Pearl") Monroe, who scored—and the Knicks were up by one. With 26 seconds left, New York got the ball and took the 24-second violation. It looked frightening as Kareem Abdul-Jabbar got the ball with two seconds left, but he missed his shot, and the Knicks had it, 87–86.

Best Game for Harlem Globetrotters. The world-famous Harlem Globetrotters are a joy to watch, with their repertoire of routines, tricks, and gimmicks. But one often forgets that the gimmicks are evolved from a body of outstanding basketball players, and the time the Trotters challenged the NBA's best in 1948, the Minneapolis Lakers, proved the point.

This would be a real test for the Globetrotters who were playing their sixth game in six nights—the fancy dribbling and through-the-legs-and-over-the-back trick shots would not daunt the likes of Jim Pollard and the high-scoring George Mikan.

Before 17,853 fans in Chicago Stadium, the Lakers

pounded into a nine-point lead by the midway mark, when the Trotters began to double- and triple-team Mikan. But Mikan missed the resulting foul shots, and the Trotters settled down and began to score.

With 90 seconds remaining, the Globetrotters began their famous "Sweet Georgia Brown" act to kill the clock, until Harlem's Elmer Robinson hit a 20-footer for the 61–59 victory.

Best Winning Streak. Well, everybody knows it was when UCLA ran up 88 in a row over three seasons, right? Wrong.

The Baskins (Louisiana) High School women's varsity team won 218 games in a row from the first game of the 1947–48 season against Ogden High School, until Winnsboro High defeated them during the 1952–53 season—and it was their only defeat that year!

Baskins is a tiny cotton town and the high school had a total enrollment of only seventy young women. Their unblemished seasonal record before that year was 38–0, 43–0, 45–0, 38–0, and 40–0.

Best Olympic Team. Without question it was the 1960 team which won the gold medal, and included Jerry Lucas, Jerry West, Oscar Robertson, Darrall Imhoff, Walt Bellamy, Terry Dischinger, Adrian Smith, and Bob Boozer. The team was so talent-laden that John Havlicek only made "alternate," and the entire roster went on to star in the NBA.

Best Attendance. The Harlem Globetrotters played an exhibition game at Olympic Stadium in West Berlin, Germany, before a horde of 75,000.

The largest indoor crowd to witness a basketball game was at the Houston (Texas) Astrodome, when the University of Texas played UCLA on January 20, 1968, before a crowd of 52,693.

Best Schoolyard Player. Although this is such a highly subjective area due to a dearth of statistical evidence upon which to base a decision, we have narrowed it down to three New York kids, all of whom played during the late fifties. One of them went on to star in the pros; the others faded, as did most playground pheenoms, into obscurity.

Our choices are Connie Hawkins, who starred for the Phoenix Suns of the NBA, and Jackie Jackson and Eddie Simmons, who grew up in Bedford-Stuyvesant in Brooklyn, became premier players at Virginia Union College, and then, unfortunately, lapsed into the mudhole of the ghetto.

Hawkins starred in the playgrounds of Brooklyn for years, constantly thrilling crowds lined up many rows deep along the fences on Saturday afternoons to see him play. Even when he was only fifteen and not yet in high school, his fame spread throughout the basketball groupies in the city. By the time he was a high schooler, he led Boys High to a New York City championship and was named All-City and All-Nation by local papers and *Parade* magazine.

But Hawkins, as great as he was, thinks that Jackson, a friend he used to "hang around" with on the Brooklyn streets, was even better.

"The greatest schoolyard play I ever saw was by Jackie Jackson," Hawkins remembers. "Jackie always had pain in his knees because of these soft lumps on them. But when he was about seventeen the lumps hardened and he became the greatest leaper I've ever seen. People would put quarters on the top of the backboard and Jackie would jump up and pick them off.

"He had this shot called 'The Double Dooberry with a Cherry on Top.' On a fast break, he'd take a pass at the foul line and jump toward the basket, holding the ball in his two hands. While he was going forward and up, hanging in the air, he would lower the ball down to his waist, raise it over his head, lower it down again, raise it back up, and *then* slam in a dunk. Nobody in the world can do that shot but him. People went crazy every time he did it."

Jackson and Hawkins played with one Eddie Simmons,

a wiry guard. David Wolf, who authored Connie Hawkins' biography, said of Simmons:

"Simmons was in the process of becoming one of the finest guards ever to play in the New York schoolyards. Even today, years after Ed stopped playing, his name is spoken with reverence in Harlem and Bed-Stuy. A trim, steely-eyed youngster, who stood only 5'9" and weighed 160 in his prime, Simmons was seriously classed with Bob Cousy and Lenny Wilkins as a ball-handler. Eddie's senior year, Boys [High] was undefeated and won the city championship in Madison Square Garden. He was voted to the All-City team."

Unfortunately, Simmons never made it to the pros. The last Connie Hawkins heard of his former friend, Simmons was attempting to kick a heroin habit, and had joined a methadone treatment program.

Best Height Advantage. Height is now commonplace on a basketball court; indeed, lack of it is more surprising. And yet, the seven-foot mark is not broken every night of the week, and the tallest player in pro basketball in the United States, according to whose program you read, is either Kareem Abdul-Jabbar, at seven feet, two inches, or Tom Burleson of the Kansas City Kings, at seven feet, two and a half inches.

But for pure towering flesh, Russia takes it all, in both sexes! Vasiliy Akhtayev, who played for Kazakhstan in 1956, was seven feet, 7.3 inches; and Ulyana Semyonova, with T.T.T. Riga, is the world's tallest woman player, at six feet, nine and a half inches.

Best Practice Dodger. Chico Vaughn, Pittsburgh Pipers. Vaughn was a highly rated defensive guard with the Detroit Pistons in the mid-sixties, but he faded from prominence and the Pistons placed him in the expansion draft of 1966. He went to the San Diego Rockets, but could not agree on contract terms, so he jumped to the American Basketball Association.

Vaughn had a penchant for practically every alcoholic beverage known to man. As a result, his training habits were not the greatest, nor was his punctuality. He would repeatedly show up late for practices, or skip them altogether. "I'm gettin' too old for practice," he would drawl. "The Chic gotta save his strength for the games."

A common Chico excuse was that there was a death in his family. "Chic lost four aunts, ten brothers, and five sisters that season," recalls Pipers trainer Alex Medich, "and his father died about five times."

At one point in the season, the president of the team, Gabe Rubin, upon hearing that Vaughn's father died, sent the family a bouquet of flowers. The father wrote a note to Rubin, thanking him for the flowers!

Best Basketball Town. Nowhere but New York City. New York is such a conglomeration of asphalt that more kids play basketball in the Big Apple than anywhere else in the country. For years New York was the recruiter's paradise. Stars such as Billy Cunningham, Connie Hawkins, Nate Archibald, and many others came out of the city's playgrounds and public schools.

The next person seemingly destined for the big time is Albert King, who graduated from Fort Hamilton High School in Brooklyn. King, if he goes on to star at the University of Maryland and the pro ranks, would only add to the already illustrious list of roundball talent who hail from Gotham.

Best Example of Basketball One-upmanship. Wilt Chamberlain signed for an estimated $100,000 in 1965, which caused Bill Russell of the Boston Celtics to disdainfully reject the $70,000 he had been offered. After all, he had won the MVP award more often and felt he was even more valuable to his team, which had won more championships.

Russell finally convinced the Celtics, and achieved the league's largest contract—$100,001!

———

Worst Game Ever Played. Two boys' prep schools in

Massachusetts, St. Michael's and Smith, played a game in the 1951–52 season, and neither team was known for its high scoring. But neither did the boys expect what happened: for three periods there was not so much as a basket or free throw scored by either team.

Finally, early in the fourth quarter, St. Michael's' co-captain, John Sullivan, received a pass from a teammate and put it in, to make it 2–0. This was St. Michael's first shot of what would be only two, and while Smith took four shots in an attempt to tie the game, that was it— 2–0!

Worst College Rout. Heavily favored Essex Community College (New Jersey) played Englewood Cliffs College on January 20, 1974, expecting to win, but unprepared to set records.

Essex scored the first 26 points of the game, and after the half it was Essex 110, Englewood Cliffs 29.

Someone on the Essex team knew that the record for points was 202, and they asked coach Cleo Hill if they could try for it. Hill was dubious, but gave the boys permission to forego defense for a scoring push. With 15 minutes left in the game, the arena announcer notified the crowd that the men were within 21 points of the record. They more than made it, as the final score was Essex Community College 210, Englewood Cliffs College 67. Essex had scored 97 out of 129 shots from the floor, 16 out of 22 free throws, and had 89 rebounds!

Worst Regulation Game (Professional). Half of the fans must have thought they were at a football game the night the Pistons squeaked out a victory over the Minneapolis Lakers, 19–18. In fact, half of the players must have thought so, too!

Worst Court. Before the new Omni arena opened in Atlanta, Georgia, the Hawks played at the Georgia Tech field house. Unlike most basketball courts, the surface was not laid over some relatively soft substance, but instead was placed directly over concrete. This meant it was

94

literally the hardest court in the NBA, and the Hawks hated it every bit as much as their opponents.

The Hawks court was so atrocious that Walt Bellamy claimed that it was "shortening careers by at least three years" and then New York Knick Willis Reed said that playing in schoolyards was preferable!

Worst Overtime Game.   The general rule of thumb about overtime games is that they are exciting cliffhangers, but this game was a paperhanger which should have been thrown over a cliff!

It was January 6, 1951, at the Edgerton Park Sports Arena in Rochester, New York, in the dark days preceding the 24-second clock, which meant that a team could stall forever if they chose—and these two teams chose.

The Indianapolis Olympians were facing the Rochester (later Cincinnati) Royals before 3,000 fans, and the game ended at regulation time tied at 65.

Each team scored only one basket in the first overtime, nothing in the second overtime, and only two points apiece in the third, followed by no score in the fourth. The basic strategy was to dribble all night, and both teams obliged so well that a newborn baby would have envied their dribbling exhibition.

Both teams woke up in the fifth overtime and each scored a whopping five points, which horrifyingly left the game tied. In the sixth overtime a Rochester player suffered a breakdown and decided to shoot instead of playing out the clock, but missed. Indianapolis' Alex Groza got the rebound and it was passed up to Ralph Bear who shot with one second left. Hurray, the Olympians won, 75–73, after four hours!

The thought of a possible repeat of the world's most soporific basketball game inspired the NBA to adopt the 24-second clock.

Worst Case of Nerves in a Coach.   Joe Lapchick has to win the award, unassisted! In 1944, while coaching St. John's University, the team played DePaul which had the

95

scoring ace, George Mikan. Mikan fouled out of the game with five minutes left and St. John's went into the lead. All of this would have been heartening for Lapchick, except that he had fainted on the bench.

Lapchick later coached the New York Knicks, and in 1952, the Knicks were playing Fort Wayne. Fort Wayne laboriously caught up to New York, and won with two seconds remaining. Lapchick collapsed at that moment, and spent three days in the hospital.

Lapchick used to manifest his nerves often against referees, but one night he got so mad at the officiating that he threw a full water bucket into the air. Unfortunately, it emptied its contents on Joe! Another night, as the Knicks played a tight one against the Boston Celtics, Lapchick took off his suit jacket and slowly shredded the lining, completely oblivious to what he was doing.

Worst Temper. In 1964–65 Bailey Howell of the NBA's Baltimore Bullets set a record for personal fouls with 345.

Worst Display of Bad Temper by a Team. Angry at what they considered unfair officiating, the players of Clayton (Georgia) Towns Country High School shot at their opponent's basket until they had chalked up 56 points for the other team, and lost the game, 129–41!

Worst-Loved Coach. To say that Jim Harding, former coach of Loyola University of New Orleans, La Salle College, and the defunct Minnesota Pipers of the old American Basketball Association, was not appreciated by his charges is making the biggest understatement since someone mentioned, "There's a little gold down in California."

Harding, a lean crew-cut man, was a perfectionist, and a stickler for fundamentals. In insisting, for example, that every player shoot fouls the same way—hands in a certain position, with the ball squarely over the head at just the right angle—he messed up more shooting styles than any coach in the history of the sport. In addition, he hated to see mistakes, especially from professionals, and the
96

slightest miscue meant a seat on the bench for the rest of the night.

Connie Hawkins, formerly of the Phoenix Suns and Los Angeles Lakers, had the extreme misfortune to play for Harding when he was a Piper, in 1968.

"He wanted us to win every game by fifty points," Hawkins remembered. "One time we were thirty ahead and Frank Card, who was a rookie, made a mistake. Harding had a tantrum on the bench. He was screaming and cursing at everybody. If a guy made one error he'd take him out of the game and yell at him. Guys got tense and nervous, afraid to make a mistake and be embarrassed."

He also had a foul mouth on the bench, and spectators sitting one or two rows behind the coach constantly complained about his language.

"He told me," said Alex Medich, the Pipers' trainer, "that when he says a profane word I should hit him in the thigh. This led to an Abbott-and-Costello scene one night in Duluth, Minnesota. He went nutty, cursing and screaming every word in the book. I'm like a machine gun, hitting him rat-a-tat-tat in his thigh. But he forgot why I was doing it. He's slapping my hand and cursing more, and I keep hitting his thigh and he's slapping away and calling everybody 'bastards' and 'c---suckers' and jumping up and down."

It is not surprising, therefore, that Harding suffered extreme tension during the season and had to be hospitalized. He was fired at the end of the 1967–68 season and immediately hooked a job coaching the University of Detroit. The players there didn't approve of his coaching methods either, and practically the entire team went on strike in protest.

Worst Professional Basketball League. The American Basketball League, begun in 1961 as an answer to the established National Basketball Association. Ill-conceived and ill-administered, it was doomed to failure before it even got started.

The ABL's founder was none other than Abe Saperstein, the major domo of the Harlem Globetrotters. Saperstein, annoyed over what he considered the failure of the NBA to grant him a franchise in that league, told the establishment to shove it and started his own league, with cities from Honolulu, Hawaii, to New York.

"However," writes author Dave Wolf, "by midseason, basketball's version of the Ship of Fools was awash in a sea of red ink. Competition was overshadowed by internecine bickering among the owners, folding franchises, bouncing checks, absurd schedule changes, last-minute cancellations and microscopic attendances. Turnstiles rusted from inactivity unless Saperstein rushed in his Globetrotters for a preliminary game.

"ABL refs didn't command a great deal of respect," Wolf adds, especially since they were hired by the local teams, in order to save the league money! "Occasionally, when teams from two close cities, such as Cleveland and Pittsburgh, played each other, refs from each city would work the games," Wolf notes. "This led to the curious sight of referees working against each other!

"One ref had to be admonished for laughing as he walked up and down the court. One owner escaped with a reprimand when he trudged into the officials' dressing room after a game and punched a referee in the mouth."

Innovations in the new league included wider foul lanes (up to 18 feet; 12 was the limit in those days) and liberal use of hands on defense. One league official was heard to say that "if the public goes for mayhem in football gear they'll go wild over mayhem in shorts."

Games were played, for the most part, in dilapidated, old arenas. The Washington team, for example, used old Uline Arena, which, it was rumored, had been built for James Madison's inauguration. The Los Angeles Jets used the Olympic Auditorium, a boxing arena, in which the floor was smaller than regulation court size.

Teams had to bus and often motor to games from city to city. The one exception was Hawaii, where flying was a necessity.

Although the competition was fairly good in the ABL— Connie Hawkins and Dick Barnett, among others, played

98

in the league—the enterprise was doomed to failure. Saperstein closed the cashbox a year later, after he had lost a million dollars.

Most Unusual Game.   The alumni of Rio Grande College held a basketball marathon which lasted 125 hours in 1973!

The "game's" final score: White 10,752, Red 10,734. There were fifteen men on each team and each five-man squad played for a backbreaking four hours at a time.

Most Unusual Basket in an All-Star Game.   In the last second of the first half of the 1957 contest, Bill Sharman whipped a full-court pass to Bob Cousy. But Cousy never touched the ball; instead, it went in for the longest basket (almost 90 feet) ever made in an All-Star game.

Most Unusual Foul Shooter.   The University of West Virginia's "Hot" Rod Hundley once went to his knees against the University of Pittsburgh, and, looking for all the world like a praying mantis, hit the shot.

Later, in a game against George Washington University, which would result in the conference championship, Hundley actually *hooked* a foul shot, in overtime!

Most Unusual Free Throw.   In early 1977 the Quenemo (Kansas) High School women's basketball team made a free throw which made both teams happy!

Poor Quenemo High. With a student body of only forty, their tallest player was a mere five feet, five inches, and in their second season of existence, they had yet to win a game. Once, against Malvern High, with only six women suited up, five fouled out. Malvern proved more than sportswomanlike, however; for each time a Quenemo player would foul out, Malvern would kindly remove a player from the lineup also—until it was two-on-two and the referee called the game. Even then Quenemo lost!

But the real humiliation came in January 1977, when

Quenemo played LeRoy High (enrollment: 93, including one six-footer). With less than a minute left, LeRoy was leading Quenemo by 83–0, when Dee Dee Neill of Quenemo stepped up to the foul line and, finally, scored a point for her team.

Most Unusual High Scorer. Pee Wee Kirkland averaged 70 points a game for the Hilltoppers in semiprofessional competition. The team used to average more than 160 points a game—but there was perhaps a reason.

Part of their success was undoubtedly because the Hilltoppers played only at home, where their highly partisan crowd probably had an unnerving effect on the opposition. You see, Pee Wee played for the Lewisburg (Pennsylvania) Federal Penitentiary team!

Most Unusual All-American. Doug Williams of Phenix City, Alabama, went to St. Mary's University in his late twenties, after a tour with the army in Korea. Despite his senior status, Williams played superior ball, and was named to the Little All-America team in 1970—at age thirty!

Most Unusual Winning Basket. In 1968 the Dallas Chaparrals of the ABA were once leading the Indiana Pacers, 118–116, with one second remaining, and the Pacers had the ball under their own net. Jerry Harkness, who was inbounds, threw the ball to the Indiana center under Dallas' net, hoping for a foul, but instead, the ball went into the basket. Normally, this would have tied the game, but since the "shot" had come from outside the 25-foot circle used in the ABA, it was a three-pointer, and the Pacers won it, 119–118.

Most Unusual Pass (Nonprofessional). Adam Coffman of Greensburg (Pennsylvania) High School made a basket from 91 feet away, against Farrell High School, in the 1953–54 season. Even more unique—Coffman was standing out-of-bounds at the time; his play was supposed to have been a pass.

Most Unusual Scoring (One Game). Birmingham Southern State College beat Florence State University (Alabama), 55–46, on January 30, 1971, thanks in part to the 25 points scored by guard Russell Thompson. Thompson did not score any of his points on field goal attempts, however. All 25 out of a possible 28 were made from the foul line!

Most Unusual Audience. The Harlem Globetrotters once played before an audience of one—in 1931, before His Holiness, Pope Pius XI.

Most Unusual Good Luck Charm. Gus Johnson, once of the Baltimore Bullets, lost an upper front tooth in a brouhaha with Walt Bellamy of the Atlanta Hawks. Johnson got a new false tooth put in, but had a gold star imbedded in the tooth—no doubt expecting to blind his rivals when he smiled!

Most Unusual Basketball Stakes. According to WPIX-TV News in New York City, a one-on-one basketball championship between neighborhood rivals was broken up when the prize was copped. By a rival gang? Nope; the local constabulary arrived to confiscate the stake— several thousand dollars' worth of narcotics!

Hockey

Best Magic Tonic. Leone's Magic Elixir, 1950–51. The brew was concocted by Broadway restaurateur Gene Leone for the oft-losing New York Rangers. Their record was well below .500 by early December 1951, when Leone perfected his formula and poured it into a large black bottle about three times the size of a normal whiskey bottle. With appropriate fanfare, "Leone's Magic Elixir" was carried into the Rangers' dressing room where players such as Don "Bones" Raleigh, Pentti Lund, and Zellio Toppazzini quaffed the brew. After drinking the mixture, the Rangers began to win and win and win. By early January they had lost only two of their eleven games. Opponents became frightened. The Toronto Maple Leafs attempted to have customs men seize the tonic when it arrived at the Toronto airport, New York *World-Telegram* hockey writer Jim Burchard was placed in charge of the brew on road trips. Once, when the Rangers lost to Detroit, Burchard explained, "The Leone brew wasn't on deck. Without it, the Rangers were under a psychological handicap." After the loss, an SOS was dispatched to

Leone, who quickly prepared more of the liquid and the Rangers whipped Toronto the next night. Eventually, the psychological value of the elixir ran its course and the Rangers faded into fifth place, out of the playoffs.

Best Team.   Montreal Canadiens, 1955–60. Coached by Hector "Toe" Blake, the Canadiens had superstars at every position and won an unprecedented five consecutive Stanley Cup championships. Goaltender Jacques Plante introduced the face mask. Defenseman Doug Harvey orchestrated the tempo of the game like no other player before or since, and the forwards, led by Maurice "Rocket" Richard, put fear in the hearts of enemy goalies. Richard was flanked by Jean Beliveau, Bernie "Boom Boom" Geoffrion, Dickie Moore, Bert Olmstead, Henri Richard, and Phil Goyette, among others. Montreal's power play was so devastating that the other five teams in the National Hockey League collaborated in the 1956–57 season to write a new rule into the record book specifically designed to limit its effectiveness. Previously, a player serving a minor penalty was compelled to remain in the penalty box for a full two minutes. The Canadiens, with their power, were often able to pile up several goals during that time. According to the rewritten rule, the player serving the minor penalty was allowed to return to the ice when a goal was scored by the opposing team. Thus, the Canadiens were limited to only one goal per power play.

Best Name.   Steve "Wochy" Wojciechowski, Detroit Red Wings, 1945–47. There may have been other big leaguers with thirteen letters in their last name but only Steve Wojciechowski of Fort William, Ontario, had his name changed so that writers and broadcasters could more easily pronounce and write it. Steve became *Wochy*.

Best Promoter.   Tom Lockhart. At one time Lockhart was general manager of the New York Rangers, president of the New York Rovers, president of the Eastern Hockey League, and president of the Amateur Hockey Association of the United States. Lockhart introduced figure skating great Sonja Henie to American audiences, having her do exhibitions during intermissions of Eastern League games at Madison Square Garden in the mid-thirties. "Some of my promotions were a little more bizarre," Lockhart recalled. "Once, when the Hershey Bears were coming to town, I was told about a live bear that could skate. So I thought it would be a good idea to have the animal lead the Bears hockey team on the ice."

Lockhart had the bear outfitted with a pair of skates, but the bear's trainer couldn't stand on his blades and it caused an uproar among the crowd.

"As soon as the bear stepped on the ice," Lockhart remembered, "the trainer fell flat on his face. The bear kept skating around pulling the trainer all over the ice."

Another time Lockhart staged "airplane races" on the Garden ice between hockey periods. "A guy was putting out toy airplanes—the ones we had as kids that you'd run with and they'd go up in the air, their wheels turning—and he wanted us to race them on the ice. So we took a couple of players, lined them up at one end of the rink, and had them skate three or four laps around the Garden and then pick a winner. That's how we flew airplanes in the Garden."

When Lockhart organized the Eastern League, the first year was complicated by a mistake in scheduling. "I couldn't accommodate all the extra games," said Lockhart, "so I had to cheat a little. I'd make up phony games; have the Crescents beating the New York Athletic Club, 1–0, and put down somebody's name for scoring the goal and add an assist or two; then I'd phone the scores in to the papers. Turned out twenty-one games were never played, but nobody noticed it. The league finished its full schedule of games played in that first year."

Best Bald-headed Referee. George "Gertie" Gravel. During the late forties, the National Hockey League boasted an official whose pate was shinier than an eight ball. Gravel, a French-Canadian, was not only extremely efficient but also equally amusing. Once, in Chicago Stadium, a fan fired a dead fish at Gravel. He picked it up by the tail in very delicate fashion, held it away from his body with one hand, held his other hand to his nose, skated over to the boards and deposited the fish near a woman spectator. With that she shouted: "Gravel, I hate you!"

Seemingly penitent, Gravel looked at the woman with soulful eyes and shook his head sadly. "Lady," he replied, "tonight I even hate myself."

Another time Ted Lindsay of the Detroit Red Wings executed a swan dive, hoping that he would inspire Gravel to penalize a Ranger player. While Lindsay remained horizontal on the ice, feigning injury, Gravel skated up to the Detroit player and calmly observed: "Ted, the ice is too hard for diving; and you can't swim in it either."

Best Present-Day Black Hockey Player. Washington Capitals' Bill Riley. Although he was preceded into the NHL by Willie O'Ree (Boston) and Mike Marson (Washington), Bill Riley of the Capitals has emerged as the best black player in the sport. As a minor leaguer, Riley had watermelons thrown at him when he played in Toledo. The fans showered him with verbal abuse, including cries of "shoeshine boy." Besides that, Riley has had to defend himself on the ice. "I was one of the bigger guys on Dayton and I was the policeman. I probably had 100 fights, but it didn't bother me. If it was racial, I knew they just didn't have any class."

Riley has one quality that was the main force in his rise to the NHL. "He just wanted to play so damn bad," explains Tom McVie, Riley's coach with the Capitals and in the minors at Dayton. "He's a smart player. A terrific dude."

Before reaching the majors Riley played in Kitimat, British Columbia. He played amateur hockey at night while he held a job in an aluminum smelting plant. After three years of hard work, Riley made it to the minors in Dayton, where he took a pay cut in order to play. "I made $245 a week the first year, $310 the second year, and $500 at the start of this season. I had a bonus for 20 goals. I had 19 when they brought me up. Could've used that bonus."

Riley has come a long way from days of poverty in Nova Scotia, where he was one of five children. His family couldn't afford to send him to a hockey school. So even though he's not making much more than the league minimum of $12,500, he's doing okay. "You know," he said, "for the first time I'm not worried about my next meal."

Best Little Guy.   Aurel Joliat. There isn't much room for 135-pounders in the National Hockey League, but Aurel Joliat was one who prospered in the league back in the twenties. Joliat succeeded with shifty stickhandling and quick moves. The Montreal Canadiens traded the popular Newsy Lalonde to get Joliat, and the little guy responded by joining with Howie Morenz and Johnny "Black Cat" Gagnon to form a high scoring line.

Joliat was no flash in the pan. He played in Montreal for sixteen years, and was good enough to win the Hart Trophy as most valuable player in 1934, and be elected to the Hall of Fame.

Today people talk about the increasing number of big men coming into the sport, and how the players are better athletes than in the past. Don't tell that to hockey's greatest little man. Joliat does not follow the sport any more—he considers it inferior.

After leaving hockey, Joliat ran a grocery store, worked for the Canadian National Railway and the Quebec Liquor Commission. He lives in Ottawa and says he has "absolutely no interest" in hockey, but does not hold the same aversion to skating.

"A couple years ago," he recalls, "on a mild night about two in the morning, I skated the whole canal in Ottawa, which is over five miles in length. I'm expecting a call from the pros any day now."

Best Long-Distance Challenge.   Dawson City, Klondike, Canada, 1905. Shortly after the Klondike gold rush had subsided, a number of rich miners from Dawson City
106

in northwest Canada decided that it was time the Klondike was represented in Stanley Cup competition. The miners assembled a team and challenged the powerful Ottawa (Ontario) Silver Seven team to a championship series in the Canadian capital. The Klondike team traveled more than 4,000 miles by the most primitive means of transportation, including dog sled. Undaunted, the boys from the Northwest invaded Ottawa in January 1905 and, to the surprise of many, almost made a contest of the first match. They ultimately were defeated, 9–2, but it was enough to kindle hopes that the second match would be even closer, if not a triumph for the Dawson City skaters. But the bubble burst in the second game. The final score was Ottawa 23, Dawson City 2. Frank McGee, the one-eyed Ottawa star, scored 14 goals, a Stanley Cup record.

Best Comeback. Toronto Maple Leafs, 1942. Trailing the Detroit Red Wings in the Stanley Cup finals, three games to none, the Leafs won the next four consecutive games in the best-of-seven series to tie Detroit and then win hockey's professional championship. To do so, Toronto's coach, Clarence "Hap" Day, made a radical lineup change after the third game. Day benched his crack scorer Gordie Drillon and ace defenseman Bucko McDonald and replaced them with raw rookies Don Metz and Wally Stanowski. Metz became an instant scoring star and Stanowski proved efficient on defense. The Maple Leafs thus became the only team in National Hockey League history ever to lose the first three games of a Stanley Cup final and win the next four for the Cup.

Best Scoring Night for Two Defensemen. November 19, 1929. Johnny McKinnon of the Pittsburgh Pirates and Clarence "Hap" Day of the Toronto Maple Leafs each scored four goals. Pittsburgh won the game, 10–5.

Best Manager. Frank Selke, Sr., Montreal Canadiens. When Selke, who had been assistant manager in Toronto, moved to Montreal in 1946, the Canadiens organization was in a state of disintegration. Selke organized a farm system which, to this day, is the best in hockey. By 1950 the system had produced such superstars as Jean Beliveau, Dickie Moore, Doug Harvey, Tom Johnson, Bernie Geoffrion, Phil Goyette, Claude Provost, and Andre Pronovost. Selke's machine was so awesome that he was persuaded to stock the weak NHL clubs with "average" Montreal players. Thus, Selke dispatched Ed Litzenberger to the floundering Chicago Black Hawks and Litzenberger soon became a star. When Selke retired in 1960, the Canadiens had won six Stanley Cup championships. What's more, he left the nucleus of a team that would win seven more.

Best Nickname. Georges Vezina, Montreal Canadiens. Because he hailed from Chicoutimi, Quebec, and was cool as a cucumber when he played, Vezina was called "the Chicoutimi Cucumber." Vezina was so accomplished that the goaltender's prize, the Vezina Trophy, was named after him.

Best Game. Detroit Red Wings vs. New York Rangers, April 23, 1950. This game combined all the elements of high drama and artistic quality. It not only was the seventh and final game of the 1950 Stanley Cup playoffs but also extended into two periods of sudden-death overtime.

The Red Wings, mighty favorites, were confronted by an underdog Rangers team that had been evicted from its home Madison Square Garden rink by a circus. As a result, the New Yorkers played their two "home" games at Maple Leaf Gardens in Toronto.

The Rangers came close to pulling off a major upset. They led the series, three games to two, and were ahead in the sixth game when Detroit rallied to win the match, forcing a seventh and final game. The Rangers led the seventh game, 2–0, but Detroit tied it at 2–2, setting the stage for the Rangers' last big opportunity. Buddy O'Connor put New York ahead once more before the Wings tied it at 3–3. The score remained tied into sudden-death overtime. Whoever scored the next goal would be the winner. Nick Mickoski of the Rangers appeared to have Detroit goalie Harry Lumley beaten, but his shot hit the goalpost and rebounded harmlessly away. Neither team scored in the first overtime. In the second sudden-death period, George Gee of Detroit was foiled on a breakaway attempt by Rangers goalie Chuck Rayner.

The Rangers were reeling after the eight-minute mark of the second overtime. A face-off was held in the New York end of the rink. Gee passed the puck to Pete Babando (one of the few American-born players in the NHL) who fired it through a forest of legs. Before Rayner could move, the puck was behind him and Detroit had won the Stanley Cup.

Best Goal. Maurice "Rocket" Richard, Montreal Canadiens vs. Boston Bruins, April 8, 1952. No athlete has ever absorbed the physical abuse in a single game suffered by Richard, nor ever rebounded to score a more spectacular goal than Richard did in the final game of the Boston-Montreal Stanley Cup semifinals of April 1952. With the score tied, 1–1, in the second period, Richard was smashed to the ice from behind by Boston's Leo Labine. The unconscious Richard was carried off the ice, his body so limp some feared he was dead. He recovered in the dressing room and insisted upon returning to the bench, although coach Dick Irvin, fearful for Richard's health, had no intentions of using him again in the game. "After receiving his stitches, Richard was in a partial coma," said a Montreal newsman. "His head was fuzzed with pain, his eyesight impaired, with dull noises ringing in his ears."

Nevertheless, in the third period Richard insisted upon playing. Late in the period, with the score still tied, he leaped off the bench, took a pass from teammate Butch Bouchard, and circled the Boston defense before shoving the puck past goalie Jim Henry. The goal was so dramatic that Richard's hard-nosed teammate Elmer Lach, who was sitting on the bench at the time of the score, leaned forward onto the sideboards and fainted. Thanks to Richard, the Canadiens had won the game.

The pain had not subsided when Richard fell on to the bench in Montreal's dressing room. His father, Onésime

Richard, walked in and put his right arm around the Rocket's shoulders and hugged his son. Hockey's greatest scorer no longer could control himself and simply broke down and cried.

Best Single Performance by a Forward. Bill Mosienko, Chicago Black Hawks, March 23, 1952. The Black Hawks' leading scorer had been the lone bright spot for the Chicago six in an otherwise unmemorable season. It was the final game of the 1951–52 schedule and pitted Mosienko's club against another nonplayoff-bound team, the Rangers.

In a span of 21 seconds during the third period, the Chicago right winger propelled his way into the National Hockey League record book by blasting three goals past substitute Ranger goaltender Lorne Anderson. The performance eclipsed the record of 1:04 by Carl Liscombe of the Detroit Red Wings in 1938. By himself, Mosienko also broke the team record for the fastest three markers by the three seconds, originally set by Hooley Smith, Babe Siebert, and Dave Trottier of the Montreal Maroons in 1932.

"The funny thing was," said Mosienko, in the dressing room after finishing the season with 31 goals, "that about 45 seconds later, I was in alone again. I faked Anderson out of position, and had an open goal to hit—and shot wide."

Best Single Performance by a Defenseman. Ian Turnbull, Toronto Maple Leafs, February 2, 1977. This steady but low-scoring blue liner treated Maple Leaf Gardens fans to a record night as he blasted an incredible five goals into the Detroit Red Wings' net. After a scoreless first period, Turnbull rocketed two shots past Detroit goalie Ed Giacomin in the second session and recorded three more goals in the third stanza at the expense of substitute goalie Jim Rutherford.

With his unexpected outburst (he hadn't scored a goal in the previous thirty games) Turnbull became the first defenseman in NHL annals to score five times in a game,
110

breaking the previous standard of four, shared by five other players—none of whom played after 1937–38. The old record had stood for forty-seven years.

Best Fight.   Montreal Canadiens vs. New York Rangers, Madison Square Garden, New York, March 16, 1947. The New York *Sun* called it "an almost endless fight." *The New York Times* classified it as "the grandest mass riot in the local history of the NHL." There was bad blood between the Canadiens and Rangers that season, and almost all of it was spilled during the contest.

Kenny Reardon, the rambunctious Montreal defenseman, had one thing in mind as he stickhandled across the Rangers' blue line with 32 seconds left in the game, which the Canadiens were leading, 4–3—freeze the puck.

As Reardon carried the puck into the New Yorkers' zone, he committed a cardinal hockey sin—he fixed his eyes on the black rubber disk and forgot to look where he was going. The next thing he knew, Bryan Hextall's hip loomed menacingly in front of him.

Reardon bounced off Hextall like a pinball right into Cal Gardner's waiting stick which obligingly bludgeoned Reardon across the mouth. "My upper lip," Ken says, "felt as if it had been sawed off my face."

The injured Canadien passed the Rangers' bench on the way to the medical room and overheard Ranger Phil Watson complain that Kenny's mangled lip was not nearly punishment enough for him. Reardon then bolted for Watson, but was intercepted by a policeman. Then up popped a balding fan brandishing a fist. "Reardon," he shouted, "I've been waiting a long time for you to get it. You louse."

"That did it," Reardon says. "I swung my stick at him— then a cop grabbed me from behind and I fell." The disturbance aroused the Rangers who rose from their seats out of natural curiosity. From a distant vantage point of the Montreal bench across the ice it appeared that the entire New York team was preparing to pounce upon Reardon.

"Get the hell over there," implored Montreal coach Dick Irvin to his players, while standing on his bench.

And the Flying Frenchmen poured over the boards like GIs at Normandy.

Montreal captain Butch Bouchard, who led the stampede, clouted the bald-headed spectator with his stick while goalie Bill Durnan and Maurice Richard sought other prospective victims. Within seconds the Rangers wiped out Montreal's beachhead, forcing the invaders to regroup at center ice, where four main events were in progress: (1) Maurice Richard versus Bill Juzda; (2) Bill Moe versus Bill Durnan; (3) Hal Laycoe versus Leo Lamoreux; (4) Butch Bouchard versus Bryan Hextall. The Marquis of Queensbury would have sanctioned the Moe-Durnan and Laycoe-Lamoreux bouts, but the others were strictly back-alley affairs.

Moe, who had been ordered not to play because of a shoulder injury, floored the heavily padded Durnan with a roundhouse right. Laycoe and Lamoreux flailed away at each other in a fierce toe-to-toe encounter that ended only because the belligerents were too tired to throw another punch.

Meanwhile, Richard broke his stick over Juzda's head, snapping the shaft in two. Juzda arose slowly and tackled Richard, bringing him down violently. Then Bouchard ripped Hextall's stick away from him and flattened him with a punch. Having dispensed with Durnan, Moe cracked a stick over Bouchard's head and Butch didn't even seem to notice that he had been hit. Juzda then excused himself from Richard, picked up a stray stick and poleaxed Buddy O'Connor, breaking his jaw.

The only players to escape unblemished were the normally violent Phil Watson of the Rangers and George Allen of Montreal. Watson says it wasn't an accident. "I grabbed ahold of Allen," Watson explains, "and said, 'Look, George, what's the sense of getting all tangled up? Whaddya say we stand on the side and watch this one?' He said okay, so we did. It was the best fight we ever saw."

Best Putdown. Hap Day worked for the Toronto Maple Leafs from the day the franchise was born, first as player, later as coach. During his coaching reign he led the club to five Stanley Cups in eight years. One would think that Day would have been rewarded for his accomplishments. However, manager Conn Smythe did not agree. Instead of rewarding Day, Smythe fired him so that he could give the job to his son, Stafford Smythe.

The story goes that Day later went into the tool handle business (what else?). A while later, he sent an axe handle to Conn Smythe, his former boss who, not knowing what to do with an axe handle, called Day to find out where he could find the blade. "Between my shoulder blades," Day replied, "where you put it!"

Best Fibbing Pep Talk. Toronto Maple Leafs manager Conn Smythe, prior to the 1949 Stanley Cup playoff round. Smythe's Leafs had won the Stanley Cup two years in a row (1947 and 1948), but the manager believed that his men were becoming complacent with success. Smythe called his players together before the series began and delivered a lecture that was worthy of Knute Rockne or Vince Lombardi. One of the more impressionable of the Leafs at the time was center Cal Gardner.

"Connie," Gardner recalled, "gave us a pep talk about the brave Canadian soldiers who were with him at Vimy Ridge in World War I, and he mentioned my father as being one of the greatest. I guess it worked on me because I played my best game of the season that night and we won. After the game, the thought struck me about the great 'con job' Smythe had done on me. My father wasn't even in the army because of a gimpy leg."

Best Flakes in Hockey. The goalies. When one thinks of flakes in hockey, one thinks of goalies. Who else would stand in front of frozen pucks flying at great speeds? The following are just some of the characters who have donned the armor of the goalies:

Charlie Hodge of the Montreal Canadiens never could pass a telephone without making a phone call. Luckily, there were no phones visible from the ice surfaces of the National Hockey League.

"Sugar" Jim Henry of the New York Rangers did not

want to suffer from varicose veins, so he declined to tighten the straps on his pads. Trouble was that the pads were sometimes spun around by a well-aimed shot so that they protected the *backs* of his legs.

Jacques Plante of the Montreal Canadiens knitted socks and underwear to pass the time between games. When the team was going bad, Plante always developed mysterious asthma attacks.

Superstition plays a big part in many goalies' lives. Roger Crozier of the Detroit Red Wings always dressed and undressed the left side first. In addition, he only wore dark clothes. Gary Smith has been known to wear twelve pairs of socks inside his skates. Between periods, he undresses and showers.

Lucien Dechene, once a goalie in the Western League, munched on hot dogs between periods. When reprimanded for drinking beer before games, Dechene replied, "What t'hell, twenty, t'irty beer before a game never hurt anybody!"

Dave Dryden liked living in Toronto so much that when he joined the Buffalo Sabres he still lived in Toronto, many miles away. The unique living arrangement became complicated whenever the Sabres played a road game against the Toronto Maple Leafs. Dryden would drive to Buffalo, ride the team bus to Toronto for the game, return to Buffalo on the team bus, and then drive home to Toronto.

Los Angeles Kings goalie Rogie Vachon uses smelling salts as a pregame pick-me-up, with a stick of gum as a chaser. Meanwhile, his onetime backup goalie, Gary Simmons, was likely to be slamming his glove into the top of the dressing room door, leaving his trademark around the league.

Angular Wayne Thomas insists on wrapping his stick with brand new black tape before every game, and then recites his teammates' names aloud when they skate by to wish him luck at the end of pregame warmups. "When they come by three at a time, it's a test of concentration," says Thomas.

As part of Ken Dryden's pregame ritual, the Canadiens'

goaltender averts his eyes when the referee tests the goal lights just before the opening face-off. "I just consider it unlucky to see the red light before a game," says Dryden. "I know it's silly and I tell myself, 'Ken, you've got to get rid of this bloody superstition.' "

Worst Stunt.   During the 1950–51 NHL season, a hypnotist made his one and only appearance in a rink to participate in a team's fortunes. The Rangers, who had encountered a series of misfortunes, decided to employ a Dr. David Tracy, who claimed to be a psychologist and hypnotist. Dr. Tracy had contacted Rangers publicist Herb Goren. He said he had been watching the Rangers lose and was convinced he could help the New York club start winning again if he had permission to do a little work with the players.

Goren approached his boss, Rangers manager Frank Boucher, and urged Boucher to let Dr. Tracy do his thing, no matter how bizarre it might have appeared. "Dammit all, Frank," said Goren, "it can't do any harm. Let's try it. For sure we'll get good publicity out of the stunt."

Boucher agreed on the theory that anything so unique might loosen up his anxiety-ridden team. Dr. Tracy was given the green light and reported to Madison Square Garden a few hours before game time. Here are Boucher's recollections of what transpired:

"He came into our dressing room an hour or so before a game with Boston. He was a burly, jowly man with sleek black hair, beautifully tailored clothes, and he had a peculiar eye. There was a white dot in it that made him look very odd indeed.

"He was particularly attentive to Tony Leswick at the beginning, staring into his eyes and talking quietly while Pentti Lund, Alex Kaleta, and Buddy O'Connor sat in front of their neighboring lockers, listening closely. He spoke to all the players, but when it came Nick Mickoski's turn, Nick fled from the room. He was afraid the guy was going to hypnotize him. Then the doctor spoke to the room at large, stressing positive attitudes, talking quietly and purposefully. He needed to; we'd lost twelve in a row.

"We played a great game, too. The Garden was jammed, after the excellent coverage accorded the Tracy experiment, and we went into the final minute deadlocked with the Bruins, 3–3. But then Bill Quackenbush, a Boston defenseman, broke the spell with a long shot that hopped crazily over Charlie Rayner's stick, and the Rangers lost, 4–3.

"Tracy told me that two things had worked against him. First, he shouldn't have undertaken his experiment at the moment of our thirteenth game without victory and, second, he should have spent more time with Charlie Rayner. The doctor said that Charlie wasn't relaxed.

"Frankly, I thought the players had responded pretty well to the psyche-prober, but when he couldn't get us past our thirteenth hurdle I concluded the experiment. Tracy couldn't put the puck in the net or keep it out any better than I could."

Worst Strike. The first antimanagement strike called by a paying spectator was launched by Brooklyn schoolteacher Marvin Resnick against Rangers manager Muzz Patrick in 1963. Resnick and some associates were angry over Patrick's handling of the Blueshirts. He first had leaflets printed and dropped from the Madison Square Garden balcony calling for Patrick's ouster. Balloons followed.

Resnick's *coup de grace* was to be a picket line outside the Garden during a Rangers–Red Wings game. Resnick did appear at 7:00 P.M. in front of the arena along with some placard-carrying picketers. They marched for 25 minutes before game time.

"Then," said Resnick, recalling how the strike failed, "we looked at our watches, realized it was five minutes to the opening face-off, tossed away our signs, and ran into the Garden." A year later Patrick was moved out of the managership and into an inconsequential front office job with the Garden. Resnick has remained a teacher to this day.

Worst Overstatement. Emile Francis, New York Rangers coach, April 29, 1971. The Rangers hadn't won the Stanley Cup in thirty seasons and, despite the fact that the Blueshirts were one of the top clubs in 1970–71, they had already made a reputation for not winning the big games.

New York fans expected different results this time, though, since their heroes had defeated the Toronto Maple Leafs in a six-game quarterfinal series, winning the final game in overtime.

The semifinal round matched the Rangers with the Chicago Black Hawks, whom they battled successfully during the regular season. But the playoffs were another story. After five head-to-head battles, the Rangers teetered on the brink of elimination from the playoffs and trailed the Chicagoans, three games to two.

The Rangers had to win game six to remain alive in the Cup chase. They quickly fell behind, 2–0, before the solemn Madison Square Garden audience. Lines already were forming at the ticket windows to return the unused tickets for the Cup finals. But the Rangers rode with Lady Luck the rest of the night.

They tied it with a pair of goals and played the Black Hawks scoreless through the end of regulation time. The tension was mounting every extra minute, the fans were emotionally drained, the skaters were physically spent, and the happy Zamboni driver was making three overtime trips around the rink.

The marathon contest finally ended at 1:29 of the third overtime period when Pete Stemkowski of the Rangers banged home a rebound of a Ted Irvine shot for his second sudden-death goal of the series, pulling the New Yorkers even in games with the Hawks. There was bedlam in the postgame dressing room celebration, even though the two clubs still had to play one more game to determine who would go to the finals.

Emile Francis, the Ranger coach, went a step too far when he bellowed in the coach's room, "This is the New York Rangers' finest hour!" He didn't have much time to enjoy their "finest hour," because they lost the seventh and deciding game in Chicago three days later.

Worst Dirty Player. Joe Desson, Philadelphia Falcons. A quiet, bespectacled gentleman off-ice, Desson was apt to go haywire at any time during a game, and frequently without warning. And heaven help the referee who happened to cross Desson's path at the wrong time. Desson's major problem was the temper he never fully controlled. When Desson wasn't fighting he was as good, as any defenseman in any league.

Early in the 1944-45 season, Desson flattened an official and was suspended for two weeks by EAHL president Tom Lockhart, though, as always, Joe was the acme of penitence after his explosion. "All I want is another chance," he said. "I will try to mend my ways."

But his niche on the notorious list was permanently carved when, as a member of the New Haven Blades, he flattened—and nearly killed—referee Mickey Slowik during an Eastern League game at New Haven Arena. This time Lockhart suspended Desson for life, one of the few times so stiff a sentence was meted out in hockey.

Worst Attempted Fix. "Did you ever hear how I tried to fix it for Convey to be a star?" Francis Michael (King) Clancy will tell enchanted listeners, recalling the time Clancy arranged to keep a former Maple Leafs player in the league by making him look good. The player was Eddie (Cowboy) Convey, a less than adequate left wing for the New York Americans in 1933 whose play constantly invited demotion to the minor leagues.

One night the Americans visited Toronto and Convey's old pals heard through the grapevine that their former teammate needed a big game to survive in the NHL. Clancy's concern prompted him to conspire with Charlie Conacher, the large, blunt right wing, and Lorne Chabot, the tall, dour goalkeeper. "Look," Clancy told them before the game, "if we get a few goals up, let's make it easy for Convey. Let's help him score a couple."

The Leafs romped ahead 4-0 in the first period, far enough for Convey to get his chance—with Clancy's skilled collusion. Convey got off the Americans' bench in the second period and, for a hilarious few minutes, it was
118

as though the stage had been manipulated. He was on against Conacher on the Toronto forward line, Clancy on the Toronto defense, Chabot in the Toronto goal.

"Now!" Clancy muttered to Conacher as Convey skated down the wing. Conacher obligingly fell down to let him through. Convey hit the Toronto blue line, where Clancy conveniently neglected to check him. Convey walked in on Chabot, who didn't move. He had a clear shot at an open side of the net—and drove the puck wide.

"One more chance!" Clancy called to Conacher and Chabot and, soon, the Cowboy again came riding down the wing. Conacher faked a bodycheck, and missed. Clancy stumbled and fell down. Convey swept in on the stationary Chabot, who left one side of the goal unprotected. Convey boomed a drive, high into the seats.

"One more time!" Clancy commanded and Convey got it, the next time he appeared on the ice. "Let him through!" Clancy shouted at Conacher, who let Convey sail past. He escaped Clancy's bogus check.

Clancy is up now, aping the Convey of many years ago. "He flew by me, really danglin', and went cruisin' in on Chabot, who was ready to step aside. He took careful aim and shot. Chabot fell to let the whole goal open, and *whap!* Convey hit him right in the Adam's apple with the puck! Down he went, chokin' and gaggin'!"

Conacher skated back to help Clancy assist the distressed Chabot. "Any more of this," Chabot said, when he could speak, "and Convey'll kill me!"

"I guess we better knock off fakin' for him," Clancy suggested.

"Right," Conacher said not concealing his disgust. "Screw Convey!"

Worst Playing Conditions During a Game. During game three of the 1975 Stanley Cup finals, the fans in Buffalo's War Memorial Auditorium got a glimpse of what hockey must look like in Foggy Old London. The Philadelphia Flyers and Buffalo Sabres were forced to decide the Stanley Cup champion in a pea-souplike atmosphere: The 70-degree heat combined with the ice and the players' movements to produce a screen of fog which made seeing the puck almost impossible—particularly for the goalies, Bernie Parent of the Flyers and Roger Crozier of the Sabres.

"I couldn't see any shots from center ice," said Parent. "I'm sure it was the same for Crozier."

The game had to be delayed eleven times because of the thickness of the fog. During each unscheduled intermission, several arena attendants were called out onto the ice to fan the fog with a sheet to make it disappear, at least temporarily.

When that failed, the players came out and skated around the fog-congested area to keep it from building up. The only players who weren't annoyed at the delays were the fourth-stringers on both teams who received more ice time than they had had in weeks.

Worst Vote of Confidence by a General Manager. Harry Sinden, Boston Bruins, October 13, 1976. Early in the 1976–77 season, Bruins defenseman Dallas Smith was holding out because of a decrease in salary. Following a victory over the Rangers in New York, Sinden was cornered near the dressing room by a New York scribe. When asked why the Bruins were giving Smith a salary cut, the irritated Sinden answered, "There's nothing wrong with a 15 percent cut if a guy's 200 percent overpaid!"

Worst Game by a Team. New York Rangers, January 23, 1944. Playing at Olympia Stadium, Detroit, the Rangers lost to the Red Wings by the record-breaking score of 15–0. Although the Rangers had been a first-place team as recently as 1942, their roster was decimated by World War II. Coached by Frank Boucher, the New York sextet employed a mediocre goaltender named Ken "Tubby" McAuley who was more a victim of his inefficient defense than his own goaltending shortcomings.

Worst Coach. Emil Iverson, Chicago Black Hawks, 1931–32. The flamboyant owner of the Black Hawks, Major Frederic McLaughlin, was determined to hire as many American-born hockey people as possible; thus,

Iverson qualified for the Chicago coaching job on the basis of one factor—he was an American. As for his other credentials, they included a stint as a figure skater and experience as a physical culturist. He had never before coached a hockey club. Fortunately, Iverson did not coach for very long. However, McLaughlin kept Iverson on the payroll with the title of physical director of the Black Hawks.

Worst NHL Rookie Award Winner. Brit Selby, Toronto Maple Leafs, 1965–66. Robert Briton "Brit" Selby was a gifted young amateur player, born in Kingston, Ontario, who played junior amateur hockey for the Toronto Marlboros of the Ontario Hockey Association's Junior A division. After the 1964–65 season, during which he starred for the Marlboros, Selby was promoted to the National Hockey League where he scored 14 goals and 13 assists for 27 points in sixty-one big league games. The sky supposedly would be the limit for young Selby, yet a year later he scored only one goal for Toronto and was exiled to the minors. He played one season in Philadelphia, was given another chance in Toronto—where he failed —and alternately was given opportunities with the St. Louis Blues, and the WHA's Quebec Nordiques, Philadelphia Blazers, and New England Whalers. At no time did Selby display the form that won him such accolades in his rookie NHL season.

Worst Stanley Cup Final(s). St. Louis Blues, 1968, 1969, 1970. When the National Hockey League expanded from six to twelve teams in 1967–68, it arranged for the winner of the established division to play the winner of the expansion division playoff. For three straight years the Blues won the expansion playoff and played the Montreal Canadiens in 1968 and 1969 and the Boston Bruins in 1970. In each of the best-of-seven series, the Blues were wiped out in four straight games, never winning a contest in the finals.

Most Unusual Hockey Hotbed. Among the faraway places with strange-sounding names, few equal Flin Flon, Manitoba, the birthplace of Robert Earle "Bobby" Clarke, center and captain of the Philadelphia Flyers. Flin Flon actually is a shortened version of Josiah Flintabbatey Flonatin, hero of a 1905 English dime novel. J. F. Flonatin explored the depths of a bottomless lake in a submarine, and later discovered a city of gold. And there his story ended.

One of the legends of Flin Flon is truth for sure: as a riotous hotbed of junior and amateur hockey, it is virtually unequaled; many major leaguers have the scars they acquired playing against a mad Flin Flon team. And people wonder how Bobby Clarke became so tough . . .

Most Unusual Goal. Deacon Perrotta, Tyngsboro, Massachusetts. A goalie for Bridgewater State College, Perrotta accomplished a rare feat for someone playing his position. Perrotta scored a goal while playing netminder in a 10–4 loss to Lowell College, in January 1977. Perrotta, on a delayed penalty call on Lowell, skated down the ice instead of going to the bench to free a sixth attacker. He made it in time to tip in a slapshot by teammate Tim Moreau. Such a feat could not have happened in the National Hockey League because rules call for a penalty for any goalkeeper who takes part in the play beyond center ice.

Most Unusual Trophy. The Pacific Plaque. During World War II, an accomplished amateur hockey player from New York, Mickey Slowik, was stationed aboard the USS *Medusa,* a 10,000-ton repair ship in the South Pacific. Slowik, who played in the Metropolitan (New York) Amateur Hockey League, found himself with considerable spare time on the *Medusa* and frequently thought about his pleasant times playing in the Metropolitan League. One day, while staying out of the way of Japanese submarines, Slowik decided to make a plaque for the New York players by hand. He crafted a lovely award which he brought home with him at the conclusion of
122

World War II and donated it to Tom Lockhart, president of the Amateur Hockey Association of the United States. Thus, the Pacific Plaque was awarded to the Metropolitan League player who scored the most assists in league play. Curiously, one of the early winners was a player with one of the most unusual names in hockey—Jim *Hatrick* of the Sands Point (Long Island) Tigers—who won the Pacific Plaque during the 1947–48 season.

Most Unusual Contract Negotiations. If not for a basic philosophical disagreement with owner Jack Kent Cooke, Scotty Bowman might have been juggling the lines of the Los Angeles Kings rather than winning Stanley Cups for the Montreal Canadiens. After Scotty left the St. Louis Blues organization in 1971, he received a call from Cooke, who wanted to discuss the possibilities of Bowman joining the Kings. Scotty agreed to meet with Cooke, but the meeting was conducted with utmost secrecy. Bowman traveled under the name of Mr. William Scott, and upon arriving in Los Angeles, hopped into a waiting limousine that took him to the privacy of Cooke's ranch.

As we know, Bowman did not take the job, but the obstacle was neither money nor deferred payments; in fact, it had nothing to do with cash. Bowman informed the Kings' owner that his philosophy on building a winner centered on the team's amateur draft picks. Cooke believed that the best way was to use the draft picks as trade bait for players who could help right away. "Cooke," said Bowman, "argued that if you dealt for players who could help you right away, you'd be finishing so high that the draft selections you gave up wouldn't be any good anyway."

Bowman did not become a King. Instead he joined the Canadiens, a club which has proven the value of draft choices by trading established players for picks in the draft which have produced players such as Steve Shutt, Doug Jarvis, and Doug Risebrough. By contrast, the Kings have been cemented in mediocrity.

Most Unusual Black Hockey Unit. The Carnegie brothers. As long as hockey relies on Canada for its talent, black skaters will remain rare because there are few blacks in Canada. The NHL has seen only three—Willie O'Ree in Boston in the late fifties and early sixties, and more recently Mike Marson and Bill Riley with the Washington Capitals. But it's unlikely that any of them will be more memorable than the all-black line composed of the Carnegie brothers, Ossie and Herbie, and Manny McIntyre, who played in Quebec's Provincial Hockey League and Senior Hockey League in the forties.

"They would have been good enough to star in the NHL today," says former NHL defenseman Larry Zeidel, who played against them in the Quebec League. "But in those days the NHL was a six-team league paying awfully low salaries. Ossie and Herbie were making terrific money in the Quebec League and had side jobs which gave them even more security. There was no reason to try for the NHL."

Nor was there a guarantee that they could have broken into the big league, which lacked an owner who possessed the determination of Branch Rickey of the Dodgers, who fought to bring Jackie Robinson into baseball. The Carnegies continued to travel by bus between towns like Victoriaville, Drummondville, and St. Hyacinthe—and later Boston and New York when the Quebec Senior League went international in 1946—playing in small arenas before 3,500 shivering fans.

Torontonians Herbie and Ossie Carnegie played center and right wing, and Manny McIntyre, of Fredericton, New Brunswick, played left wing. One of the few existent chronicles of their career was written by Richard Wilson, who in 1945 was a sportswriter for the *Sherbrooke Daily Record* when the Carnegies hit their peak playing for Sherbrooke Rand in the Provincial League.

"Believe me, black was beautiful long before it became a civil rights slogan," Wilson wrote. "That all-black hockey line on the white ice was one of the prettiest sights anybody could ever hope to see in sports. Sure, they played in a small league, in small buildings, but there was nothing small about the excitement they generated.

"Herbie Carnegie, who centered the line, was as good as any hockey player around. He had all the standard moves plus a couple of his own specialties. He excelled in all departments—stickhandling, passing, playmaking, shooting, forechecking, backchecking, penalty-killing, and speed.

"On the right wing, Ossie didn't have the speed, flash or dash of Herbie, but he always did a workmanlike job with 100 percent effort. He was stronger, physically, than the other two, possessed a blazing shot, and played excellent positional hockey. Ossie was particularly effective in the corners where he could hold his own with any defenseman in the league.

"Manny worked left wing with the same discipline that Ossie showed on the right. He was a fine positional player, good in the corners, and willing to mix it with any challenger. A big man, McIntyre could hold his own when the going got rough; which sure was often in the Provincial League. If Manny had a weakness it was to pass instead of shoot. He was a good passer and playmaker and had twice as many assists as goals. His talents complemented the Carnegie brothers' perfectly.

"As an all-black forward line, they were an instant gate attraction. Transcending that novelty, however, their individual and combined hockey talents never failed to excite the fans. Ovations from partisan home crowds around the circuit were not uncommon.

"The best way to describe the line is to say that they always were in tune. You might call it three-part harmony. They knew each other's moves and anticipated each other so well it was impossible for a checking unit to hold them off the scoreboard very long.

"During that 40-game season they were held scoreless in only five games. They had a total of 84 goals and 98 assists for 182 points, an average of 2.1 goals or 4.6 points per game. Their 84 goals made up 44 percent of the team's 189-goal total. Likewise, it would be redundant to say that they were the best line in the league and, as a result, they were marked men. Every team played its best checking line against them, naturally. The opposition's game plan was always bottle up the black line and everything will fall into place.

"It worked, briefly, but then the Carnegies and McIntyre asserted themselves, adjusted their strategy, and Sherbrooke went on to win the league championship with 24 wins, 12 losses, and four ties. In 15 of those wins, the black line equalled or exceeded the opposition's score. A typical night for them was the home opener against the St. Hyacinthe Saints.

"What follows is the newspaper report of Herbie Carnegie's first goal of the season, significant because it symbolized the way the line operated: 'With four seconds to go in the second period, Herbie Carnegie took the puck from McIntyre at the St. Hyacinthe blue line, wormed his way through the defense with a beautiful display of stickhandling, drew the goalie out of position, and slammed a shot past him that never left the ice. This gave Sherbrooke the lead, 4–3, in a game they eventually won, 6–5.'

"Ossie and Manny also scored their first goals of the season in that game—eight seconds apart—and the report of it went this way: 'At 19:11 Ossie parked himself at the corner of the Saints' net and detoured McIntyre's pass into the twine. On the ensuing face-off, Herbie passed to McIntyre who sailed in on goalie Thifeault and made the score 3–2 for Sherbrooke.' The date was November 25, 1945.

"On January 12, 1946, Sherbrooke hosted the Lachine Rapides and won, 8–4. Each member of the black line scored again. Herbie opened it at 8:34 of the first period. Here's how the paper described it: 'Herbie, master of the art of stickhandling, backhanded in the first goal after ragging the puck around in the Lachine end for several minutes, then set up brother Ossie for the second.'

"His uncanny puck control was put to good use in killing penalties, too. One occasion stands out in my mind. Just after Sherbrooke had been penalized, Herbie won the face-off and kept control of the puck in the center ice zone with some masterful stickhandling. His route took

126

him to the right boards where he crossed the visitors' blue line. He sidestepped a bodycheck by one of the defensemen, then headed straight across the ice in front of the net, about 45 feet out.

"He didn't shoot. Instead, he faked the other charging defensemen, stickhandled around them, and circled back to the neutral zone, still in possession of the puck. In other words he had stickhandled completely around the opposing defensemen. While this was going on, 90 seconds of the penalty had expired before he passed to a teammate to take a breather. For that he won a standing ovation from the crowd.

"Herbie had a couple of other tricks that would baffle the opposition. One was running on the toes of his blades, like a figure skater, to get out of heavy traffic or elude a bodycheck along the boards. He had one move I've never seen any other player use. He would go after a loose puck in the corner at full speed, head straight for the boards, then brake slightly and reverse his blades in a manner that gave him a backward motion. With this tactic, he would back out of the corner, dragging the puck while the pursuing defenseman—bent on destruction—would splat himself against the boards. To keep them guessing, Herbie would mix up the maneuver and sometimes do it in the other direction. He made a lot of defensemen look foolish with that one.

"It would be gross sensationalism to compare the Carnegies' situation with that of Jackie Robinson. The fact of the matter was that they experienced little if any discrimination, mostly because the attitudes of Canadians toward blacks always have been more liberal. Canadians, more or less, have a 'live and let live' philosophy. Any rumbles involving the three were the same that anyone else might face playing in that tough league. One thing is vivid: none of them ever backed down."

Most Unusual Called Bluff. In 1947–48 the Detroit Red Wings had Fern Gauthier, who once had been a prolific scorer, but who had fallen into a dreadful slump. A

Detroit writer said that Gauthier couldn't put the puck into the ocean even if he was standing at the end of a pier.

Rangers publicist Stan Saplin heard about the allegation and realized that there are no known oceans near Detroit, but there is the Atlantic Ocean off New York City. He contacted the Red Wings and asked their front office if they'd mind letting Gauthier in on a publicity stunt.

The good-natured Detroiters agreed, and a few weeks later, when the Red Wings came to New York, Saplin got together with Gauthier and explained his project. Saplin, Gauthier, a couple of other Detroit players, and a photographer would take the subway down to the tip of Manhattan Island. They would take a pail full of hockey pucks and a stick. With the pucks sitting at the edge of the pier, Gauthier would then prove that he could shoot the puck into the ocean.

When the group arrived at the appointed spot, a number of New Yorkers looked on in amazement at a young man shooting round black disks in the direction of the water. There is photographic proof that Gauthier did get the pucks into the ocean, although rumor has it that he missed on his first two tries, the first landing on a passing barge and the second one nabbed by a low-flying sea gull.

Most Unusual Press Agent. Hockey has had its share of classic press agents and one of the best was Jack Filman, a native of Hamilton, Ontario, who became the Rangers' publicist in their first season. Filman was given to poetic license and, like many press agents, was wont to stretch the facts. In a publicity release he once explained the origin of hockey, claiming that North American Indians invented the game, and called it "hogee." Pressed about the veracity of the term, Filman insisted that it was the correct word. " 'Hogee' in English," said Filman, "means 'it hurts.' "

Jack always started a day with a *mouthful* (not a *drink*) of gin while making up the Rangers' program. It's been said that one of the funniest sights was watching Filman in consultation with the printer's son when he came to collect the copy for the program. Since the printer's son
128

Homestead Grays catcher Josh Gibson once slugged the ball 500 feet and only got a double for his effort . . . in the "Best Hit for Fewest Bases."

Buffalo's Danny Gare (right) shoots into an open net in one of the clearest moments of the NHL's most fog-ridden Stanley Cup series between the Philadelphia Flyers and the Sabres in 1975.

Ms. Billie Jean King in the process of defeating Bobby Riggs in the "Most Unusual (Tennis) Promotion" for a winner-take-all purse of $100,000.

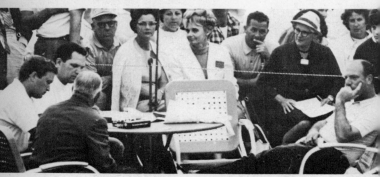

Roberto De Vicenza (right) sits glumly by as officials confirm the fact that he has just committed the "Worst Mistake to Cost a Masters Tournament."

Johnny Weismuller as
"Best Male Swimmer" and
as Tarzan, his most
famous movie role.

Paavo Nurmi exhibiting the style which qualifies him as "Best Long-Distance Runner."

"Babe" Didrikson Zaharias, "Best Woman Golfer," on her way to becoming the first American to win the British Women's Championship, 1947.

Kelso, horse racing's all-time winningest horse, shows his stuff before retirement.

Jack Johnson posed in one of the quieter moments in a stormy career as boxing's "Best Heavyweight."

Cassius Clay (about to become Muhammad Ali) raises his hand in victory after his first-round KO of Sonny Liston before the "Worst Crowd for a Heavyweight Championship" (2,434) on May 25, 1965.

Pro tennis player Ilie Nastase of Rumania exhibits his best-known
trait on the court—bad temper.

Hilda Chester, the "Best Brooklyn Dodger Fan."

Sixty-four-year-old Elzear Duquette, the "Most Unusual Olympic Fan," pulling his coffin behind him on the way to the 1976 Montreal Olympics.

Tennis immortal
Helen Moody shows her
"best volley" form.

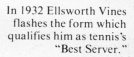
In 1932 Ellsworth Vines
flashes the form which
qualifies him as tennis's
"Best Server."

Basketball's "Best College Player"—Clarence "Bevo" Francis—goes up for one of his famous jump shots for Rio Grande College.

Ethiopia's Abebe Bikila winning the Olympic Marathon in 1964, becoming the first to win the Marathon twice.

St. John's University coach Joe Lapchick belies here his reputation for having the "Worst Case of Nerves in a (Basketball) Coach."

Chicago Black Hawk Bill Mosienko exults after scoring the fastest three goals in hockey history on March 23, 1952.

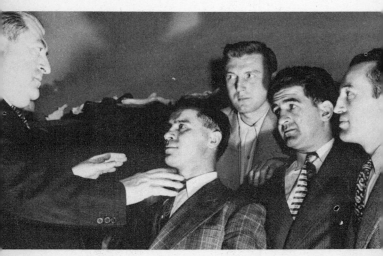

Dr. David Tracey "hypnotizes" New York Rangers Tony Leswick, Eddie Slowinski, Chuck Rayner, and Edgar LaPrade, during the NHL's 1950-51 season. (It didn't do them any good—they still lost!)

Bert Haas, third baseman
for the 1940 Brooklyn
Dodgers, literally huffed
and puffed a ball over the
foul line, devising the
"Best Way to Foil a Bunt."

Gene Sarazen, golf's "Best
Come-From-Behind
Player," in the process of
winning the 1932 British
Open.

Things were not all "rosy" in the 1929 Rose Bowl for USC captain-elect Roy "Wrong Way" Riegels, who carried the ball 70 yards toward his *own* end zone before being downed by a teammate.

Pete Gray actually played a full season with Cleveland Browns (1945), despite the fact that the outfielder had no right arm!

Amos Alonzo Stagg (extreme left), "Best Collegiate Coach," with his 1899 undefeated University of Chicago club.

At the 1954 Cotton Bowl, Alabama's Tommy Lewis gained dubious notoriety when he tackled Rice's Dick Moegle *from the bench*, in football's "Worst Tackle!"

was deaf and dumb and Filman had a mouthful of gin, nobody spoke. "With signs and gestures," said a Ranger official, "the two of them labored over the layout, shaking their heads vigorously and pointing furiously with never a sound emanating from either one of them."

Boxing

Best Argentinian Fighter. Pascual Perez. Although Luis Firpo ("the Wild Bull of the Pampas") got the most publicity, thanks to his bout with Jack Dempsey, Perez was the more accomplished boxer. In 1948 Perez won the Olympic Flyweight Gold Medal and emerged as a proficient professional. Fragile in appearance (four feet, eleven inches, 106 pounds), Perez was the first Argentinian to win a professional championship when he outpointed Yoshio Shinai in Tokyo on September 9, 1954, thereby gaining the flyweight title. Perez scored fifty consecutive victories before losing a decision in a nontitle bout to Sodao Yarouta, the Japanese champion, in January 1959. Perez ultimately lost his world title to Pone Kingpetch of Thailand in April 1960.

Best Hockey-playing Fighter. Murray "Muzz" Patrick, who played defense for the 1940 Stanley Cup–winning New York Rangers, was regarded as one of Canada's greatest boxers in his time. Before becoming a regular in the National Hockey League, Patrick was amateur heavyweight champion of the British Empire. He also was a basketball, track, and six-day bike race star.

Best Versatile Champion. Henry Armstrong of Columbus, Mississippi, is distinguished as the only fighter ever to hold three championship titles simultaneously. During a four-month period in 1938, Armstrong was universally recognized as featherweight, lightweight, and welterweight champion. Armstrong finally relinquished his featherweight title in 1938 when he could not dip to the prescribed weight of 126 pounds.

Armstrong made his debut in October 1936, defeating Mike Belloise, the New York Athletic Commission featherweight champion. He received worldwide recognition as featherweight titleholder on October 29, 1937, when he beat Petey Sarron in the sixth round. Armstrong next won the welterweight crown, outpointing Barney Ross on May 31, 1938. His unprecedented third championship was the annexation of the lightweight championship when Armstrong outpointed Lou Ambers on August 17, 1938, in New York City.

In a return match with Ambers in August 1939, Armstrong lost the lightweight championship and in October 1940, Fritzie Zivic outpointed Armstrong for the welterweight championship before a packed Madison Square Garden on Eighth Avenue in Manhattan. The fight was stopped in the twelfth round when it appeared that Armstrong was blinded.

Armstrong announced his "retirement" shortly after losing to Zivic, but made a brief comeback, losing to Willie Joyce, Beau Jack, and Sugar Ray Robinson before finally calling it quits for good in 1945.

Best Attendance. Milwaukee, Wisconsin, August 18, 1941, Tony Zale vs. Billy Prior. A live audience of 135,132 watched Zale knock out Prior in the ninth round. Despite the awesome attendance, neither the fighters nor the promoters made a penny profit. The match was a free exhibition which had been staged by the local chapter of the Fraternal Order of Eagles.

Best Bare-knuckle Fighter. Jack Broughton, Great Britain. Born in Gloucestershire, Broughton preceded "The Great" John L. Sullivan who later became known as "the father of boxing." Broughton became English champion in 1734, defeating George Taylor at London in 20 minutes. Apart from his innumerable victories, Broughton made many contributions to boxing including the invention of the boxing glove. He also wrote the first set of boxing rules and remained the premier Britsh champion until he retired from the ring to become a landowner. Broughton died at the age of eighty-eight.

Best Little Heavyweight Champion. Tommy Burns, 1906. Weighing in at 180 pounds (and five feet, seven inches), Burns won the heavyweight championship by defeating Marvin Hart in Los Angeles on February 23, 1906. Burns retained the title for two years, finally losing it to Jack Johnson on December 26, 1908, in Sydney, Australia.

Best Australian Fighter. Albert Griffiths (alias Young Griffo). Born at Sydney in 1871, Griffo developed into one of the best defensive boxers of all time. British fight historian Maurice Golesworthy regarded Griffo as a classic stylist in the "old and professional art of self-defense."

Griffo's first title was the world featherweight championship, which he won in 1890 by outpointing Billy Murphy at Sydney. Although Griffo had beaten the American champion, Ike Weir, the Australian failed to gain recognition in the United States. However, in 1893 Griffo toured America, winning twelve consecutive bouts until losing to Jack McAuliffe in a disputed decision. He then won the hearts of American fight fans by battling the American featherweight ace, George Dixon, three times in two years (1894–95) and each time to a draw. Boxing critics regard those bouts as among the finest displays of the art of self-defense. Griffo died in 1927.

Best Comeback. Sugar Ray Robinson. The middleweight champion and one of the most exciting boxers of the post–World War II era, Robinson announced his retirement in December 1952 so that he could launch a career on the stage. However, the lure of the ring became irresistible and Robinson decided to make a comeback two years later. Normally, comeback attempts in boxing prove disastrous because the fighter inevitably falls out of condition and is unable to regain prime form. Robinson was the exception. Upon his return, he won five out of six fights including the middleweight championship. Sugar Ray and Carmen Basilio then engaged in a tug-of-war for the crown over the next few years in what developed into one of boxing's best rivalries. Robinson finally retired for good in 1959.

Best Losing Effort Against Joe Louis. After defeating James J. Braddock for the heavyweight championship in 1937, Joe Louis soon became the most feared heavyweight of the post–Jack Dempsey era and perhaps the most devastating boxer of all time. His nickname, "the Brown Bomber," was hardly a misnomer. It seemed that Louis could dispatch any foe, whether it be Lou Nova and his then notorious "Cosmo Punch" or "Two Ton" Tony Galento and his big, cushiony belly.

But Louis appeared to have met his match on June 18, 1941, when a young Irishman from Pittsburgh named Billy Conn entered the ring at the Polo Grounds for a crack at the Bomber's title. By the end of the twelfth round—the championship was a fifteen-round bout— Conn appeared headed for one of boxing's most startling upsets. He had dazzled Louis with his footwork and was well ahead on points as he left his corner for the start of the thirteenth round.

Abruptly and with no apparent forewarning to his handlers, Conn switched his style. For twelve rounds he had frustrated the heavier but slower Louis with his peripatetic defensive dancing and jabbing that obviously was wearing down the Bomber. But as the thirteenth round ticked off, Conn began trying for the haymaker. In the process of seeking the knockout blow, Conn took chances that he had conspicuously avoided in earlier

133

rounds. Eventually, he left himself open and the still alert Louis connected with the knockout punch. World War II intervened to prevent an immediate rematch. But Conn and Louis did enter the ring again in Yankee Stadium on June 19, 1946. This time Louis knocked out his foe in eight rounds.

Best French Fighter. Georges Carpentier. Born in Pas de Calais, Carpentier owned one of the fastest rights in the ring. At age sixteen he won the French lightweight championship. Two years later he won the European championship. His most widely publicized fight, however, was a defeat. Carpentier and Jack Dempsey attracted boxing's first million-dollar gate on July 2, 1921, at Boyle's Thirty Acres in Jersey City, New Jersey.

Best Lazy Champion. James J. Jeffries. After winning the heavyweight title from Bob Fitzsimmons on June 8, 1899, Jeffries fought only ten more times in his entire career. He retired in 1905.

Best Night. Tommy Burns, March 28, 1906, San Diego, California. Defending his heavyweight championship, the volatile Burns wiped out challenger Jim O'Brien in one round. Noting that another first-rate heavyweight was in town, Burns invited Jim Walker to take a crack at the crown *that same night*. Unruffled and hardly perspiring, Burns also knocked out Walker in one round.

Best Corruption of a Name. Al "Bummy" Davis, Brooklyn lightweight. In the late thirties, a young fighter named Albert Abraham Davidoff was too young to obtain an Amateur Athletic Association card. He assumed another (but older) teen-ager's name, Giovanni Pasconi. As Pasconi, Davidoff won several bouts until he was old enough to use his real name. But the name of Albert Abraham Davidoff never made it to the big time. A notoriously mean fighter, Davis was thought to have obtained the nickname Bummy because of his street-fighting tactics in the ring. Actually, it was because of his

134

Yiddish name Ahvroom, which became corrupted to Boomy, then Bummy!

Best Brother Combination. Joe and Vince Dundee. Boxing has enjoyed precious few brother acts. Those who have made it to the professional level rarely have reached championship status. The Dundees were an exception. Joe won the World Welterweight Championship in June 1927, when he won a fifteen-round decision from Pete Latzo in New York. He lost his title on a second round foul to Jackie Fields in Detroit on July 25, 1929.

His brother, Vince Dundee, was the American middleweight champion from October 30, 1933, when he decisioned Lou Broillard, until losing to Teddy Yarosz in Pittsburgh on September 11, 1934.

Best Tall Fighter. Jess Willard. The six-foot-six-and-a-half-inch Willard won the heavyweight championship from Jack Johnson on April 5, 1915. He remained champ until July 7, 1919, when he lost the title to Jack Dempsey.

Best "Jewish" Heavyweight. Max Baer. Heavyweight champion in 1934 and 1935, Baer remained a foremost contender for many years during the reign of Joe Louis. Although he wore a Star of David on his trunks, Baer's "Jewishness" was more publicity than fact. Legend has it that Baer originally became a boxer after he knocked a farmhand, who had been making advances to his girl friend, through a door. Baer won the heavyweight championship on June 14, 1934, from Primo Carnera. He lost it on June 13, 1935, to James J. Braddock.

Best Swedish Heavyweight. Ingemar Johansson. In 1959, a relatively unknown Scandinavian boxer knocked out heavyweight champion Floyd Patterson in the third round of their New York bout. Previously, Johansson had disposed of Eddie Machen in a bout at Gothenburg, Sweden, in 1958. Johansson remained the golden boy of boxing for one year.

In a rematch on June 20, 1960, Patterson knocked out

Johansson in the fifth round. The pair boxed again on March 13, 1961, in Miami. This time the Swede was eliminated by a knockout in the sixth round. He never again was a factor on the heavyweight scene.

Best Heavyweight.   Jack Johnson. One of the most controversial athletes, Johnson was the first black man to become heavyweight champion. According to the late boxing historian Nat Fleischer, publisher of *Ring* magazine, Johnson was the most accomplished heavyweight champion. Once Johnson reached the top, a campaign was launched by promoters to find a "White Hope" to dethrone the superb Negro fighter. One by one, Johnson disposed of the best opponents, including Jack O'Brien, Tony Ross, Al Kaufman, Stanley Ketchel, and Jim Jeffries before fleeing the country to escape a warrant for his arrest.

In Europe, Johnson continued to box, defeating André Spaul in two rounds and Frank Moran in twenty. He knocked out Jim Johnson in the first of two bouts and fought Jim Johnson to a draw in their second meeting, claiming he had broken his arm. American promoters finally persuaded Jack Johnson to meet Jess Willard for the heavyweight championship on April 5, 1915, in Havana, Cuba.

In a bout which, more than sixty years later, raises unresolved questions, Willard knocked out Johnson in the twentieth round and won the championship. At the time of the decisive blow, a broiling sun was scorching the ring. Photos taken at the time of Willard's knockout punches reveal Johnson shading his eyes against the sun. Some critics have suggested that Johnson had planned to take a dive; a charge which he denied until the day he died.

Although Johnson remained an active boxer until 1928, the Willard bout finished him as a major contender. The question of his alleged "dump" has continuously been revived. It played a major part in the Broadway hit play (and later movie) starring James Earl Jones, *The Great White Hope*.

136

Best Knockout Punch. Jack Johnson vs. Stanley Ketchel, October 16, 1909. In a bout at Colma, California, Johnson struck his foe with a roundhouse right that sent Ketchel reeling to the canvas. Apart from the damage to Ketchel's psyche, his mouth was significantly missing several teeth, several of which were later discovered well embedded in Johnson's boxing glove.

Best Nonknockout Punch. Luis Firpo vs. Jack Dempsey, September 4, 1923, at the Polo Grounds in New York City. In the first round, Dempsey had pummeled Firpo to the canvas seven times, but each time the Argentinian rebounded and counterattacked with a vicious right that catapulted Dempsey through the ropes and onto the working press section below. Cushioned by typewriters and aided by a friendly corps of newspapermen, Dempsey was able to return to the ring in time and held off Firpo long enough to recover his senses. In the second round Dempsey scored a knockout.

Best Promoter. George Lewis "Tex" Rickard. Father of the Madison Square Garden Arena (of Eighth Avenue and Fiftieth Street), Rickard came to Broadway after making a fortune in the Alaska gold rush. Shortly after moving from Texas to New York, Rickard and a group called "the Six Hundred Millionaires" joined forces to build the sports palace that was to be Madison Square Garden.

It was not difficult for an investor to be persuaded by Rickard. Tex had already staged the Joe Gans–Battling Nelson fight in Goldfield, Nevada, and cleared a net profit of $13,215. Four years later in Reno, Nevada, he promoted the Jack Johnson–Jim Jeffries bout that produced a record gate of $270,775 and a crowd of 15,760. (The five-game baseball World Series that year had gross receipts of $174,000.)

Boxing writer Barney Nagler observed: "Rickard's success as a promoter was remarkable in the sense that he was a novice. He had only seen one fight before staging the Gans-Nelson bout."

Once Madison Square Garden was completed, Rickard lured some of the world's best boxers to New York. Rickard's idea was to feature boxing at the "new" Garden and fill it at other times with such diverse events as the circus, track meets, and six-day bicycle races. However, Rickard soon was persuaded that he also could make a pretty penny on ice hockey. Hence, he invested in a National Hockey League team appropriately named (Tex's) Rangers. Although the Rangers were an immense success, Rickard's heart was in the boxing ring. He continued to promote successful fights and helped pave the way for the legalization of boxing in New York State.

Best Match That Never Materialized. London, England, June 1722. A feud between a pair of British women culminated with the following ad placed in a London newspaper:

"Challenge—I, Eliizabeth Wilkinson of Clerkenwell, having had some words with Hannah Hyfield and requiring satisfaction, do invite her to meet me upon the stage and to box for three guineas; each woman holding half a crown in each hand, and the first to drop the money to lose the battle."

Police authorization was required in London for all boxing matches. Wilkinson could not obtain such a permit and, as a result, the bout never materialized.

Best Honor. Jack Broughton, one of the most revered boxing figures in England, was buried at Westminster Abbey, burial place of British nobility, although Broughton was not a member of English royalty.

Best Prognosticator. Bob Fitzsimmons. Onetime heavyweight champion, Fitzsimmons was an inordinately superstitious athlete and one who placed great faith in the validity of dreams. Fitzsimmons frequently observed that he had dreamt the night before the fight that he would lose his championship to Jim Jeffries. Jeffries did, in fact, win the bout.

"I believe in dreams as I do the Gospel," said Fitzsimmons. "My reason for this strong feeling is that almost every dream I have had has come true."

Fitzsimmons liked to place good luck charms in his dressing room prior to his bouts. Once, when he was about to fight "Gentleman" Jim Corbett in Atlantic City, New Jersey, Fitzsimmons—a blacksmith by trade—made two horseshoes and placed them on his dressing room floor. "I made two horseshoes every week that I was in training and gave them away to newspapermen and my handlers," Fitzsimmons recalled. "When I had made the thirteenth horseshoe I decided to keep it for myself.

"One morning I was out on the road. My wife was following me on horseback. Suddenly, I got a hunch. I stopped running and said to her: 'Rose, I'm going to stop Corbett in the thirteenth round. This horseshoe had told me so!'" This time Fitzsimmons was wrong. He stopped Corbett in the fourteenth round.

Best Poet. Muhammad Ali (formerly Cassius Clay), composer of innumerable verses about himself ("float like a butterfly, sting like a bee"), was once invited to lecture on poetry at Oxford University.

Worst Conditions. When boxing still was illegal in New York State, a clandestine bout between Johnny Regan and "Nonpareil" Jack Dempsey (not to be confused with the later champion) was held in secrecy on an island off Long Island Sound on December 13, 1887. The winner would be heavyweight champion. A few well-chosen friends were invited to the secret bout which, unfortunately, was held perilously close to the shore.

In their haste to stage the fight, the promoters overlooked the possibility of rapidly rising tides. The tide began rising as the bout began and, soon, the boxers were flailing at each other while waist-high in water. Finally, the promoters called a halt and moved the ring further inland.

By the time the new site had been found and the bout

resumed, the weather had taken an abrupt turn for the frigid and Dempsey and Regan now found themselves fighting in a snowstorm. The bout ended in the forty-fifth round when Dempsey knocked out Regan with a right. The winner died a year later.

Worst Denial of a Title. Fred Apostoli, 1937, 1938. A middleweight who attained boxing maturity in the late thirties, Apostoli somehow ran afoul of the International Boxing Union, then the designator of champions. In 1937 the IBU recognized Marcel Thil as middleweight champion and Freddie Steele as the American titleholder. Apostoli was ruled the leading challenger.

In September 1937 Apostoli, who had been Golden Gloves champion, defeated Thil in ten rounds. However, the IBU denied him the championship because he had signed a prebout agreement stipulating that the fight with Thil would be a nontitle match. Shortly thereafter Thil resigned the championship whereupon Apostoli defeated Steele (January 7, 1938) and Glen Lee (April 1, 1938) in championship contests.

Not only did the IBU slight Apostoli but the National Boxing Association, the governing body of American boxing at the time, refused to award him the title, naming Al Hostak instead. No reason was given.

Worst Bloodbath. Sam McVey vs. Joe Jeannette, April 1909, Paris, France. Starting with a first-round knockdown, McVey floored Jeannette twenty-one times in the forty-nine-round bout. Nevertheless, despite the battering, Jeannette continued to counterattack and finally deposited McVey on the canvas in the thirty-ninth round. By the forty-ninth round, McVey had been floored nineteen times and at the start of that fateful round, McVey rose from his stool and abruptly collapsed, ending the fight.

Worst Heavyweight Champion. James J. Braddock, 1935–36. Considering that he was heavyweight champion for two years, Braddock was a well-defeated boxer, having suffered twenty-two losses in less than ninety bouts.
140

Worst Reward for a Champion.　John L. Sullivan, 1899. In a seventy-five-round bout at Richburg, Mississippi, "The Great" John L. defeated Jake Kilrain for the world heavyweight championship. At the end of the bout, both boxers were arrested—boxing was then illegal in Mississippi—and charged with assault and battery. Kilrain was sentenced to two months in jail while Sullivan was ordered to serve one year. The champion was released on bail and later won a new trial. Ultimately, he paid a $1,000 fine for winning the championship!

Worst Referee.　Wyatt Earp. Renowned for his quest for law and order as marshal of Tombstone, Arizona, Earp was considerably less effective in the boxing ring. Following his job as marshal, Earp moved to San Francisco where he did some work as a boxing official. Observers considered Earp less diligent with the law than he had been in Tombstone.

Once, Earp refereed a bout between Bob Fitzsimmons and Tom Sharkey at the National Athletic Club on December 2, 1896. Although Fitzsimmons pummeled Sharkey through most of the bout, it appeared that Earp had fixed the fight so that Sharkey (no relation to Jack Sharkey) would win. In the eighth round, with Sharkey barely able to stand, Earp stopped the fight and awarded the decision to Sharkey—on a foul claim.

The suitably irate Fitzsimmons started toward Earp to, at the very least, argue the decision. But the former marshal abruptly ended any further discussion by pulling out a loaded revolver. Fitzsimmons then staged an orderly retreat.

Worst Treatment of a Referee.　Pete Muller, German middleweight champion, vs. referee Max Pippow. During a bout with Hans Stretz of Cologne on June 1, 1952, the high-strung Muller took exception to the referee and punched Pippow to the canvas. For the swing, Muller was disqualified and banned for life by the German Boxing Association.

Worst Weight Discrepancy.   Tommy Loughran vs. Primo Carnera, March 1, 1934. Weighing in for their heavy-weight title bout in Miami, the goliath Carnera tipped the scales at 267 pounds, 86 more than his opponent. Notoriously clumsy, Carnera nevertheless outpointed Loughran in their fifteen-round match to retain the championship.

Worst Jinx.   Tom Sharkey, an Irish boxer, was paranoid about peacocks. While training for a bout with Gus Ruhlin, Bob Fitzsimmons, unaware of Sharkey's peacock phobia, sent him a flock of peacocks as a gift. "When the birds arrived," said Sharkey, "I nearly passed out. I remembered an old Irish woman once telling me that the owner of a peacock never had any good luck. I wanted to send those birds back to Fitz, but I loved him like a brother and didn't want to offend him. All through training camp I wept, thinking about those unlucky peacocks. When I lost to Gus in the eleventh round I blamed it on those Jonah birds."

Worst Crowd for a Heavyweight Championship.   Sonny Liston vs. Cassius Clay (later known as Muhammad Ali), Lewiston, Maine, May 25, 1965. In this rematch for the heavyweight championship, Ali retained his title with a first-round knockout over Liston. The attendance was 2,434.

Worst Jinxed Title.   The middleweight championship. More middleweights have suffered ill luck after winning the title. "Nonpareil" Jack Dempsey (no relation to the heavyweight champion), the first middleweight champion, lost his crown to Bob Fitzsimmons and was soon forgotten by friends and family. He was buried, a pauper, in an unmarked grave.

Stanley Ketchel, one of the best middleweights of all time, was murdered. Kid McCoy, middleweight champion from 1914–17, was imprisoned for murdering his girlfriend. Upon his release from jail, he committed suicide. Harry Greb, "the Pittsburgh Windmill," died on an operating table. Mickey Walker, "the Toy Bulldog," won almost a million dollars, but died broke. Marcel Cerdan, middleweight champion in 1948–49, died in a plane crash.

Worst Win for Jack Dempsey. Tommy Gibbons vs. Dempsey, at Shelby, Montana, July 5, 1923. Dempsey was the heavy favorite to demolish his challenger well before the fifteenth round, but, for inexplicable reasons, the heavyweight champion fought so poorly that even Dan McKettrick, a member of the Dempsey troupe, told the press corps after the fifth round: "The champ ain't fightin'." At the end of the twelfth round, a newspaperman said: "It's a good thing Dempsey has his own referee with him." Referee Jimmy Daugherty raised Dempsey's hand after the fifteenth round, announcing that Dempsey had won the decision. But it marked the first time since Dempsey had become champion that he failed to knock out his challenger. Some observers, including Warren Brown of the Chicago *Herald-Examiner,* blamed the surroundings for the fiasco. An arena, which was built for 47,000, was sprinkled with only 8,000 fans as the fighters entered the ring. "The crowd showed up for the fight all right," wrote Brown, "but not until a last-minute cut in prices was authorized, and $25,000 worth of customers came in at the reduced rates. Later in the afternoon, the gates were thrown open and the entire town of Shelby and visitors from outlying districts swarmed in to take advantage of the first chance ever given the American public to see a world's championship prize fight without laying down the old dough in one bunch or another."

Dempsey's effort was so disappointing that the fans soon began to take out their hostility on the press, which had picked the champion to win by a knockout. A shower of straw cushions fell on the reporters, who earlier had been bedeviled by the mosquitoes of Shelby. However, by the first round, the mosquitoes, inexplicably, had disappeared. "Perhaps," said Brown, "the insects, like most of the folks who had been asked to pay from $20 to $50 for seats, could not decide whether it was worth it. The mosquitoes, off stinging in another part of the state, did not hear about the free list until it was too late."

Most Unusual Referee's Exit.   Ruby Goldstein, June 25, 1952, at Yankee Stadium. Handling the World Light-Heavyweight Championship between Joey Maxim and Sugar Ray Robinson, Goldstein was compelled to retire from the bout because of the intense heat. Although the bout was held in the evening, the temperature hovered in the high eighties. Goldstein, tiring rapidly after having to separate the two fighters, was exhausted by the end of the tenth round and made his unceremonious exit.

Most Unusual End to a Career.   Al "Bummy" Davis. Famous for his four-round knockout of Schoolboy Fried-kin at Madison Square Garden in 1938, Bummy Davis became a boxing headliner in his early twenties. He fought a bitter fight with Fritzie Zivic at Madison Square Garden and remained one of New York's most exciting headliners until he met sudden death at the age of twenty-five. Davis had sold a bar to a friend in a tough Brooklyn neighborhood. One night two gunmen entered the bar while Davis was visiting his friend. One of the gangsters used profanity in ushering Bummy to the wall. Furious, Davis wheeled and uncorked his formidable left hook, breaking the stickup man's jaw in two places. But the gangster held on to his gun and shot Davis through the throat. Davis chased the gunman out the door, but collapsed dead on the sidewalk.

Most Unusual Knockout.   Ad Wolgast vs. Joe Rivers, July 14, 1912. World Lightweight Champion Wolgast and Rivers connected simultaneously with equally potent blows in the thirteenth round of their title bout. The equally stunned boxers collapsed to the canvas while referee Joe Welsh began his count. When Welsh realized that neither boxer would be able to survive the ten count,

144

he lifted the favorite, Wolgast, to his feet, propped him up and, finally, counted Rivers out.

Most Unusual Punch. Ike Williams. The lightweight champion from 1947 to 1951, Williams employed a devastating "Bolo Punch" with great effect. Williams' weapon was a wide, swinging punch brought up, seemingly, from the canvas. Its origins were in the Cuban sugar fields where workers, harvesting the cane, swung their machetes cutting a similar swath.

Most Unusual Knockdown. Charles Weinert vs. André Anderson, 1916. Despite his youth, Weinert was one of the best heavyweights, having defeated the likes of "Battling" Levinsky and "Porky" Flynn. Matchmaker Billy Gatson staged the bout at the old Manhattan Opera House, putting the ring on the stage.

In the second round, Weinert hit Anderson with a left hook and then an uppercut to the jaw. Anderson was catapulted through the ropes, rolled off the Opera House stage, and fell into the orchestra pit amid an assortment of musical instruments. "He landed seat first in the wide, inviting mouth of the big bass horn," said *Ring* magazine publisher and historian Nat Fleischer. "Tightly wedged into the horn, Anderson strove in vain to extricate himself while the referee reached through the ropes and tolled off the fatal ten."

Most Unusual Treatment. Victor McLaglen. Later to become an actor and Hollywood film star, McLaglen had been a boxer and once was nearly killed, accidentally, during a bout with Phil Schlossberg in Vancouver, British Columbia, in 1908. The incident developed after Schlossberg split McLaglen's lip with a punch and blood flowed freely down his throat. When the round ended, McLaglen returned to his corner to be treated by an extremely nervous and absentminded trainer. "He asked me to toss my head back," McLaglen said, "and then poured some lotion down my throat. I immediately collapsed, unable

145

to catch my breath, and was carried to the dressing room. The guy had poured ammonia down my throat—and a good dose of it, at that. I never again took a mouthwash without smelling it to be sure it wasn't ammonia!"

Most Unusual Comeback. Nava Esparza, December 15, 1947. A Mexican welterweight, Esparza was belabored by Rocco Rossano of Brooklyn at the St. Nicholas Arena. Within 26 seconds of the opening bell, Esparza was horizontal, taking the ten count. When, at last, he was revived, Esparza climbed out of the ring. But, instead of proceeding to the dressing room, he picked up his water bucket and went back to the ring—to await the next fighter. The punch-shocked Esparza had attempted to become a "second" for the next match!

Most Unusual Delayed Knockout. Babe Herman (a Californian and no relation to the baseball player of the same name) once fought Irish Johnny Curtin at New York City's Pioneer Club. A split second before the bell sounded ending the fifth round, Herman landed a hard right to Curtin's jaw. As the bell went off, the fighters headed for their respective corners. Curtin took two steps and then, feeling the effects of the blow, pitched forward and fell, unconscious, to the canvas. He was unable to answer the bell for round six.

Most Unusual Standing Knockout. Benny Leonard vs. Freddie Welsh, May 28, 1917. As Leonard battered Welsh into a corner, Freddie clung to the ropes for support. Leonard followed through with a right to the jaw and a flurry of jabs that sent Welsh back across the ropes, glassy-eyed but not horizontal. Referee Kid McPortland ushered Leonard away from his groggy foe. Although Welsh was not on the canvas, McPortland began counting him out. At precisely the count of ten, Welsh dropped to the canvas and soon was carted out of the ring.

Most Unusual Technical Knockout. John C. Morrissey

vs. Yankee Sullivan, October 1953. In the thirty-seventh round, Sullivan was ruled the loser on a TKO because he failed to answer the bell. Sullivan was not physically incapacitated, but he had been taken up with some between-rounds activity. He had used the rest period to beat up a group of Morrissey's rooters who had been needling him throughout the match.

Most Unusual Undefeated Champion. Theagenes of Thasos. According to historians, Theagenes was the most successful warrior in pre-Christian Greece. At a time when one-on-one battles required a fight to the death, Theagenes reportedly obliterated 1,425 challengers in a row.

Most Unusual Sparring Partner. In preparation for his bout with Harry Gibbons, Jack Dempsey once recruited J. Paul Getty, who became one of the richest men in the world.

Most Unusual Dedication. John McNeil, New York State boxing commissioner, 1924–36. During his term of office, McNeil saw 30,000 fights, worth 70,000 rounds.

Most Unusual Undefeated Streak. Hal Bagwell, Gloucester, England. Although he fought 183 consecutive bouts without losing (including five draws), between August 10, 1938, and November 28, 1949, Bagwell remained in virtual anonymity.

Most Unusual Major Bout. Jim Mace vs. Joe Coburn. Billed as "The Fight of the Century," the bout between the English champion, Mace, and Coburn, the onetime American champion, went three hours and 48 minutes, but hardly a punch was thrown.

Most Unusual Boxer-Wrestler. Abe "the Newsboy" Hollander. Between 1905 and 1918 Hollander alternately participated in 1,309 boxing matches and 387 wrestling matches.

147

Most Unusual Postponement. Billy Conn vs. Bob Pastor, May 11, 1942. Following his superb thirteen-round performance against heavyweight champion Joe Louis, Billy Conn became the darling of boxing. However, since Conn ultimately lost the bout, he was compelled to earn his way back to a second challenge by facing other boxers. A bout, therefore, was lined up with heavyweight Bob Pastor. Conn was a favorite to rout Pastor until, as New York *Herald-Tribune* boxing writer Caswell Adams noted, "Billy broke his left hand on the granite head of his father-in-law, Jimmy Smith, at an Irish post-christening party." The shattering of Conn's metacarpal bone meant that his bout with Louis had to be postponed—not to mention his bout with Pastor. "Bob Pastor," said Adams, "got the break of his life when Conn hit Smith."

Boxing promoters, upon hearing the details of Conn's bout with his father-in-law, wished they could have booked the two relatives in the ring instead of Conn and Pastor. "Billy suffered a severe cut," said Adams, "when one of his right-hand swings at his father-in-law went wild and through a kitchen window."

Soon news of the bout at the christening obtained almost as much newspaper space as a regular boxing match between Conn and a foe. Billy, himself, was quoted at length, describing how he had hoped to make peace with his father-in-law.

"As the rest of the family were talking and shaking hands," said Conn, "I went into the kitchen. The old man started right away to bring up old sores. I said that I didn't come to argue and he started to holler. And I told him not to holler at me, that I wasn't deaf and I kept smiling through it all. Finally, the yelling gets so loud that I asked him if he was trying to scare me and he shook his finger at me and I said I wasn't scared of anyone and he said that he waited long enough to get me.

"Well, he punched me and then I punched him and right away I felt a funny feeling in my left hand after I hit Smith on top of the head and then I threw my right, but through the window and then we both went down on the floor, with him scratching at me and giving me this.

148

And then the place was a madhouse, with everyone coming in from the other room. . . . It's a hell of a thing that whenever you get in a fight your friends grab and hold you. Why don't they hold the other guy?"

Apart from Conn, the man who suffered most from the postponement was veteran fight promoter Mike Jacobs, who figured to make a lot of money from the bout. When Jacobs heard about the circumstances leading to Conn's injury, he replied: "You could have called the turn on a thing like that happening at a christening. That's the way those things go!"

Horse Racing

Best Bet. John W. Gates, a gambler so rich he could—and did—bet on anything, once amassed a mind-blowing $2 million in one race. Gates pulled his miracle betting coup by placing his stake, appropriately enough, on a horse named Royal Flush in the Stewards' Cup.

This obscure horse opened at odds of 100 to 1, but Gates turned his claque loose on the bookies, and after the ensuing orgy of betting, the odds had dropped to 10 to 1.

Royal Flush won by a handy six lengths, over Americus; and "Bet-a-Million" Gates, normally a blasé gentleman, threw off his poker-face exterior for once. He clutched his wife in a mighty bear hug, lifted her high in the air, then waltzed her all over the grounds!

Best Undefeated Horse. The famed Eclipse, one of three foundation sires (the others being Matchem and Herod), who first appeared in 1769 to win every race he entered that year, including the King's Plate, the Salisbury, and the Lichfield. By the end of this year, odds on Eclipse were often put at 1 to 100!

But the single race for which Eclipse was undoubtedly best remembered was a special one against sixteen of England's greatest thoroughbreds. Dennis O'Kelly, who had purchased this fabled beast for a paltry 1,100 guineas, bet friends that he could predict the exact finish of the race. His boast helped to make this event one of Britain's most-talked-about matches ever.

Eclipse demolished the competition, not only "distancing" them—surpassing the field by a lap—but double-distancing them, a feat which has never been duplicated.

And O'Kelly's prediction? "Eclipse first," he had written on a sealed sheet of paper, unsurprisingly enough. But O'Kelly's scribble went on to say . . . "the rest, nowhere."

Best Mare.   There is no doubt that modern racing lovers fell for the late Ruffian, whose fiery life ended so tragically in July 1975, after an injury she suffered in a match race with Foolish Pleasure. One of the gamest fillies ever to put hoof on turf, the rangy black mare could well have become a legend in racing history. But since her life was snuffed before the world could decide her true greatness, our choice instead is Kincsem, the Hungarian mare who swept to eighteen consecutive European victories in the 1870s.

Born to Waternymph, owned by Prince Paul Esterhazy, and later sold to a reluctant and unidentified owner, Kincsem won her first race at Hanover, Germany, against a field which included Double Zero, that year's German Derby winner. During her first trip to the British Isles, Kincsem suffered a terrific bout of *mal-de-mer* (seasickness), but recovered in time to win the Goodwood Cup. Kincsem's victory had been so decisive and her performance so impressive, that the Prince of Wales offered to buy her. His Royal Highness to be had to be turned down, however, rather than incur the wrath of the entire Hungarian nation for having sold their favorite.

Kincsem, which means "my treasure" in the Magyar tongue, died at the age of fourteen, and on that date a national day of mourning was declared throughout Hungary. Newspapers ran black borders around their pages, and people wept openly on the streets of Buda and Pest.

Best Won-Loss Record. Again, it's our choice for greatest mare, Kincsem. She was unbeaten in fifty-four incredible races between 1877 and 1880, including the aforementioned English Goodwood Cup of 1878.

Best Money Winner. Kelso, who won a total of $1,977,896 between 1959 and 1966. During his career, he won thirty-nine of sixty-three races, placed in twelve, and showed in two.

Best Money Winner in One Year. Secretariat, who won an astounding $860,404 in 1973 alone, including, of course, his prizes in taking the Triple Crown—Kentucky Derby, Preakness, and Belmont. His total winnings throughout his short but record-breaking career were $1,176,781!

Best Ploy by an Owner. The closest thing to a sucker punch in horse-racing history came when several Australians, eager to test their talent in the States, brought in what they called two of their best in horseflesh—Winooka, a strong, fine-looking animal, and Travallion, a rather gangly creature.

Winooka, after appearing in several races, was a disappointment. Travallion was an even bigger nothing, seemingly just a pacer for Winooka, consistently finishing behind him.

Then, strangely, the Aussies entered Travallion in the last event of an afternoon in which Winooka had squeaked out a third in an earlier race. Bookies gleefully took bets on the horse, who had done absolutely nothing in workouts, and odds on Travallion went to 15 to 1 by post time.

Imagine the touts' chagrin when Travallion breezed to

a huge lead before the race was even in the backstretch, and subsequently coasted home. It was only then that the bookies realized they had been dunned. Winooka's image as the star of the pair had been a ruse—Travallion had been the kicker.

The sucker punch—feint with the left, then attack with the right—had been all too neatly delivered right to the chins of the American bookies.

Best Longshot. Dragon Blood, a British horse, ridden by Lester Piggot in the Primio Naviglio at Milan, Italy, on June 1, 1967, started the race at odds of 10,000 to 1 . . . and that's a lotta lira for some lucky winner!

Best Payoff. Forgetting about combination bets, such as the Daily Double, Triple, Exacta, etc., the best payoff on a single $1 ticket to win is $941.75, on Wishing Ring at Latonia in Kentucky in 1912.

Best First Prize. Rheingold came in first at the 1973 Arc De Triomphe race in Paris, and was rewarded with 1,497,400 francs, or $382,651.

Best Price for a Thoroughbred. Mrs. Penny Tweedy and a syndicate of twenty-eight other members, each of whom forked over $190,000, paid a total for Secretariat, in February 1973, of $6,080,000!

Secretariat—as virtually everyone knows—went on to win the Triple Crown of American racing, breaking records along his way. When "Big Red" was put out to stud, however, it looked as though Mrs. Tweedy and her syndicate might have bought a very fast pig in a poke, for the large stallion's fertility tests were questionable. Secretariat settled down to his "chores" eventually, though, and his offspring are already bringing fancy prices.

Best Price for a Standardbred. Nevele Pride, thought by many to be the greatest trotter in history, brought a price of $3 million from Louis Resnick and Nevele Acres, in 1969.

Best Winnings by a Standardbred. Une de Mai carted his gig to a total of $1,851,424, until he was retired at the end of the 1973 season; and Albatross, a pacer, brought in $1,201,470 until he was put to stud in December 1972.

Best Thoroughbred. Man o' War, right? Wrong. Well, then, maybe Citation, or Secretariat, or even Nashua? Wrong again!

Based strictly on winning—and isn't that what it's all about—the best ever has to be Kingston, son of Spendthrift, owned by Mike Dwyer. Kingston won more races than any animal which ever put hoof to turf—89 of 138 races.

Best Harness Farm. The Hanover Shoe Farm of Hanover, Pennsylvania, has bred such champions as Bret Hanover, Adios, and the fabled Nevele Pride, only three among what might well be dozens of winners throughout the country on any given day.

Best Thoroughbred Farm. The consensus, even with the Thoroughbred Breeders Association, is that Spendthrift Farm of Lexington, Kentucky, has produced the most of the best of the winners over the years. Spendthrift steeds have included Majestic Prince, winner of the 1969 Kentucky Derby; and Caracolero, a champion colt who raced and won in Europe.

Best Mile. Considering that the course in Brighton, England, slopes downhill for two-thirds of a mile, it is no big surprise that the record for the fastest mile was set there, by Soueida, on September 19, 1963. Furthermore, that record was tied three years later by Loose Cover, on June 9, 1966. Both horses ran the mile in one minute, 31.8 seconds, clocking 39.21 miles an hour!

Best Two Miles. The most common distance run at American tracks today seldom exceeds a mile and a quarter, with many races of a mere six or seven furlongs, but the longer races are still common in England,
154

Australia, and New Zealand—where the record for two miles was set in Trentham, Wellington. Il Tempo managed that distance in three minutes, 16.75 seconds, on January 17, 1970.

Best Stretch Drive. The Thornton Stakes was a marathon four-mile race which used to be held annually in California. These long races, based on the European models, were once run often in the States, but have been discontinued in favor of the "sprint" type race, often as little as six furlongs.

But on the occasion of this running of the Thornton Stakes, one jockey by the name of Willie Martin had been given strict orders beforehand concerning his horse, Star Ruby. No matter what, Martin was not to prod Star Ruby until the last mile of the race.

This looked to be a horrendous strategy, as the horse, favored before the race, fell 100 lengths behind, to bettors' distress. Miraculously, though, Star Ruby began to close, without prodding: 100 lengths behind at the half-mile pole, she had closed the gap to 20 lengths as they came into the stretch.

"Then," writes turf historian Horace Wade, "with one final stroke of the bat, the mare's colors leapt up to engulf the leaders and soar away to an easy victory. Star Ruby ran the last mile of that grueling race in the most incredible time of 1:43. It was as game a stretch drive as the sport has ever seen."

Best Endurance. Logan raced an incredible seventy-three times in 1893, winning twenty-one, placing in nine, and earning third in nineteen!

Best Breeder. King Darius of Persia (522–485 B.C.) is fabled to have had more than fifty thousand brood mares. Of course, it is also true that the horses of that era were half the size of today's throughbred, but that still makes one heck of a brood herd!

Best Investment. Alsab was purchased for $700, but

won $350,015 during his career. Not many people can get a 500 percent return on their investment today!

Best Horse at Overcoming Injury. The modern racehorse, bred entirely for speed, is much like a rare concert violin: the slightest maladjustment and an entire career is ruined. A minor cold, for example, renders the thoroughbred incapable of running.

The story of My Dandy, a chestnut gelding which raced in the twenties and early thirties, is therefore remarkable, for he returned from not one or two injuries, but *four,* when he should, by tradition, have been destroyed.

My Dandy's first mishap was shipping fever, a type of pneumonia, which he contracted en route from the Midwest to New Orleans. Veterinarians claimed the colt would never recover, but the horse's trainer, Jack Carter, protested.

"I know this colt," he insisted. "He'll fight this thing out, and win over it." And win he did: $40,000 that year!

My Dandy was next injured in a freak accident, when a nail in his stable punctured his eye. "The right eye is gone," said the track vet. "The left eye may follow in sympathy. He'll never race again. My advice is to shoot him."

Again the advice was ignored, and the game colt finished in the money twenty-seven times out of thirty-two starts that year, with only one eye!

When the horse developed lameness, he was retired. It was obvious that My Dandy was bored with the easy life, however, and astoundingly, he was brought out of retirement. His fourth injury occurred in a workout and it was again recommended that he be destroyed, and again, the recommendation was ignored. And all My Dandy did, when he first raced after his fourth injury, was to come from dead last to win!

Best Blind Pacer. Sleepy Tom, billed as "The World's Toughest Piece of Horseflesh," captured the fancy of the American racing public in 1879, helping to draw crowds by his appearances. Why? Sleepy Tom was blind in both eyes!

Best-Named Horse. Just has to be Upset, who beat Man o' War—that legend's only defeat—in the 1919 Sanford Memorial Stakes at Saratoga Springs, New York. William Knapp, who rode Upset on that shocking day, recalled his victory with something close to regret.

"Sure, Upset beat Man o' War, but looking back on it now, I know that Man o' War surely was one horse which should've retired undefeated. Never was a horse like him. He could do anything—and do it better than any other horse that ever lived.

"If I'd moved over just an eyelash that day at Saratoga, he'd have whipped me from Dan to Beersheba and never had a losing scratch against his amazing record.

"Sometimes, thinking back, I'm sorry I didn't do it!"

Best Rescue. When the racehorse Moifaa was being shipped from Australia to England, the ship was wrecked, and he was given up for dead. The plucky animal swam to shore, however, and was found by a fisherman. Returned to his trainer in time to be reconditioned, Moifaa was entered in the Grand National Steeplechase, the reason for which he had originally been shipped to England, and won, against 25 to 1 odds!

Best Single Day for a Jockey. He's not exactly a household name, but one Hubert S. Jones, riding the mounts at Caliente, California, in the forties, won eight races on June 11, 1944. As if that weren't cause enough for cardiac arrests among the touts, five of Jones's wins were photo finishes!

Best Year for a Jockey. How do you call it—most wins or most moolah? Well, in 1974, Chris McCarron, a mere stripling of nineteen years, won a total of 517 races for a record; but in that same year Laffitt Pincay, Jr., set a high money mark, by galloping for a tidy $4,231,441.

157

Best Race by a Kid. It may appear that jockeys today are starting out younger and younger, but in fact, the youth mark was set many years ago, between 1909 and 1912, by one Frank Wootton. Frank was the English champion jockey for those years, and Wootton had ridden his first winner in South Africa at the incredible age of nine years, ten months!

Best Reason to Diet. The lighter the jockey the better—right? A gentleman known to the world only as Kitchener (no relation to the famous British general) would undoubtedly agree, since he rode Red Deer in England's Chester Cup in 1844, weighing but 49 pounds!

Best Comeback by a Jockey. There have been jockeys who have returned to the top of their profession from serious injuries, but only one, Ralph Neves, returned from the dead!

At Bay Meadows, on May 8, 1936, Neves' mount tripped going into the stretch, and Neves was flung head-first into the rail. After examining the inert form, the track doctor announced that Neves' heart had stopped. Nevertheless, the jockey was rushed to the hospital, where efforts to revive him were futile. Neves was pronouncd dead by one doctor, and covered by a sheet.

"I was never so surprised in my life," Neves later related, "when I heard the doctor say. 'He's dead.' I knew I didn't feel dead, even if I was sore all over. So I decided it was time to open my eyes and say to the doctor, 'How about a shot of pop, Doc?'

"He jumped a foot and a half and got as white as the sheet he had covered me with. I was rushed to a hospital bed, which seemed silly to me when I knew I was billed to ride Instigator in the seventh race!"

Finally left alone in his room, Neves dressed, sneaked out of the hospital, hailed a cab, and returned to the track, where he suited up for the seventh race. It was just a bit unsettling for his *confrères* when Neves strolled into the jockeys' quarters at the precise moment they were taking a collection for his funeral wreath! Imagine, too, the shock to Ralph's wife, who was just returning from a tearful meeting with the track president, who had given her his condolences, when Ralph entered. The poor "widow" fainted dead away!

Neves returned from his "death" to become one of America's top jockeys.

Best Example that Life Begins at . . . Sixty! Victor Morely Lawson won the first race of his career on October 16, 1973, as he rode Ocean King to the winner's circle in Warwick, England. There was nothing unusual in this, except that Lawson was sixty-seven!

Best Driver. Canada's Herve Filion, who races at New York's Yonkers and Roosevelt Raceways, won 637 races in 1974, establishing a record of 5,147 career victories. Every race won since, has, of course, added to that illustrious total.

Worst Bet. Mike Dwyer, a colorful figure in the sport of kings, once bet a quarter of a million dollars on one of his nags, Harry Reed. Dwyer shipped the flat sprinter to England for the sole purpose of making a killing, and once in the British Isles, Dwyer ran from bookie to bookie, laying on bet after bet.

Discomfited by Dwyer's un-English antics, the staid Britishers were delighted, therefore, when Harry Reed abruptly wheeled at the race's start, and stood immovable, tail pointing in the direction he should have been heading!

Dwyer not only did not get a run for his quarter-million-dollar wager, he didn't even get a walk!

Worst Track Investments. Emil Schwartzhaupt was a wealthy man who decided he wanted a Kentucky Derby winner—at any cost. Thus, he spent $30,000 for Tommy Ganty from Blue Larkspar/Mame O'Hara; $26,000 for Hilar out of Bull Dog/Epitome; and another $25,000 for Dancing Margot out of Challenger II/Bay Appointment.

Tommy Ganty never saw a starting gate; Hilar never returned a penny; and Dancing Margot, the most successful of the three, returned a paltry $3,125.

Worst Reason to Lose a Kentucky Derby. Head Play, second to Broker's Tip in the 1932 Run for the Roses—a race touted by some as the dirtiest ever—might have won but for the whim of his owner, Mrs. Silas Mason. Unable to attend the Derby because she was in England, Mrs. Mason, an avid follower of spiritualism, consulted a medium to see how her horse would fare in the match.

"Your horse," responded the medium, "is the best, but I see a cloud in the crystal. You are in danger of being crossed by a crooked clique."

"What shall I do?" asked the stunned Mrs. Mason.

"Change jockeys," immediately suggested the medium.

Unfortunately, Mrs. Mason put her jockeys where her medium's mouth was, and switched from the veteran Charlie Kurtsinger to an unknown, Herb Fisher. More unfortunate still, Fisher didn't have the experience to counter the tactics of Broker's Tip's jockey, Don McCade, who slashed at Fisher when the two entered the stretch. Kurtsinger would have known how to handle the situation, and would probably have brought what was undoubtedly the best horse in the field from a disappointing and unfair second, to the winner's circle.

Worst Fix. The 1926 Champlain Handicap, in Aurora, Illinois, never was run, after it was discovered that six of seven entries had been poisoned!

Apology and Elizabeth K were killed, and four others ruined by a gang who had planned to make a bundle on a horse named Fayenza, the only animal not poisoned. They made a "killing" all right, but overdoses of strychnine revealed their plot, and W. W. Young, president of the Day and Night Bank of Charleston, West Virginia, was convicted and sentenced to reimburse the owners a total
160

of more than $40,000. His lethal partners were given jail sentences.

Worst Curse. The bookie's dream is the absolutely sure bet, and during the thirties there was one sure thing *never* to bet on in the Epsom Derby—and that was any horse whose name began with the letter *w!* A bet on such a horse was a lesson in throwing money away, and the reason, according to turf legend, is because of a gypsy curse!

Gypsy Lee (no relation to Gypsy Rose Lee!), a member of the Romany family, is said to have placed her whammy on the *w*s after she had predicted the winner of that year's Epsom Derby would be a horse named "Blew Gown." An owner chided Gypsy Lee for her ignorance by pointing out that "blue" was spelled with a *u*, not a *w*. Furious for being made a fool, Gypsy retaliated by stating that she would place a curse on any horse whose name began with a *w*—such a horse would never win the Epsom Derby while she lived.

True to the gypsy's curse, no such horse did win the Derby. Gypsy Lee died in 1934, and, come time for the Epsom Derby, her relatives eagerly scanned the field for a horse with a name beginning in *w*. Windsor Lad, owned by the Maharaja of Rajpipla, was entered and the gypsies placed all of their holdings on him.

Somewhere in the Great Beyond, Gypsy Lee must have smiled a knowing smile: Windsor Lad won the Epsom Derby, paying 7 to 1!

Worst Star-crossed Horse. The famed Black Gold was born under the eerie light of a comet.

"It's an ill omen," mourned H. M. Hoots, the colt's owner. "It bodes ill to the colt and evil to those who handle him."

As though echoing his very words, Hoots contracted pneumonia that very night, after a lifetime without a single illness, and died soon after. But that was merely the onset of what would be a celebrated, but tragic, life for Black Gold:

161

• He developed a weak left foreleg, inherited from his dam, Useeit, but won the 1923 Bashford Stakes running on the bad leg.

• He was the favorite in the 1924 Kentucky Derby, and won, paying 10 to 1. The bettors were left empty-handed, though, when the bookies ran off with the bets!

• After being put out to stud following the 1924 Chicago Derby, it was discovered that Black Gold was sterile, so he was raced again. Horribly, he broke down on his first start, and had to be destroyed.

And the people who surrounded Black Gold during his ill-fated life fared no better:

• Jockey J. D. Mooney, Black Gold's mount in the Kentucky Derby, soon became overweight and lost his meal ticket. So did the horse's trainer, Stanley Webb, who ignored advice from veterinarians that the leg would be unable to take the strain of racing after prolonged inactivity.

• Waldo Freeman, the stable agent, had three wins in one day immediately after Black Gold was put down, which looked as though he had escaped the negative influence of the colt. However, he suffered a heart attack and died that same day!

Today Black Gold is buried in the infield of the New Orleans Fair Grounds, where he had started his strange career—fortunately the fair grounds seems unaffected by the star-crossed horse's past.

Worst Brother of a Winner. Playfellow was the son of Fair Play, and a full brother to the unique Man o' War. While his sibling's feats were legend, playful Playfellow did not follow his brother's hoofsteps: he won no races as a two-year-old, two races as a three-year-old, and none as a four- or five-year-old.

Oh, brother!

Worst-looking Derby Winner. Morvich, an ungainly and angular foal, was named by his breeder, Adolph Spreckles, after a similarly clumsy character Spreckles was reading about at the time of the colt's birth.

Luckily, Morvich was singularly unaware of his appearance or his nickname, "the Ugly Duckling." In fact, he won eleven races as a two-year-old, and the 1922 Kentucky Derby as well. After his win at Churchill Downs, Morvich was toasted by Edward P. Morrow, governor of Kentucky:

"I congratulate the man who bred the winner; the trainer, who, with skill and enthusiasm, directed this thoroughbred; and the owner who brought him a great distance to the soil of Kentucky, who entered him as a sportsman and won in a fashion truly worthy of the commendation of all . . .

"But above all, I congratulate, thank God, the horse!"

Worst Mistreatment of a Horse in a Race. One race in Idaho featured cow ponies carrying riders a distance of 100 miles! Six horses dropped dead from the strain, and the race was eventually shortened to 85 miles.

Worst Start of a Jockey's Career. Eddie Arcaro, one of the greatest jockeys in turf history, rode 250 losers before he won his first race!

Ultimately, Arcaro won 4,779 races—including five Derby winners, six in the Preakness, and six in the Belmont Stakes, on such horses as Whirlaway, Citation, and Kelso.

———

Most Unusual Horse's Birthday. Any day other than January 1, which is the universal birthday of all registered horses. Standardbreds become a year older on that date, even if the foal is born the day before, on December 31!

Naturally, this has an effect on the breeding patterns for horses, since it would be absurd to breed for a fine race horse, and then have the foal born near January 1, which would force it to train and race in an age category nearly a year more mature than its actual age. On the other hand, the closer to the first of the year on the January side, the more development a foal has when it begins its racing career as a two-year-old.

163

Most Unusual Betting Story.   Philip Pine, author of *The Complete Book of Harness Racing,* relates what has to be one of sport's most eccentric betting tales:

"A faithful fan at Bay State Raceway, who commuted regularly from the track to Salem, Massachusetts, parked his car in a darkened corner of the parking lot on a warm summer evening. He wasn't quite ready for what was to happen to him.

"A bent, ugly old woman whose voice crackled and rattled when she spoke approached the man out of the shadows. A black shawl covered her head and a cloak-like dress clung to the ground as she shuffled toward him. A crooked finger wagged in his face as she cracked: 'Would you like to know all the winners for tonight's races?'

"The man remained silent, but finally shook his head up and down.

" 'Well, I'm a witch, young man, and I have powers to look into the future. I can tell you who's going to win tonight. You can become rich, but first, you must do something for me.'

"The shaken man's sudden thoughts of easy riches stirred him out of his fears and he blurted, 'What do I have to do?'

" 'Kiss me,' came the raspy reply.

"The man could think of nothing worse.

" 'Hug me and kiss me and riches will be yours,' crooned the crone.

"A wave of revulsion washed over the man. But his greed for easy money overcame the distasteful decision placed before him. Without a word, he grabbed the old woman and planted a kiss below her warted nose.

"Wiping his lips with his right sleeve, he asked, "Okay you got what you wanted. Now gimme the names of those winners tonight.'

" 'How old are you, sonny?' queried the woman.

" 'Thirty-five,' he said.

" 'Sonny, ain't you a little old to be believing in witches?' And she shuffled back into the shadows."

Most Unusual Betting System. Horace Wade, dean of turf historians, recalls one fellow's unique system:

"There was one fan in Arlington Park, Chicago, who used to arrive at the track an hour or two before post time. He would sit there, watching with entranced vision, the broad sweep of the sky. A bird would flutter past. Instantly his pencil would ring up Horse Number One to win. Perhaps later a flock of five English sparrows would wing past. His pencil would circle Horse Number Five and then two birds would fly by and Number Two Horse would be spotted for show money.

"I confess to watching that race with an intense interest, and, sure enough, those horses came galloping home, red, white and blue, exactly as he had played them.

"Before the season closed, the 'bird system' had many ardent disciples. I asked its ingenious owner what he did if more birds flocked by at one time than were horses in the race.

" 'Play the field to win,' he answered, laconically."

Most Unusual Stroke of Luck. Two soldiers once pulled up to Thistledown with a paltry $2.19 between them. This was in the good old days when a uniform was a symbol for respect, so they were admitted free, and with a dime they purchased a program, deciding to bet the Daily Double.

The two chose their bets by rolling a pebble onto the program sheet, noting upon whom it stopped. Unhappy with the stone's choices, they rolled the pebble again. Incredibly, the pebble rolled to a halt on the exact same horses!

Wary of toying with fate, the GIs bet their last two dollars on the two nags chosen by the pebble's roll, leaving themselves with a riproaring nine cents in their collective pockets. One hour later they strolled away with a check for $2,400 in their hands, courtesy of the Daily Double!

Most Unusual Ploy. The "chicken game," an effort to convince bookies that a horse was a "bleeder," was common practice immediately following the Civil War.

Bleeding in a horse is hemorrhaging from the nostrils, caused by the horse choking with exertion, which in turn causes the horse to "pull up." The phenomenon is quite common, and no more harmful than a nosebleed in humans, but a "bleeder" is a poor betting risk, because they pull up quite often.

And the "chicken game"? An unscrupulous bettor would acquire a freshly killed fowl, cut it open, collect the blood in a small pouch, and insert the pouch in the horse's mouth. When the pouch burst in the heat of the race, the horse would appear to be a bleeder, putting it in low esteem with the bookies. Having increased the odds against the horse, the nefarious bettor would then bet on the nag and often clean up.

The "chicken game" died a worthy death when investigators and bookmakers cottoned on to the chicanery.

Most Unusual Promotion. In 1910 the Secretary of the Charleston, South Carolina, racetrack, Martin Nathanson, devised a means of boosting sagging track attendance—by running a camel race! The animals were provided by a local carnival passing through town; the riders were from among the carnival performers.

Five camels were entered and since the bookies had absolutely no track record upon which to give odds, each beast was rated at 4 to 1. However, one animal, Ben Ali, became the early favorite of several Arabs working in the carnival, and by post time, odds on Ben Ali had softened to 8 to 5.

Things began to smell a mite fishy when the very men who mounted the camels were the very same Arabs who had bet so heavily on Ben Ali. The track steward assured the bookies that he would keep a close eye on the proceedings, stating that all bets were off if any irregularities were detected.

There appeared to be no foul play, as each driver urged his mount inexorably. Yet Ben Ali won the four-mile race going away, and the bookmakers, needless to say, took the real beating.

Later that evening, at a Charleston saloon, several of

the bookmakers ran into the Arab jockeys, and New York bookie Tom Shaw approached the reveling riders. "All you fellows knew at the start who was going to win," ventured Shaw. "I want to know how—they had never raced before!"

"Effendi," answered one of the Middle Easterners, "there could be no other result. Ben Ali is what we call the bell camel. All their lives other camels are taught to follow the bell camel. You couldn't have driven them past Ben Ali with a bullwhip!"

Most Unusual Grudge. A Chicago alderman named John J. Coughlin owned a horse called Roguish Eye, entered in the 1928 Belmont Futurity. Coughlin brashly claimed to the world, "I own the best colt in America," in the absolute certainty his horse would win the race.

The race, run before the invention of the high-speed camera now used at every track to determine close finishes, was seemingly won—closely—by Roguish Eye, with High Strung second, and Jack High third. However, moments later the board lit up with High Strung as the winner, and the race was official. Coughlin, to put it ever so mildly, was nonplussed.

Coughlin never forgave, or forgot. The following year, his best colt was dubbed "Who Won?" and his favorite the year after that was "Oh, Yeah?"

Most Unusual Race. It was a cool September 11 in the year 1750 at Epsom Downs, England, when Mr. Godwood ran his horse, Crop, against Mr. Hams's roan. Mr. Godwood obviously thought a lot of Crop, for the conditions of the race were that his horse would travel 100 miles before Mr. Hams's roan could do 80, and a side bet of 100 guineas was bet on the contest.

Post time for the race was 6:30 A.M., and within an hour Crop had run ten laps around the track and was exhausted, while the roan was in no better condition. By the thirtieth mile the toll was so severe that the two animals had subsided to a walk, and they strolled the remainder of the way. Despite the efforts of spectators who walked out onto the track with bags of oats and hay as enticement, the horses were simply too far gone.

After the race had been called to a limping halt, it was discovered that the roan had indeed traveled his required 80 miles, but poor Crop had failed his 100 by six miles, thereby losing the 100 guineas for his master, the cocky Mr. Godwood!

Most Unusual Steeplechase Victory. Never Mind II won the steeplechase held on December 29, 1945, despite the fact he had refused the fourth jump, his rider had given up, and he had been returned to his paddock!

The rider was then told that all the other horses had fallen or given up also, so out he went with Never Mind II and "raced" around the two-mile course, finishing in 11 minutes and 28 seconds what normally took a mere four minutes.

Most Unusual Kentucky Derby Winner. Spokane, winner of the 1889 Run for the Roses, had to have the most unusual background of any Derby winner. Instead of the indolent life of the normal thoroughbred, being nurtured in the security of a breeding farm, Spokane was born to Interpose in the heart of the wild Rocky Mountains. Interpose had escaped the confines of her owner's ranch, but was captured six years after her "jailbreak," and remained long enough to be successfully mated.

But Interpose broke free once again, and her foal was born in the wilds of the mountains. Soon after, she was once again snared and her colt was returned with her to the farm where he was taught the wiles of the track. He was then entered in the 1889 Kentucky Derby, where he nosed out Proctor Knott, the favorite, in a thrilling run.

Spokane next won the American Derby in Chicago, to prove he was no fluke, and became one of the most romantic winners in racing annals: "the Wild Horse of the Rockies," who captured the hearts of racing fans everywhere.

Most Unusual Training for a Thoroughbred. Most racehorses are carefully bred and matured for a sole reason: to be fast. But one horse, named Chase Me, who raced in the twenties and thirties, began his life far removed from the comfort and isolation of a thoroughbred breeding farm.

Chase Me was originally a saddle horse for the children of Mrs. Elizabeth Bosley, for whom he even learned tricks! Later he was a show horse for the eldest Bosley daughter, winning sixteen blue ribbons. Chase Me was thus a bit elderly when he began his racing career.

Chase Me was being used as a pace horse one day when it was noticed that he continually outdistanced the horse he was supposed to pace. Thus, at the advanced age of four years, he ran his first race at Havre de Grace, Maryland, winning by an astounding fifteen lengths.

There were many more races won by Chase Me, but true to his background, each time he entered the winner's circle, he would nuzzle anyone who brought him a lump of sugar.

This was a racehorse?

Sadly, the friendly children's pet had to be destroyed after he broke down during the 1934 Metropolitan Handicap at Belmont Park.

Most Unusual Training Diet. Nickel Coin won the 1951 Grand National Steeplechase, despite odds of 40 to 1 and the absolutely nauseating diet of duck eggs and beer!

Most Unusual Reaction to Exercise. Every racehorse must be continuoally exercised to be kept in shape. Although few of them may like it, no other horse reacted to the daily torture quite like Primer, who raced in the forties.

Primer's most common tactic was to suddenly wheel on the track, often separating rider from saddle, but one day's antic became track legend: on this morning he simply plunked himself down in front of the track kitchen, and lay there, motionless and unblinking. Word soon spread through the compound—"There's a dead horse out there!"

Everyone tried, unsuccessfully, to nudge, tug, and rout the supine steed. Finally, Primer's trainer pushed through the perplexed throng, shook his head in resignation, threw up his hands, and walked back to the barn. Whereupon Primer, satisfied, rose, shook himself off, and trotted obediently after his trainer!

This feat, among many others, earned Primer the nickname "Old Screwball."

Most Unusual Jockey. One of the most tried truisms of horse racing is that jockeys watch their weight as closely as touts watch tote boards, with the consequence that most of them live on a light diet. But not so for one Paul Keiper, who not only ate as much as he wanted without gaining weight, but he literally ate *anything,* period!

A legend in racing circles, Keiper ate both edible and inedible objects of all types and varieties, including razor blades, light bulbs, and green bottle flies—and washed down with a bottle of India ink (no doubt an indelible, as well as an inedible, experience!).

One such Keiper story came out of Suffolk Downs in Boston. A wasp, it seems, flew into the riders' quarters, and, naturally, Keiper chased and captured it.

"He swallowed it like it was candy," said one amazed colleague. "Paul said later it buzzed around inside of him all night and kept him awake, but none of us believed him. Still," he conceded, "it mighta been true."

Keiper retired in the late fifties. "I'm ready to retire on my laurels now," he admitted in 1955. "I think my luck has switched, and I'm going back to pineapple salad and chicken meat—with maybe an occasional chicken bone tossed in, just to whet my appetite and precipitate my palate!"

Tennis

Best Comeback at Wimbledon. Henri Cochet, France. During the 1927 championships, Cochet lost the first two sets in the semifinals to Frank Hunter of the United States, but suddenly found his groove and ran off a series of winning games to ultimately defeat Hunter. In the semifinal round, Cochet trailed "Big" Bill Tilden of the United States by two sets, 2–6, 4–6. Again, Cochet tapped his resources and counterattacked to defeat Tilden, 7–5, 6–4, 6–3. Cochet's foe in the finals was Jean Borotra of France. This time, with the match tied at two sets apiece, Cochet fell behind, 2–5, in the fifth and final set. After surviving *six* match points, Cochet rallied to win the set, 7–5, and the Wimbledon championship.

Best Analysis of Ilie Nastase. Ion Tiriac, Rumanian tennis coach. After working for years with Nastase and watching his protégé suffer innumerable tantrums, Tiriac observed: "I feel sometimes like a dog trainer who has taken his little puppy and taught it everything: all manners,

171

graces, and tricks. Then, just when training is finished, the dog makes a puddle in the middle of the floor!"

Best Volley. Helen Moody and Howard Kinsey, January 7, 1936. During a mixed singles exhibition in San Francisco, Moody and Kinsey volleyed for 78 minutes, hitting 2,001 consecutive strokes. It is possible that their record could have continued indefinitely were it not for Kinsey's impatience. "I must leave immediately for a tennis lesson," he explained. Kinsey, who organized the United States Professional Tennis Association and was the first American to turn pro, had been unaware of the record until later informed by referee Henry Roberts, Sr.

Best Old-timer. William J. Moore. Founder of the Cape May (New Jersey) School, Moore died at the age of one hundred and one in 1973, but continued playing tennis actively almost until his death. Moore was compelled to spend his one-hundredth birthday in the hospital; he was recuperating from injuries suffered while playing tennis.

Best Bad Player. Herbert Flam. Although born in Brooklyn, Herbie Flam grew up in Beverly Hills, California, where he was a contemporary of Pancho Gonzalez, and a winner of the National Junior Championship. Owner of an abominably weak service and a herky-jerky forehand, Flam nevertheless was one of the gamest competitors tennis has known.

During the 1950 national championships at Forest Hills, Flam met the wily veteran Gardner Mulloy in the semifinals. On one occasion Flam executed what many believe was the most "impossible" return in championship tennis. Flam charged the net only to be met by a Mulloy lob that landed directly at the base line. Thinking he had won the point, Mulloy turned his back on Flam and strode to his serving position. Meanwhile, Herbie charged after the ball, reached it in time, and whacked a perfect crosscourt forehand past the startled Mulloy. Flam received a three-minute standing ovation. Because of his technical deficiencies as a player, Flam frequently compensated with unorthodox play. When he faced a strong server, Flam would play ten feet in back of the base line. Despite his deficiencies, Flam was a member of the United States Davis Cup team and a frequent finalist in major tourneys. (1950 United States nationals).

Best Big Service. Michael Sangster, Great Britain. In June 1963, Sangster's service was scientifically timed at 154 miles per hour. At the point where the ball crossed the net, it was timed at 108 miles per hour.

Best Uncollected Winnings. Chris Evert. In 1972, the princess of American tennis won $50,000 on the tournament trail. However, because of her age (eighteen), Miss Evert was unable to collect any of the money.

Best Male Left-hander. Rod Laver, Australia. The only two-time winner of the "Grand Slam" (Wimbledon, Forest Hills, French, and Australian Open tournaments), Laver in his prime lacked a weak spot in his repertoire. "Laver," said former tennis champion Don Budge, "can do everything on a tennis court. He's got all the shots, and he's a fine competitor." Tennis critic Bud Collins of the Boston *Globe* once remarked: "If Laver wore a top hat you'd think he was Mandrake the Magician." Or, Pancho Gonzalez: "Laver hit winning shots when you thought you had him out of position." According to Julius D. Heldman, a tennis critic, "His [Laver's] shots are breathtaking, his talent is enormous and his drive made him the most successful player in the world in his day."

Best Slavic-American Tennis Community. Hamtramck, Michigan. An auto-making center, Hamtramck had a population in the fifties that was, according to tennis ace Fred Kovaleski, "99 percent second-generation Slavic." Hamtramck's tennis-orientation was due to Mrs. Jean Hoxie, a tennis coach, who enjoyed an insatiable appetite for grooming young players. "She used to drum up trade for the tennis courts," said Kovaleski, "by invading the schools and picking out the best handball players. When I was eleven, I won the grade school handball championship and was immediately collared by Mrs. Hoxie and whisked off to Hamtramck's asphalt court." Kovaleski eventually made it to Wimbledon (1950) and was among a long line of successful tennis players developed in Hamtramck by Mrs. Hoxie. Where once there was but a single court, Hamtramck built eight and even boasted an indoor court. "The Polish town of Hamtramck," said Kovaleski, "was Australianized by a fiery, enthusiastic Irish woman!"

Best Male Doubles Combination. Adrian Quist, John Bromwich, Australia. First-rate stars both before and after World War II, Quist and Bromwich were adept at singles and doubles. As a doubles combination, they were winners of eight consecutive Australian doubles championships from 1942 through 1950.

Best Pre-Nastase Tantrum Thrower. Earl Cochell. As early as 1948, Cochell was demonstrating his effectiveness. In that year he defeated the fast-developing Frank Sedgman at Newport and would continue to excel until he faced Gardner Mulloy in 1951 during the fourth round of the United States nationals at Forest Hills. Cochell, at the time, was twenty-nine years old and ranked seventh in the United States. Were it not for his temper, there is no telling how much higher Cochell might have advanced. However, in his match with Mulloy, Cochell erupted in a manner that would have made Ilie Nastase proud, or, perhaps, envious, since Cochell was banned for life. According to one story, it happened this way: "When the crowd booed him for serving underhand, snapping at linesmen and conspicuously tossing away points, he demanded the mike from the umpire to talk back to the crowd. The request was denied." It was charged that, during the intermission, Cochell used "profane and obscene language" to a referee who asked him in the locker room to change his conduct.

Cochell's opponent, Mulloy, once described the episodes that led to the banishment of his foe for "unsportsmanlike conduct detrimental to the welfare of the game."

In an interview with Bill Verigan of the New York *Daily News,* Mulloy recalled the incidents on Forest Hills' center court:

"We split the first two sets, and I led the third 4–1 and 30–love. So he decided to throw the set, then make a fight of it after intermission. We all do that but he was unsporting. He wouldn't move on my serves and wouldn't try on his. When the crowd booed, he made motions at them, and they booed more.

"Then he got into an argument with the umpire and grabbed the mike to tell the crowd 'I want you to hear my side, too.' When the set ended, he shouted obscenities at the referee, an older man, Dr. Elsworth Davenport, in the locker room, and when I told him to calm down, he shouted them at me. I told him I'd punch him in the nose, so he went to work again on Davenport."

In retrospect, Mulloy said he believed the punishment was too severe on Cochell. "Earl," said Mulloy, "was an actor, but he was never as bad as Nastase. If Cochell had appealed after a year, he would probably have been reinstated, but he just disappeared."

Best Prize Money. Jimmy Connors vs. John Newcombe, April 26, 1975, at Caesar's Palace, Las Vegas, Nevada. An unprecedented $500,000 was put in the pot for the so-called battle of the titans. The winner was Connors, 6–3, 4–6, 6–2, 6–4.

Best Family Team. Nancy and Cliff Richey of Dallas, Texas. The children of tennis instructors, George and Betty Richey, Nancy and Cliff developed into two of the top amateur players in the world. In 1965, for example, both were ranked in the top ten in the United States. "The Richeys of Dallas are a family consumed by a single passion," said author Frank DeFord of *Sports Illustrated.* "The passion is tennis and it binds them together and gives meaning to their lives. The Richeys are singularly proud of themselves and their accomplishments. They are straightforward, pragmatic people, firmly believing that discipline, competition and victory offer greater rewards than a more prosaic life. The results seem to bear them out." As for foreign family teams, the Ulrichs of Denmark —Torben, Jorgen, and their father, Esner—combined for one hundred and seven Davis Cup victories.

Best Career Comeback. Art Larsen. A tennis player before he joined the army for World War II, Larsen landed on Omaha Beach at "D-Day" plus thirty minutes with the 17th Calvary Squadron of the 9th Army. It was doubtful, then, that Larsen would ever touch a tennis racket again. Most of Larsen's buddies were killed upon landing, but Larsen fought his way to Brest, France, as a tommy-gunner. "Suddenly," Larsen recalled, "out of nowhere, a fleet of bombers began strafing and bombing us. Our own air force had mistaken us for Nazis. Before the holocaust was over, half the group was killed, ambulances were lined up for miles." Miraculously, Larsen came through unhurt—physically.

The episode, not surprisingly, was traumatic and Larsen became radically superstitious. "I'd figured I'd done something lucky that day," he recalled. "I remembered that I'd changed my socks, putting the left on first, and ate breakfast at a certain hour. The next day I followed the same routine, and the next, all through France, Belgium, and Luxembourg." When Larsen eventually made it home to California, he was considered too nervous to hold a job. Eventually, a Veterans Administration doctor suggested tennis as therapy. It worked, although Larsen continued to be superstitious.

"I wouldn't step on any kind of chalk line," Larsen admitted. "I always had to have the winning ball to put back in play. I'd cross on the opposite side of the net from any opponent, tiptoe over base lines, even in competition, tap the base line three times before serving, stand for a second with my back to the court. The doctor told me my 'jinxes' were 'compulsory suggestiveness' and he convinced me of one thing: I was wasting a heck of a lot of energy on them."

Only five feet, nine inches tall and 150 pounds, Larsen possessed boundless energy. He also became a top-ranking
176

tennis player and, in 1950, he reached the finals of the United States nationals at Forest Hills. Despite—or, perhaps, because of—his wartime adversity, Larson defeated Herbie Flam to win the nationals. "He didn't sleep a wink the night before he played Flam," wrote sportswriter Jeanne Hoffman, "Yet he was raring to go after the fifth set while Flam was near collapse—triumphant testimony that Art recovered from his war experiences and a sickly childhood."

Best Wimbledon Final (Female).   Mrs. Lambert Chambers vs. Suzanne Lenglen, 1919. The winner was Lenglen by a score of 10–8, 4–6, 9–7, the greatest number of games played by women (and a record that never can be broken because of the new tiebreaker system). "I felt on top of the world that day," Mrs. Chambers recalled. "Then, Suzanne went ahead, 4–1, and later, 5–3. Meanwhile, we were having strenuous rallies. In the ninth game she came to set point, but I managed to recover and stretch out the set. In the second set I hung on desperately and finally got my backhand working just as forcefully as my forehand and I ran out the winner, 6–4." In the third set, Lenglen went ahead, 4–1, but Mrs. Chambers came back to tie the set at four apiece. Lenglen eventually won the set, 9–7, and the match.

Best Wimbledon Match (Male).   Henri Cochet (France) vs. Bill Tilden (United States), 1927. Cochet was the victor, 2–6, 4–6, 7–5, 6–4, 6–3. Trailing 1–5 in the third set, Cochet lost only two points in rallying to a 6–5 lead. "Point after point went to Cochet," said referee F. R. Barrow. "He actually won 17 aces serving and the spectators were too spellbound to applaud. But when the little Frenchman at last got the set at 7–5, he got a round of cheers that seldom have been heard."

The total disintegration of Tilden's game was awesome. "Personally," Tilden said, "I have no satisfactory explanation. All I know is my coordination cracked wide open and I couldn't put a ball in the court."

Al Laney of the New York *Herald-Tribune,* and one of

the most insightful tennis reporters, spoke to Tilden immediately after the match. " 'Maybe you were right,' Tilden told me," said Laney. "He was referring to a statement that he had passed his best years and could no longer call on that matchless stamina."

Best Player Never to Win Wimbledon. Richard "Pancho" Gonzales. A winner of the United States nationals at Forest Hills in 1948 and 1949. Gonzales turned professional before winning Wimbledon. Once a pro, he was banned from playing at the English court. When the antipro ban eventually was lifted at Wimbledon, Gonzales was past his prime.

Best Youngster to Win Wimbledon. Charlotte "Lottie" Dod. In the summer of 1887, fifteen-year-old Charlotte Dod won the women's singles championship. "By horse and carriage they sped to Wimbledon to cheer the Little Wonder," said the London *Sunday Express*. Miss Dod won the title again the next year and every time she entered, in 1891, 1892, and 1893.

Best Crowd. Billie Jean King vs. Bobby Riggs, Houston Astrodome, September 20, 1973. An audience of 30,742, not to mention a television audience in the millions, watched tennis' most ballyhooed "Battle of the Sexes" in which King routed Riggs by a score of 6–4, 6–3, 6–3. The match had been publicized for several months in advance of the event, much in the manner of a heavyweight title bout. The largest crowd for an orthodox match—25,578 fans filled White City Courts in Sydney, Australia—was lured by the Davis Cup challenge round between the United States and the Australians on December 27, 1954.

Best Female Player. Suzanne Lenglen, France. The Mademoiselle from Compiegne won the Wimbledon singles championship from 1919 through 1923, and again in 1925. Lenglen was a doubles champion from 1919 through 1923 and again in 1925. In addition, Mlle. Lenglen was mixed doubles champion in 1920, 1921,

1922, 1923, 1925, and 1926. She was Olympic champion in 1920, as well as the Olympic mixed doubles victor. Suzanne also was the world hard court singles champion in 1914 and also 1921, 1922, and 1923.

Best Animal Therapy for Championship. Central Park Zoo, Gussie Moran, 1949. In 1949, Miss Moran, one of the leading American female tennis performers, was a house guest of Mickey Falkenburg Wagstaff, the mother of tennis aces Bob, Tom, and Jinx Falkenburg. At the time, Gussie was entered in the National Indoor Tournament in Manhattan. Apparently, Miss Moran was so overcome with nervousness that Lee Falkenburg, Mickey's husband, urged her to visit the Central Park Zoo. According to *World Tennis* magazine, Gussie was steered to the lion cage to "pick up a little courage from the lions." Miss Moran accepted the advice. "She watched the lions every day," said *World Tennis*, "then went to the courts and played like a tiger. She won the tournament, and from then on she was a zoo addict."

Best Server. Ellsworth Vines. According to *New York Times* tennis expert Allison Danzig, Vines's serve was devastating. "No one hit a forehand flatter or harder or kept the ball so close to the net. He was murderous overhead. He hit so hard, so close to the lines that few of his shots came back. They either won or were in the net or out of the court for the next part.

"Wimbledon galleries were aghast at the force of his attack as he beat John Crawford in the semifinal and Bunny Austin in the final in 1932, allowing only six games and sending service after service beyond their reach."

Another respected tennis critic, Julius D. Heldman, described the style of Vines's service thusly: "I have always likened Elly's wind-up action on the serve to that of a writhing snake. His body seemed to amass energy as he stretched up to maximum height for the first ball. Think of an Indian fakir piping a snake into standing erect and you can then visualize Vines climbing up to the top of his swing. It was a beautiful motion which was followed by a stinging, heavy whip at the ball.

"I ballboyed for Vines when I was twelve years old. He was playing Fred Perry in the finals of the Pacific Southwest. A very vivid recollection is that of catching one of Vines's aces as it whizzed by Perry. It was leaden—heavy and hard, with enough spin to hurt. My hand stung for an hour."

Best Performance by a Professional. Rod Laver, 1971 Tennis Champions Classic, January 2–March 19, 1971; thirteen matches in seven arenas against eight opponents.

The 1971 Tennis Champions Classic took Rod Laver from New York to Los Angeles and back in eleven weeks. When it was over, Laver had won all thirteen matches in seven different arenas, and prizes totaling $160,000. Most importantly, he had accomplished a tennis feat that astounded most observers—himself included.

"At the very outset," said Laver after defeating Tom Okker at Madison Square Garden to end the Classic, "I totally agreed with everyone that it was virtually impossible for any one player to go through this Classic undefeated. I have done just that—and I do not believe it either."

Laver, then thirty-two, had defeated the field including Ken Rosewall, John Newcombe, Tony Roche, Roy Emerson, Arthur Ashe, Tom Okker, Roger Taylor, and Dennis Ralston. As a result, he was compared to the likes of Bill Tilden, Don Budge, and Pancho Gonzales. Rod Laver had arrived.

Laver won the Classic's first match—and his first $10,000—against Rosewall on January 2 at Madison Square Garden. Laver won, 6–3, 6–2, 7–5, with Rosewall coming on strong at the end. "It's just that whatever I hit," said the Forest Hills champion, "Rod hit better." Laver, who was visibly nervous when the set started, said after the match that he doubted he could perform that well throughout the Classic. Events would prove otherwise.

A week later, at Rochester's War Memorial Auditorium, Laver picked up another $10,000 by defeating Wimbledon champion John Newcombe. The match was an exhausting five sets—6–4, 6–2, 4–6, 5–7, 6–4—and Newcombe later paid tribute to Laver's clutch play. "When I make a truly great shot," said Newcombe, "I look up and thank God. Rod takes his for granted."

On January 13, at Boston Garden, Laver's earnings reached $30,000 when he defeated Tony Roche, 7–5, 4–6, 3–6, 7–5, 6–1. Roche actually had Laver at match point in the fourth set, but Laver's cross-court volleys evened the score and set up an easy fifth set, leaving Roche in the dust.

January 16, the Philadelphia Spectrum, and long-time friend off the court and foe on the court Roy Emerson. Laver won the first two sets handily, 6–2, 6–3; Emerson pushed the third set to tie break, but Laver hung on for a 7–5 victory. "I don't understand how Rod can win all that money," said Emerson of the $10,000-a-match purse. It was time to return to Madison Square Garden, where the Classic began and where it later would end.

At the Garden five days later, Arthur Ashe pushed two sets into sudden death, but Laver was not to be denied. "He takes advantage of everything," said Ashe, winner of the 1968 U.S. Open and a rookie professional, after the 7–5, 6–4, 7–5 match.

Laver faced Okker for the first of their three matches, at Olympia Stadium in Detroit, on January 23. Again it was a squeaker, with Okker winning the first two sets, 7–5, 7–5, on tie breaks. Laver's stamina prevailed, and the last three sets went to Rod by identical 6–2 scores.

Ashe and Laver had their return match at Madison Square Garden on January 28. "It's getting easier as I go along," Laver said, as it occurred to him that he just might go all the way. After all, what could be more difficult than his ordeals against Roche and Newcombe? But Ashe took the first set, 6–3, in what was, in Laver's words, "a poor match on my part. I was much too relaxed in the beginning." Laver turned it around by taking advantage of Ashe's five double faults, and took the last three sets, 6–3, 6–3, 6–4.

Victories over Roger Taylor and, again, Okker, followed. Laver swept Taylor, 6–3, 7–5, 6–2, at the Los

Angeles Forum, and also swept Okker, 6–1, 6–4, 6–3, at Madison Square Garden, but the Okker score was deceptive. Okker forced Laver to play his best tennis ever, and at one point, aghast, dropped his racket after being caught flat-footed in the forecourt. Laver ran around the ball after catching up with it and put it past Okker.

"I couldn't believe some of those shots," said the Dutchman later. "He couldn't believe them himself."

Laver defeated Ralston at Madison Square Garden, 3–6, 6–1, 6–4, 6–3, and then Emerson, in a long match at New Haven, 6–3, 5–7, 6–3, 3–6, 6–3. Laver's prizes now totalled $110,000 and the stakes increased for the last two matches.

Match 12, against Ralston, was worth another $15,000 and took place at Madison Square Garden almost a month after the New Haven match. The score was 6–3, 6–4, 7–5. Laver was unstoppable by now. "I don't feel unbeatable," he said, "but if my opponents feel I am—well, that's terrific."

Match 13 took place the next day, March 19, and the opponent was the same Okker who had given Laver the hardest time in the Classic. Laver won the furious first set, 7–5, in sudden death with the Dutchman almost equal to everything Laver had to offer. But with Laver drawing first blood, the momentum was with him, and amidst growing applause, Laver took the last two sets, 6–2, 6–1, ending the greatest string of victories in tennis history, and one of sport's most awesome performances.

"The applause began to grow at the end of the second set," recalled Fred Podesta, veteran sports promoter and former Madison Square Garden official. "Applause in a special way—applause as a salute to what the fans saw happening as game after game dropped into Laver's column, bringing him to the ultimate victory. When it was over, applause and awe surrounded Laver as he accepted the final check.

"What happened was not only unusual, it was one of the greatest of all performances in any sport—and assuredly the greatest ever in the sport of tennis."

182

Best Little Man. Bryan M. "Bitsy" Grant. Known as "the Mighty Atom," Grant weighed in at 120 pounds, yet frequently was more than a match for the giants of tennis. At five feet, four inches, Grant took the measure of such aces as Don Budge and frequently went up against the likes of Frank Parker, Frank Shields, and Bobby Riggs. He won the National Clay Court singles championship in 1930, 1934, and 1935. Grant frequently was chosen to the United States Davis Cup team and, in 1937, scored victories over Australia's John Bromwich and Jack Crawford, beating both of them without loss of a single set. "Pound for pound," wrote *New York Times* tennis expert Allison Danzig, "Grant has been as great a tennis competitor as the world has seen."

———————

Worst Conditions for a Major Match. Helen Wills vs. Suzanne Lenglen, Carlton Tennis Club of Cannes, France, February 17, 1926. "Atrocious conditions," wrote John R. Tunis in the Boston *Globe,* "is an understatement of the case."

Miss Wills, champion of the United States, and Mademoiselle Lenglen, champion of France, meeting each other on the same court were worthy of only the most lavish trappings. Instead, they played at a club that didn't even have a press stand, let alone a press box. The Carlton Club was located in a small space between four mean back streets of Cannes. Nearby was a sawmill which produced, as Tunis recalled, "a raucous buzzing that was anything but soothing to the nerves in the middle of an important match." The clubhouse contained no towels, no electric light, and a shower bath that did not shower. The Carlton Club was unable to contain all the spectators who had come to see what was considered the greatest match between two women tennis players ever. As a result, fans were shunted onto a nearby garage roof where they were sold "seats." Others stood on ladders or mounted motor buses which had conveniently been drawn up behind the court. When the match began, workers who had failed to complete the makeshift grandstands kept hammering away as the women stroked the balls across the court.

"Never," wrote Tunis, "was any sporting event played under such conditions. Never such a lack of preparation, of arrangements, of any attempt at caring for and handling the press, the crowds, for the thousand and one incidental things that arise at times like these."

Adding further confusion to an already bizarre scene was the fact that the match actually was won twice—once officially—by Mlle. Lenglen. She had Miss Wills at match point when the American's shot crashed into her forehand corner. Suzanne thought it was out, tossed the balls to the court, and rushed to the net to shake hands with the American. The ball, however, was not out; although the umpire thought so and already was descending from his chair. But a determined linesman insisted that the shot was good. Unfortunately, a horde of cameramen already had stormed on the court and they had to be waved off so that the match could continue. This time Miss Wills rallied, but in five more minutes Mlle. Lenglen reached match point again and, this time, the umpire remained in his seat and Suzanne retained her title as the greatest woman player in the world.

Worst Weather for a Match.   December 26, 1947, New York City. Until Christmas Day-plus-one, 1947, the Great Blizzard of 1888 had been regarded as the definitive New York snowstorm. But by midafternoon of December 26, 1947, the snowfall had exceeded the total footage of 1888 and it was still snowing. Unfortunately for promoter Jack Harris, that very night he was scheduled to present Jack Kramer against Bobby Riggs at Madison Square Garden for what he dubbed "the tennis match of the decade." It was, in fact, the professional debut of Jack Kramer, whose serve was the mightiest in tennis. His smallish opponent, Riggs, was acclaimed as the finest defensive player in the game at the time. By midafternoon, 20 inches of snow had fallen and still more to come. Harris, urged by his aides, was tempted to call off the match as word of choked traffic, delayed subways and buses, and general confusion seeped into his office. "No one," insisted Harris, "will go out to see a tennis match in this weather." But postponing such a well-touted event at the well-booked Madison Square Garden was a formidable feat in itself and Harris decided to go ahead with the match despite the fact that 25.8 inches of snow had piled up by 9:39 P.M. when Kramer and Riggs walked out to center court.

"The fear," said writer John M. Ross, "was that they would settle the score in comparative privacy."

Yet, inexplicably, despite the blizzard, the hardship, and the potential threats to their return home, 15,114 fans filled Madison Square Garden. "It was a testimonial to Riggs and Kramer and to tennis," said Ross. "But it was a night that the performers had to take a back seat to the spectators. They really stole the show!"

Jimmy Powers, sports editor of the New York *Daily News,* was so stunned by the turnout that he wrote: "It was the greatest tribute to an indoor athletic event in the history of sport."

Riggs won the match, 6–2, 10–8, 4–6, 6–4.

Worst Mishap. In a 1961 match between Danielle Wilde of France and Carole Rossen of Great Britain a sparrow was killed after being struck by a ball hit by Ms. Rossen.

————————

Most Unusual Entrant in a Major Tourney. In 1893, "Mr. X," Joshua Pim, a London doctor, refused to use his correct name in the Wimbledon tournament. He believed that it would bring embarrassment to his medical practice. Nevertheless, he won the Wimbledon tournament playing under his assumed name.

Most Unusual Personal Turnabout. Dr. Richard Raskin. An ophthalmologist and superb tournament player, Dr. Raskin frequently was mentioned in newspaper dispatches because of his competent play which never reached superstar status. However, in 1976, Dr. Raskin willingly underwent a sex change and was renamed Dr. Renée Richards. As Renée Richards, she encountered more than the normal amount of controversy. Many female players objected to Dr. Richards' participating in tournaments as a woman. Nevertheless, the former Dr. Raskin continued to play regularly on the tennis circuit until 1977.

Most Unusual Match. Wimbledon, 1904, F. Resely and S. H. Smith. The match was tied at two sets apiece when the players agreed to toss a coin to decide the victor, because they also were doubles partners and wanted to preserve their energy for a match the next day. Resely won the toss and the match.

Most Unusual Promotion. Billie Jean King vs. Bobby Riggs, Astrodome, Houston, Texas, September 20, 1973. Billed as the supreme tennis "Battle of the Sexes," the fifty-five-year-old Riggs (who had previously beaten Margaret Court in a television spectacular) faced thirty-year-old King, one of the best women players of all time. The purse was $100,000 winner-take-all in a match that was nationally televised and promoted many months in advance. Riggs, who had displayed a complete mastery of Court, was easily dispatched by King, 6–4, 6–3, 6–3. Associates of Riggs argued that Bobby took the match with King too lightly. Bobby, himself, confided that unless he ceased his partying a month before the widely heralded match, he would be in trouble. But Bobby, according to friends, partied to the very end and then capitulated with unaccustomed futility to King. Riggs's pleas for a rematch were ignored by the female winner.

Most Unusual Player. Jaroslav Drobny. Formerly a championship hockey player in his native Czechoslovakia, Drobny made his first Wimbledon challenge in 1938. He gave up his hockey career after World War II, concentrating on tennis. In 1953 he participated in tennis history, defeating Budge Patty at Wimbledon, 8–6, 16–18, 3–6, 8–6, 12–10. The match lasted more than four hours and required ninety-three games, the longest singles contest in Wimbledon history to that point. When it was over, Drobny uttered the deathless squelch: "It's the first time I ever had a cramp!"

Most Unusual Tournament. The Adirondack (New York) Mountain Invitational Tourney. A clever New York press agent named Spencer Hare was anxious to lend some prestige to one of his accounts, the Adirondack Mountain resort, Scaroon Manor on Schroon Lake. He decided to stage an annual tennis tournament and, somehow, received the sanction from the Eastern tennis officials. The tourneys, which reached their popularity in the late fifties, featured low- to medium-grade players, but received considerable publicity in the New York papers. However, when Scaroon Manor went bankrupt so did the Adirondack Mountain Invitation Tournament. "Since I didn't have the client," said publicist Hare, "there was no point having the tourney."

Golf

Best Description of Golf. "An attempt to place a small little sphere . . . in a slightly larger hole . . . with utensils totally unsuited to the task."—Woodrow Wilson, twenty-eighth president of the United States, and an avid amateur golfer.

Best All-Time Golfer. Although an argument could be, and no doubt will be, made for golfing immortals such as Bobby Jones, Sam Snead, Arnold Palmer, and Ben Hogan, Jack Nicklaus must be considered the best golfer of all time.

Nicklaus has won sixty PGA-sponsored events, including sixteen major tournaments (five Masters, two British Opens, two U.S. Amateurs, four PGAs and three U.S. Opens), and is rapidly approaching $3 million in career money winnings.

To clearly illustrate the dominance "the Golden Bear" has over the sport, one simply has to glance at Nicklaus' 1975 season record: he won the Masters and the PGA, finished two strokes behind in the U.S. Open and one stroke back in the British Open. Jack missed the pro golfer's dream, the never-before-won Grand Slam, by a mere three strokes.

Best Woman Golfer. This has to be a three-way tie between Mildred "Babe" Didrikson Zaharias, Mickey Wright, and Joyce Wethered.

Joyce Wethered won the English Women's Championship five consecutive times, between 1920 and 1925; was the British women's champion four times, and one season finished second only once in five outings.

Mickey Wright was the leading money winner in the LPGA tour from 1960 through 1964, winning thirteen tourneys in 1963 for a record. Wright also won four Women's U.S. Opens and four LPGAs.

"Babe" Zaharias may well have been the female athlete of the century, but still ties with Wethered and Wright when it comes to golf. After starring in the 1932 Olympics, Babe became the first American woman to win the British championship, in 1947.

It was only a year later, 1948, that Babe got the idea for the first Ladies' Professional Golf Association, and that organization was born early in 1949, with Babe being the premier money winner in the LPGA circuit in her first four years as a pro, 1949 through 1952—including three U.S. Opens. Zaharias was also voted the woman athlete of the year in 1932, 1945 through 1947, and again in 1950. Incredibly, she was voted the "Woman Athlete of the Half Century" by Associated Press in 1949.

Best Composite Golfer. Combining the drive of Jack Nicklaus, the long iron play of Hale Irwin, the short iron play of Gene Littler, and the chipping of Lee Trevino with the putting of Johnny Miller, would produce the world's only almost-perfect golfer (and the whole rest of the pro circuit could go into involuntary retirement!).

Best Come-from-Behind Player. Gene Sarazen practically made a career of it, first in 1922 when he finished

189

the U.S. Open with a winning 68, after being completely out of the picture for the whole tourney. In the 1932 Open, after again coming from nowhere, Sarazen won the contest by finishing his last twenty-eight holes in 100 strokes! In 1935 he took the Masters from an astounded Craig Wood by overcoming a three-stroke deficit with a double eagle (three under par!).

Best Pro Driver on Tour Today. If a relative unknown named Jim Dent could perform all of his shots the way he drives, he'd challenge Nicklaus as the leading superstar in golf today. Dent consistently drives the ball past the 300-yard mark, and often hits beyond even the 350-yard limit, with ideal conditions.

Best Record of Continuity. There have been more tourneys won by individuals, others have been more spectacular—or even more consistent in a shorter span of time—but any pro will have to go far to achieve Gene Sarazen's record of thirty-one consecutive U.S. Opens (1920–54) for continuity. Sarazen won the Open in 1922 and 1932.

Best Brother Act (One Tournament). In the 1910 U.S. Open, brothers Alex and MacDonald Smith tied with John J. McDermott for the title. In a playoff the next day, Alex Smith shot a 71 to win the open, followed by McDermott's 75, and brother MacDonald Smith's 77.

Best Brother Act (Lifetime). Harry and Tom Vardon. Harry was one of the sport's all-time best (the Vardon Trophy for the lowest average on the pro tour is named after him), with a lifetime record which includes winning the British Open a record six times (1896, 1898–99, 1903, 1911, and 1914), and the U.S. Open in 1911.

Brother Tom never won a title, but placed as runner-up to Harry in the 1903 British Open and in the British Pro Match Play Championship in 1905. Tom actually turned pro before Harry, helping his brother into the game.

Best Year (Tournaments Won). In 1945 Byron Nelson won eighteen tourneys, including eleven in a row! (See *Best Winning Streak by a Pro.*)

Best Year (Money Won). With today's inflation, this may be a short-lived record, but in 1974 Johnny Miller won eight tournaments, earning himself a tidy $353,021 for the season! Now, how many people do you know take home more than $44,000 for each job they perform?

Best Winning Streak by a Pro Golfer. From the Miami Four-Ball tournament on March 8–11, 1945, until the finish of the Canadian Open on August 2–4, 1945, Byron Nelson had one of all sport's most incredible winning streaks. Nelson won the Miami tourney, the Charlotte Open, the Greensboro Open, Durham Open, Atlanta Open, Montreal Open, the Philadelphia Inquirer Invitational, the Chicago National, the PGA, the Tam O'Shanter Open, and the Canadian Open. His total prize money for the eleven tourneys was $34,849.33—less than average first-place money for a single tournament today!

Best Prize Money (One Tournament). With a total purse of half a million dollars, the 1973 "World Open" at Pinehurst, North Carolina, was won by Miller Barber, who finished the 144 holes with a score of 570, to take first prize of $100,000.

Best Year on the Circuit (Average Score). Sam Snead won the first Vardon Trophy, awarded annually to the golfer with the lowest average on the tour. This was back in 1950, when Snead had a 69.23 average, a seasonal low which has never been duplicated.

Best Performance in a Masters. Jack Nicklaus shot a 271 in 1965 for the lowest four-round Masters total in history.

Best Performance in a PGA. The popular number seems

to be 271, regardless of which tournament—for Bob Nichols shot that 72-hole total in 1964 for a record which still stands today (this is also the record total for the Masters!).

Best Performance in a U.S. Open. The magic number is 275 in the Open, but that record has been set by two superstars—Jack Nicklaus in 1967 and the smallish Lee Trevino in 1968.

Best Comeback in a U.S. Open. In 1966 at Olympic Golf Course in San Francisco, Billy Casper trailed Arnold Palmer by a whopping seven strokes, with nine holes remaining in the tournament. Casper suddenly came to life and became the hottest thing since chili peppers, and shot a 32 on the final nine holes. Palmer, shaken by Casper's mad charge, fell apart, and finished with a closing 39, leaving the two men in a tie. Casper won a playoff the next day.

Best U.S. Open Record. Jack Nicklaus has won the Open three times, and several have won it twice, but for true consistency, the best record goes to Walter Hagen, who won the Open in 1914 and 1919. Even more impressive, Hagen finished in the top ten in the Open a record-setting sixteen times, something no one else has ever accomplished. Too bad it doesn't win the prizes!

Best Competitive Round in a Tournament. The lowest round ever shot in the U.S. Open was recorded by Johnny Miller in the last circle of the 1973 tournament. Miller stormed from six strokes behind the leaders to shoot a 63, vaulting over a dozen players to win at Oakmont, California.

Best Birdie Streak. It was the final round of the 1961 St. Petersburg Open, under the swaying Florida palms, when Bob Goalby proceeded to knock home eight birdies in a row. And, you ask, did Goalby win after his remarkable feat? Yes, with a four-round total of 261.

Best Recorded Drive. Mr. E. C. Bliss must have been in a state of his namesake after he drove the 445-yard ninth hole on the Old Course at Herne Bay in Kent, England. Bliss, a twelve handicapper, let loose his lengthy lob in August 1913. To present some comparison, Jack Nicklaus, one of the modern game's best drivers, has barely hit within 100 yards of Bliss's record.

Best Drive in a Hurricane. This is not the easiest way to improve one's driving, but in 1934, F. Lemarchand stood unperturbed upon the tee of the thirteenth hole at Devon, England, and, with gale force winds at his back, proceeded to blast one the 483-yard length of the hole. Wonder what it did for his putting?

Best Putt. In the 1955 Masters tournament, veteran pro Cary Middlecoff, at the height of his career, placed an 86-foot putt on the thirteenth green of the Augusta National Course, no doubt surprising himself as much as he did the onlookers.

Best Weird Putt. Long before Middlecoff was out of short pants, R. W. Bridges made a hole in one on a 196-yard hole at Woodlawn Country Club in Kirkwood, Missouri, during the summer of 1931. Well, so what, you say, there have been lots of holes in one, and longer ones to boot. But the whole point of this little ditty is that Mr. Bridges used his putter off the tee!

Best Hole in One. In 1965 a mere broth of a stripling, twenty-one-year-old Bob Mitera, made a hole in one on the 444-yard par four at the Miracle Hills Course in Omaha, Nebraska. Well, different strokes for different folks . . .

Best Drive (Not in Tournament Play). Anyone who has played a bit of golf has heard the many stories about fanatics who take their clubs with them no matter where they are, just in case they have a moment to practice their chipping, or whatever. But Nils Lied has got to be the all-time golf freak.

Lied, an Australian, was working as a meteorologist at Mawson Base, Antarctica, in 1962, when he whipped out one of his clubs and drove that undoubtedly frigid ball 2,640 yards (or one and a half miles) across solid ice! Once again, not the easiest way to improve one's drive . . .

Best Clutch Putt. During the 1975 Masters tourney, Jack Nicklaus assured himself of his fifth green blazer (and some healthy long green for his pocket, too) with a superb putt on the sixteenth hole. The Golden Bear sank a hard-to-believe 40-footer, moving into the lead for good on the par-three hole.

Best One-Hole Performance in the Clutch. Gene Sarazen had a characteristic way of handling the fifteenth hole at Augusta. It's one of the toughest holes in the world of golf—a par-five monster, and Sarazen usually drove off the tee, popped close to the pond which protected the green, chipped to the green, and putted twice.

But this was the 1938 Masters tournament; Gene was losing, and he couldn't afford to play it the conventional way. Instead, he smashed a 300-foot drive straight down the fairway, then used his four-wood to clear the pond. Incredibly, the ball kept rolling after it bounced onto the green, and plunked right into the cup. Sarazen came up with a double eagle, tied the round, and proceeded to defeat Craig Woods the next day.

Best Intentional Hook. In 1924 Joe Kirkwood was leading the field in the Texas Open at the Breckenridge Golf Club by a couple of strokes in the last round. Unfortunately he had badly misjudged one shot and landed in some trees near a creek which trickled sluggishly past the green. There was no way Kirkwood would be able to get the ball over those trees, and he couldn't afford the penalty for lifting the ball—it was too close a match.

But, taking three-iron in hand, Kirkwood stood facing

the creek, with the green far to his left behind the trees, and took a whack. The ball went across the creek, boomeranged sharply to the left, looped around the entire grove of trees, and like a little puckered miracle, landed a few feet away from the pin, on the green! Need it be mentioned that Kirkwood won the match?

There is a monument erected at the very spot where Joe smote iron to gutta-percha, thanks to money collected by spectators who saw him do it that day.

Best Trick Shooter. Lee Trevino, before he became a golfing superstar and performer for TV commercials, used to do tricks with a golf club. Trevino actually made a living out of placing bets with fellow golfers, particularly by betting he could win under the strangest of conditions. Lee once triumphed over one poor sap who was allowed to use the full panoply of clubs, while Trevino played only with a lone soda bottle!

Best Intellectual Golfer. Boyishly blond Jack Nicklaus was given an honorary degree by Ohio State University, gracing him with the title "Doctor of Athletic Arts."

Best Nine Holes with One Club. An amateur champion from Long Island, New York, John J. Humm by name, one day shot a 34 on a nine-hole course, using only his three-iron. Would that be called a "hummdinger"?

The very next day Humm played the same nine holes with all fourteen clubs, and only managed a 40!

Best Golf Bet. Alvin C. "Titanic" Thomas once bet an acquaintance that he could drive a ball more than 500 yards. Naturally, the friend jumped at the bet, no doubt thinking that Thomas had become a victim of duffer's dementia. But Titanic was no fool, and it was on a chill winter's day that he stopped at a frozen water hazard on a Long Island golf course. Titanic teed off and the ball skidded across the frozen lake, gathering momentum. Not only did the ball make the 500-yard mark, but it stopped almost a half-mile away.

Best Golf Course. According to a poll taken by the editors of *Golf* magazine, the Shinnecock Hills Golf Club in exclusive Southampton, Long Island, New York, is the *primus inter pares* of courses in the United States.

Designed by Willie Dunn in 1891, the par 35-35-70 course sports great "character" in each and every one of its eighteen holes.

Best View from a Course. The Tuctu Golf Club in Peru —the highest in the world at 14,335 feet above sea level—offers the player a view extending well over 50 miles. Of course, one has to dig an endless panorama of snow-capped peaks.

Best Example of "Here Today and Gone Tomorrow." Comedian Groucho Marx was an avid, although at best an erratic, golfer. The mustachioed cigar smoker once made a hole in one at the Brae Burn Country Club outside Boston. Next day's Boston *Globe* reported Groucho's feat, printing three photos side by side—Groucho plus Bobby Jones and Walter Hagen—with the caption "Groucho joins the immortals." Marx played the same course again the following day, followed by a small army of *paparazzi* who hoped he might repeat his performance.

On that same hole Groucho opened by muffing his drive and then blew the hole completely, taking twenty-two shots to put it in the cup. The subsequent edition of the *Globe* again printed the Hagen and Jones pictures, but left a blank space where Groucho's mug shot had been, with the caption "Groucho leaves the immortals!"

———

Worst One-Hole Performance. Naturally this has to be a professional-only category, since any duffer sets this record on any given day!

But, in the 1938 U.S. Open, at Cherry Hills in Denver, Ray Ainsley had inordinate difficulty with a nearby brook. When poor Ainsley was through hacking his way to the pin, he had shot a 19 on the par four sixteenth hole!

Worst Choke in a Major Tourney. In 1939, at the beginning of his remarkable golfing career, Sam Snead entered the National Open at the Spring Mill course in Philadelphia. Snead, Craig Wood, and Denny Shute were tied for first, when Shute and Wood each finished with a 284, while Snead was still on the seventeenth green. Sam needed only nine shots for the last two holes to take the title.

Snead bogeyed the seventeenth, leaving his last chance on the last hole. Sam's drive went into the rough, his second shot landed in a trap, the third in a furrow, the fourth in another trap, and poor Snead eventually took eight shots on the normally par four hole, blowing the tourney.

Worst Mistake to Cost a Master's Tournament. In 1968 Roberto de Vicenzo of Argentina was in the competition, along with Gary Player and Don January, and the match was up for grabs after the third round. On the fourth round, with a mere two holes left to play, de Vicenzo and Bob Goalby were locked in a dead heat. De Vicenzo bogeyed the eighteenth and final hole, but so did Goalby, and the tourney appeared to be headed for sudden death. Ironically, the *seventeenth* hole was what did de Vicenzo in.

Tommy Aaron, keeping score for de Vicenzo under the pairing system (when two golfers are paired, one keeps score for the other, and vice versa), had added an extra stroke to de Vicenzo's total back on the seventeenth. De Vicenzo had actually birdied the hole, but Aaron marked a four on the scorecard, and de Vicenzo unthinkingly signed it. Under professional rules, if a golfer signs the card, the result—right or wrong—stands, and cannot be changed. De Vicenzo's total showed 66, when in fact he had shot a 65, but there was nothing to be done.

De Vincenzo, horrified after realizing his mistake, commented: "Stupid! Stupid! I play golf all over the world for thirty years. Now all I think of is what a stupid I am to be so wrong in this wonderful tournament. I must be too old to win!"

Worst Clutch Putt. Doug Sanders faced a simple one-and-a-half-foot putt for a sure win of the 1970 British Open. Incredibly, Sanders missed, forcing a playoff with Jack Nicklaus, which Nicklaus subsequently won. It was the last time Sanders has challenged for a major title, and he has never won one.

Worst Performance by Amateurs in the U.S. Open. In both 1963 and 1969, there was not a single amateur golfer who was able to complete the full seventy-two holes for the tournament.

Worst Year on the Pro Tour. In 1934 Paul Runyan was the top money winner on the pro circuit, with $6,767—a modestly respectable salary in those halcyon days. Unfortunately, Runyan's expenses for the season were $6,765, leaving poor Paul with a net profit of $2!

Worst Swing by a Good Golfer. This category presents a three-way tie between Lee Trevino, Gay Brewer, and Doug Sanders. Trevino has a flat, unorthodox swing and appears often to attack the ball; Brewer has a long, peculiar loop at the top of his swing; and it has been said of Sanders' swing that he could do it in a phone booth and not crack the glass!

Worst Golfing Torture. Colonel Bill Farnham played 376 holes at Guilford Lakes, Connecticut, which is normal golfomania for perhaps an active month in the summer. But Farnham did it in twenty-four hours and ten minutes, playing from 2:40 P.M. on August 11, until 2:50 P.M. on August 12.

Worst Man to Play Ahead of. Ken Bowsfield played eighteen holes at Burnham Beeches, England, on September 30, 1938, shooting a 69. Unfortunately for anyone who was attempting to play a leisurely game in front of Bowsfield, quick Ken played his full round in an astounding 91 minutes, averaging only about five minutes a hole!

Worst Hole to Walk. It is not uncommon at the Black Mountain Golf Club in North Carolina, to see golfers wrapping up their round after the sixteenth hole. No, it's not because the place is solely inhabited by doctors making emergency calls, but rather because the seventeenth hole at Black Mountain is more than half again as long as the average hole—a par six, 745-yard-long killer.

Worst Single Hole in the World. By golfer consensus it is a tiny hole only 155 yards long, and it resides at the Augusta National Country Club in Georgia, home of the Masters tournament. This bane of amateur and pro alike is the twelfth hole, but Lloyd Mangrum called it "the meanest little hole in the world."

The twelfth tee at Augusta is at an elevation, making it difficult to judge the prevailing winds, which seem to prevail capriciously and endlessly on this hole. Once the duffer has survived the winds, there is a deceptively fast green, causing many a miscalculated putt. Even "the Golden Bear" of golf, Jack Nicklaus, hates the twelfth at Augusta: "That . . . hole has jumped up and grabbed a lot of people."

Worst Sand Traps. By unanimous consent, the Pine Valley Golf Club in Clementon, New Jersey, wins the prize for worst traps, clubs down! And not only does it have the worst traps overall but one in particular has become legend.

Robert Trent Jones, a noted golf architect, once—almost poetically—described the course:

"The sandy wastes are terrifying, for unlike ordinary trapland, they bristle with small pines, low-growing juniper and other troublesome bushes and shrubs. Moreover, the sand is mottled with footprints—since there is too much sand to be raked, none of it is."

Furthermore, the trap on the seventh hole at Pine Valley is known, not so affectionately, as "Hell's Half Acre." It is, literally, a half acre of sand which is nearly always confronted if one attempts to play the hole safely. But, if one tries to gamble instead and avoid the trap, the rough is the result! The trap is so horrid that a sand wedge, especially designed just for traps, is virtually useless.

Most Unusual U.S. Open Winner. Orville Moody won the 1969 Open, with a 281, coming from complete obscurity to win the championship. Then, just as rapidly, he returned to limbo, never playing another important role in a major tournament.

Most Unusual U.S. Open. In the 1931 U.S. Open, winner Billy Burke had to play the equivalent of two tournaments in order to stagger off with his prize. After seventy-two holes at Inverness golf course, Burke and George Van Elm were tied at 292 apiece, which forced a thirty-six-hole playoff. Incredibly, after that playoff, the two were tied at 149 apiece, necessitating a second thirty-six-hole playoff! Burke, who no doubt didn't want to see a club again for a year, finally won the tourney by a stroke, 292–293!

Most Unusual Animal Interference. It was 1950 during the U.S. Open at Merion Course in Philadelphia that Lloyd Mangrum really got bugged!

Mangrum, George Fazio, and Ben Hogan were engaged in an intense battle for the lead coming into the sixteenth hole. Mangrum's shot to the green landed sixteen feet from the cup, and he marched up to play it. Looking down, he noticed that there was an insect perched on the ball, and somewhat impatiently, Mangrum waited for the creature to depart. But since the insect appeared quite content to remain until the following year's Open, Mangrum finally used his putter to mark the ball's position, picked it up and brushed the offending mite off the ball.

Disastrously, that move cost him what might well have been the tourney, since he was penalized two strokes for lifting the ball, and lost his lead.

Most Unusual Mishap in the Rain. Once during the

Southern California Women's Open there was a sudden downpour, but it was decided to continue the match. Mary K. Brown putted the eighteenth hole, but the cup was full of water!

Brown's putt rolled right across the cup over the water, and then went down a hill in a wee rivulet caused by the torrent. Luckily for Mary K. Brown, however, officials saw the water journey of her ball, and allowed her to take the putt over again—which she made.

Most Unusual Putt. During the U.S. Amateur championship at Newport, Rhode Island, in 1895, one player attempted to putt with a billiard cue! The case was instantly referred to the U.S. Golf Association officials present, who ruled against it.

Most Unusual Lie. The following two incidents must tie for strangest lie in professional play, and as with most things in life, one of them is good news, the other bad!

In 1920 Bobby Jones was playing in the Southern Amateur Tournament in New Orleans, when one of his drives landed in a shoe resting in a wheelbarrow! Loath to lift his ball and take the subsequent penalty, Jones elected to give the shoe a boot, so to speak. The ball flew out of the shoe, rolled onto the green and Jones parred the hole.

On the fifth hole during the second round of the 1949 British Open, Harry Bradshaw found his ball perched inside half a broken beer bottle. Bradshaw also elected to play the ball where it lay, shattering the bottle and his hopes for a championship, for he took six strokes on the normally par four hole.

Most Unusual Birdie. At the Shawnee-on-Delaware course during the 1938 PGA tournament, Sammy Snead and Jimmy Hines were neck and neck coming into the par three thirteenth hole. Hines's drive was further from the pin than Snead's, so he took his chip shot first. Hines's ball smacked Snead's . . . and both balls rolled into the cup. Both players were credited with a birdie 2 on the hole, and

Snead ultimately beat Hines by one stroke—although both men lost the tournament, to Paul Runyan.

Most Unusual Self-Inflicted Accident. During the 1934 U.S. Open at Merion Course in Philadelphia, Bobby Cruikshank made a difficult shot over a creek on the eleventh hole, and kept himself in contention. Wild with joy over his shot, Cruikshank threw his club elatedly into the air. It promptly crashed down, smack on Bobby's cranium, knocking him cold. Cruikshank recovered almost immediately and finished the tournament, but he had obviously destroyed his own composure, and finished tied for third.

Most Unusual Spectator Interference. In that very same 1934 U.S. Open, one hole later—on the twelfth—"Wiffy" Cox's drive struck a foreign object. One of the spectators had left a coat thoughtlessly on the fairway, and when he saw Wiffy's ball adorning his attire, he ran onto the fairway in embarrassment, and whisked away the offending garment. Unfortunately, he also whisked away Wiffy's ball, which then rolled into the rough.

Most Unusual Course. It was a lazy day in New York City between tourneys when Walter Hagen and Australian trick shooter Joe Kirkwood got the absurd idea of using the city streets for a golf course.

The two teed up a few streets away from their Central Park South hotel, playing through the concrete fairways into their hotel lobby, up the elevator, down their corridor and into their room. Lacking any other receptacle, the toilet bowl became the cup and Kirkwood always won, because he could always chip the ball into the porcelain "pin," while Hagen couldn't!

Most Unusual Course Rule. At Hillcrest Country Club in southern California, new patrons are sometimes startled to find that one of the club's rules is that players must wear pants (long or short doesn't matter . . .) on the course at all times.

It seems that Harpo Marx and George Burns were playing a few holes one hot, desertlike day, and the two decided to doff their shirts. The two were unaware that this was against club rules, until an irate member complained to management and the two were told to put the shirts on their backs again. The irrepressible flakes decided that since there was no rule about playing pantless, they would proceed to strip off their trousers. They did, and the club immediately passed the ruling about pants!

Most Unusual Con. Bob Hope, an inveterate golfer, and his chum, producer Sam Goldwyn, were playing golf one day when Goldwyn missed an easy two-foot putt. In a rage Sam threw away his putter, vowing never to use the blankety-blank thing again. As Goldwyn stomped off, Hope quietly picked up Sam's discarded putter and put it into his own bag.

A few holes later Hope used Goldwyn's putter to put away a lovely 20-footer (Hope happens to be a fine putter).

"That was very good," exclaimed Goldwyn. "Let me see that putter a minute." Sam examined it carefully then took a few practice swings.

"I like this putter very much," said Goldwyn. "Will you sell it to me?"

"Sure," said Hope with a perfectly straight face. "It'll cost you fifty dollars."

Goldwyn happily bought his own club back, thinking he'd gotten a real deal; and it wasn't until many years later that he found out what Hope had done to him.

Most Unusual Golfing Superstitions. Golfing superstitions abound as with any other sport. Some golfers are very superstitious about the order in which their clubs are placed in the bag, about the sighting of an animal or bird just before taking a drive (this is a "bad" omen). Many golfers insist that the ball's trademark name be on top at the tee; others will not use a new ball on a tricky hole, or feel that they have to use a new ball merely to change their luck. Some have to take new balls out of their wrapping before they get to the tee, and many favor odd numbers on

203

the balls. There is hardly a golfer living, it sometimes seems, who doesn't have a superstition about the color of clothes, or a "favorite" shirt.

Golfing superstition even extends to caddies, and it is many an unfortunate caddy who has lost out on a high-tipping patron simply because the golfer had a disastrous round that day . . . and was absolutely certain that the new caddy was to blame! In fact, golfing superstitions are just about as crazy as the game itself!

Olympics

Best All-Around Athlete. Usually the winner of the grueling ten-event Decathlon is considered the best athlete in the world. Therefore, on the basis of his stunning 8,618-point performance in the 1976 Montreal Games, United States' Bruce Jenner should be the choice, right?

Wrong!

Theagenes of Thasos was a champion boxer, sprinter, and wrestler who won over 1,400 Grecian championships in his long and distinguished career.

In addition, Theagenes competed in an event known as the pancration—a combination boxing and wrestling event—held to the death, with no holds barred. And he won them all!

Best Wrestler. Although Ivan Yarygin of the Soviet Union established his dominance in the freestyle wrestling events at the Montreal Games in 1976, he would be hard pressed to better the record of a Greek, Milo of Croton, who lived in the sixth century B.C.

Milo, according to legend, was the strongest wrestler

ever to compete in the ancient Olympic Games. Besides constantly dominating the wrestling events, Milo added some of his own unique twists; to wit: he carried his own life-size statue up the mountain where the statues of athletic heroes were kept, and placed it there himself! Another of his feats was to wrap a leather cord around his forehead and snap it by swelling the veins in his forehead!

Naturally, Milo ate a king-sized meal; his dinner was rumored to be seven pounds of meat, seven pounds of bread, and he drank four or five quarts of wine!

Unfortunately, Milo met with an untimely end. He was walking in the forest one day when he happened upon a tree with an ax mark in it. Unable to resist temptation, he proceeded to try to chop it down with his own hands! However, he miscalculated and his hand became entrenched in the hole! By and by a pack of hungry wolves entered the scene and, refusing to acknowledge Olympic greatness, proceeded to devour the ill-fated champion.

Best Jumper.   Ray Ewry of Lafayette, Indiana. Ewry recovered from a childhood bout with polio, taking up calisthenics and jumping in an effort to strengthen his legs. The exercises worked so well that he completely dominated the standing jumping events—which no longer are on the Olympic program—at the 1900, 1904, and 1908 Games.

In ten events from 1900–08, including the high jump and standing broad jump, Ewry won ten gold medals. His best performance came on July 16, 1900, when he easily won the standing broad jump and the standing high jump for the first time in his Olympic career.

"His leap in the standing high jump was almost unbelievable," writes Dick Schaap in his history of the Games. "From a stationary start, Ewry cleared the cross bar at five feet, five inches. No other contestant came within four inches of his height."

Ewry's records will stand forever, since the standing jumping events were discontinued after 1912.

Best Long-Distance Runner.   Paavo Nurmi, Finland. The "Phantom Finn" dominated the long-distance running events, including the 1,500 meters, 2,000 meters, 3,000 meters, 5,000 meters, 10,000 meters, and 20,000 meters in the Olympic games of 1920, 1924, 1928.

It was rumored that Nurmi developed his strength by running after a mail train in his native Turku, Finland. James Loudeau, director of athletics at a British university, commented:

"This was not a very hot specimen as trains go. It went along at a careful eight to ten miles an hour; still it had good breeding and stamina and nobody else in Turku thought of running races with it."

Besides setting world records in those events, Nurmi also set records for the one-, two-, three-, four-, five-, and six-mile runs.

Many of the long-distance runners who have gained Olympic notoriety have been Finnish, including Lauri Lehtinen, who broke Nurmi's 5,000-meter world record in 1932, and Lasse Viren, who won both the 5,000- and 10,000-meter events in Montreal in 1976.

One wag, trying to explain why the Finns are such strong runners, commented: "They spend their entire lives speaking Finnish. If they can cope with that they can cope with anything!"

Best Male Swimmer. Although Mark Spitz set the Olympic world atwitter with his classic seven-gold-medal performance in Munich in 1972, our choice is not Spitz, but another American of an earlier age, Johnny Weismuller, who is more familiar to those under fifty as Tarzan of movie fame.

Weismuller set world records in sixty-seven different swimming events, both Olympic and non-Olympic, from the 50-yard dash to the 880-yard endurance test.

His coach, William Bachrach, noted that "Johnny didn't give a damn what the event was, just as long as they had a tank, timers and a finish line."

Weismuller remembers about Bachrach that he was a stern taskmaster. "He told me, 'Kid, with me you'll be swimming for months, and against nobody. I'll grind you down and you'll probably learn to hate me, but I guarantee that when I get through with you you'll be a first-place swimmer!' "

Weismuller was. In the 1924 Games, held at Paris, he won the 100 meters in 59 seconds flat, beating the great Duke Kahanamoku of Hawaii, the two-time champion in the event, and Arne Borg, the so-called Swedish Slugger who, until that day, had never lost a race.

Then, in the 400-meter freestyle, Weismuller shaved *20 seconds* off the world record. He also was a member of the team which won the 800-meter relays and gained a fourth gold as a member of the United States water polo team.

In the 1928 Weismuller repeated his performance of the last Olympics, winning again the 100-meter freestyle and helping the United States win the 800-meter relays for the second consecutive time.

Weismuller's durability, winning events in two Olympics, and his diversity give him the nod over Spitz who, although he had a brilliant 1972 Olympics, had been a disappointment in his 1968 appearance.

Best Olympic Ice Hockey Team. Not the vaunted Russians of 1972 nor the Czechs of 1976, but the Canadians of 1924.

The first year the winter games were held, 1924 in Chamonix, France, ice hockey went on the program. But at that time, only the Canadians were ardent practitioners of the sport; and they proved it, by slaughtering their opponents.

In the opening round they beat the Czechs, 30–0! Then came the Swedes, 22–0; Switzerland, 33–0; and England, who finally solved the Canadian netminding, 19–2. Their toughest match was with the Americans in the finals, but even the star-spangled skaters went down to defeat, 6–1. There has never again been a domination by one team like that in Olympic annals.

Best Figure Skater. Undoubtedly the incomparable Sonja Henie of Norway. Sonja, who broke into Olympic competition when she was only twelve, astonished the world with her style, which was likened to ballerina Anna Pavlova's.

"Sonja," writes Dick Schaap in his history of the Games, "was one of the first figure skaters to transform the sport into an art. She adopted the 'Dying Swan' sequence from 'Swan Lake' and patterned her performance after Anna Pavlova."

Said another reporter: "Music and her skating are inseparable. With a quick movement she glides down the ice gradually gaining speed. Before the onlookers realize it, Sonja is moving in her natural pace, spiraling down the ice on one skate with her arms extended to each side, her head thrown back and a confident smile on her face."

Incredibly, she dominated three separate Olympics—1928, 1932, 1936, amassing more scoring points than anyone else in Olympic history. She brought the art of skating to America, and popularized the sport—or the art, if you will—in her many motion pictures and public appearances.

By the time she retired as a professional in the forties, she had made more than $5 million, and was still making a million a year.

Best Coxswain. These unheralded crew members often can turn defeat into victory, and that's just what Don Blessing did for the 1928 United States rowing team, which won the eight-oars competition.

Whythe Williams, who covered the Holland Games for *The New York Times,* described Blessing's exuberance in the cox's seat:

"Blessing's lungs are magnificent, and for the entire 2,000 meters he gave what, by unanimous accord, was one of the greatest performances of demoniacal howling ever heard on a terrestrial planet. Never for a second did he cease. . . . What magnificent flights of rhetorical vituperation! One closed his eyes and waited for the crack of a cruel whip across the back of the galley slaves."

The crew, from the University of California, all received gold medals. Blessing also received a case of laryngitis.

Best Female Athlete. Babe Didrikson, who won only two gold medals in the 1932 Olympics at Los Angeles— but women at that time were allowed to enter only three events!

Babe decided to enter the javelin throw, hurdles, and high jump, and won the first two events, setting world records in both. She also set a world record in the high jump—but surprisingly did not win the event.

Didrikson and Jean Shiley of the United States tied in the finals with record marks of five feet, five inches, and the two entered a jump-off for the purpose of awarding the gold medal. Shiley was declared the winner, however, because Didrikson's head went over the bar before her feet, therefore violating the rule against "diving."

The late Paul Gallico, then of the New York *Daily News,* once asked the Babe, who later became a world champion golfer, if there was anything she did not play.

"Yeah," said Babe, looking him straight in the eye, "dolls!"

Best Show of Courage. The greatest acts of heroism do not necessarily take place on the field. Nor do they necessarily involve athletics.

In the 1936 Olympics, held in Berlin during the height of the Nazi influence, Hitler's propaganda decried the American teams, especially the "black auxiliaries." The members of the German team, as good examples of a master Aryan race, naturally were not supposed to fraternize with the inferior subhumans.

But Luz Long, a German sprinter, told Hitler to take his propaganda campaign and shove it. During the trials for the broad jump, the great Jesse Owens, who was to embarrass Hitler in other ways, had fouled twice, leaving him only one more attempt to qualify. Long befriended him and advised the black star to start farther back, therefore giving him enough leeway so that he wouldn't foul, noting that Owens would easily be able to clear the needed distance.

Owens, of course, easily qualified and went on to set a world record for the broad jump. "At the instant I landed for my final jump," Owens remembers, "Luz Long was at my side, congratulating me. It wasn't a fake smile, either. He was a wonderful guy. It took a lot of courage for him to befriend me in front of Hitler."

Of course the war put an end to any friendship Owens and Long might have cultivated. Long, in fact, was killed during the war in Sicily, but Owens and Long's widow corresponded regularly.

"She told me," Owens remembers, "that when she saw Luz congratulate me after that jump that she was the proudest person in Germany that day."

Best Olympic Romance. Harold Connolly and Olga Fikotova. Connolly, an American hammer thrower, who won a gold medal in the 1956 games, took a liking to Olga, who won a gold medal for the Czechs in the discus throw. They started seeing quite a bit of each other in the Olympic Village, until they went home, Connolly to Boston, Olga to Prague.

However, love cannot be separated by anything as flimsy as an Iron Curtain, and they started corresponding by mail. Finally, a year later, Connolly visited Czechoslovakia on a ten-day visa, and requested permission to bring Olga back stateside so he could marry her. At first the Czechs refused—after all, they were losing one of their best discus throwers and getting nothing in return.

After much discussion—and a push by the U.S. State Department—permission was granted and the two were married. Czech marathoner Emil Zatopek acted as the best man.

Three years later, in 1960, both Connollys were in the Olympics again—on the same team this time, but marriage could not bring either of them a gold medal.

Best Olympic Film. There have been few commercial films made about the Olympic Games, but the games have been a great source of documentaries. Our choice for the best film about the Olympics is Leni Riefenstahl's *Olympische Spiele 1936*.

Riefenstahl, the German who made the famous propaganda film *Triumph of the Will*, put more time, effort, and equipment into filming the Olympic film than David O. Selznick did into making *Gone With the Wind*.

Riefenstahl used over fifty cameras, and shot more than a million feet of film for the production (70 percent of which went on the cutting room floor). In addition, Riefenstahl lent her magnificent editing techniques, for which she is most famous, to the entire production, spending more than six months editing it.

Ken Vlaschin, program director of the National Film Theatre of London, calls the movie "the finest film ever made about sport of any kind. It is much more than a factual diary of the Games, it is a hymn to physical health, to the human body and to the glory of youth.

"The first part—'Festival of the People'—is a symbolic paean to the human body, concentrating on track and field, culminating with the Marathon. The second part—'Festival of Beauty'—has to do with the more poetic aspects of the Games, gymnastics, yachting and riding.

"Each event has been superbly photographed and the individual shots have then been combined in the editing with a particular rhythm."

Best American Shooter. Gary Anderson became the first American in forty years to win the free rifle event in two consecutive Olympics, 1964 and 1968. He also was the first lefthand shot to do it. In non-Olympic international competition between 1963 and 1968 he won ten gold medals.

Best Marathoner. Abebe Bikila was the only man in the history of the Olympic Games to ever win this grueling event two consecutive times. In 1960 Bikila knocked ten minutes off Emil Zatopek's Olympic record, winning the event in two hours, 15 minutes, 16.2 seconds.

The following Olympics, 1964 in Tokyo, Bikila bested

his own record, beating it by fifteen minutes. It appeared that nothing would stop him from copping his third straight Marathon in Mexico City—but he was injured in an automobile accident and never raced again.

He died at only age forty-one, in 1973. His funeral attracted almost the entire city of Addis Ababa, who paid last respects to the first gold medalist from black Africa.

Best Woman Gymnast. Not Olga Korbut nor Nadia Comaneci, but a young lady named Larisa Latynina of the Soviet Union. The difference between Miss Latynina and the other two gymnasts—who some said were the creations of a hero-conscious media—is time. Although Olga stunned the world with her performance in 1972 and little Nadia was near-perfect in 1976, they still have to prove they can repeat in later Olympics.

Larisa did. Combining the 1956 and 1960 Olympics, Larisa won seven gold medals, three silver, and one bronze. She won the combined exercises both years, as well as the floor exercises, and twice was on the Soviet team which won the combined exercises.

In international competition, including the annual World Championships and European Championships, Larisa won 24 gold, 15 silver, and 5 bronze medals.

. Of course, Nadia Comaneci, being only eighteen when the 1980 Moscow Olympics roll around, has a chance to equal Miss Latynina's marks. But until she does, Larisa Latynina still has to be counted as the number one female gymnast.

Best Fencer. This little-heralded sport, which may be the hardest to master, has as its champion in Olympic competition Nedo Nadi of Italy. He won five gold medals in the 1920 games at Antwerp, Belgium, the only time that ever has been accomplished in fencing events.

Nadi started with the foil, teaching himself at an early age. From the foil he moved to the sabre and the epee—all weapons of different size and strategy. In 1912, before he won his five gold medals, he proved his skill in the foil competition, winning the event without a single defeat.

This very difficult accomplishment—somewhat like going undefeated throughout an entire baseball season—is considered one of the greatest accomplishments in the history of fencing.

Best Athlete to Take Advantage of His Success. When Mark Spitz won seven gold medals in the 1972 Munich Olympics, entrepreneurs from all over the world were eager to get his name on endorsements of myriad products. One of the most famous Spitzian mementos was the poster showing him in his star-spangled racing trunks laden with his seven gold medals. That poster brought him a tidy sum, estimated at well over a million dollars.

Spitz, who also tried to become an actor—and failed —decided that it was worth it to rest on his wet laurels, deciding not to swim again.

"I used to work out every once in a while," admitted Spitz in 1975, "but I don't think I have the time to start seriously training again for tough competition."

Worst Reaction by a Snubbed Champion. Legend has it that one Oebotar of Achaia, a champion chariot racer back in the days of the ancient Olympics, was not satisfied with the honors bestowed on him by the good people of Achaia—normally at least a statue and a lifetime kingship —and he decided to take his revenge.

He did it not by "jumping" cities, as modern-day athletes would, but by putting a curse on the city! No Achaian, he said, would win in the Olympics for the next three hundred years! And none did.

Finally, the good citizens of Achaia, hungry for a winner, decided to swallow their pride. They erected a statue of Oebotar and hoped that the curse would be lifted. It was; Sostratos of Achaia won the sprint for boys in the following Olympics held in Athens.

Worst-Planned Olympics. The 1900 Olympics held in Paris almost wrecked the revival of the Games before they even were able to catch on. They were held along with a major industrial exposition and were carried on, according to one reporter, "as a sideshow, almost as an afterthought."

The French government decided to keep the Olympics completely out of the spotlight, to the point of not displaying the official Olympic banner anywhere and refusing to use the word "Olympics" in the program of events.

"It was so ludicrous," described one observer, "that the athletes competing were not even sure that they were competing in the Olympics!"

In fact, it was a wonder that the competition—called simply "international championships"—was even held at all! The running track was situated in the middle of the Bois de Boulogne, the main park in the city of Paris. The only problem was that there was no track, because Parisian officials did not want to desecrate the grass! The pits for the jumpers also were inadequate, and there were many bad falls, especially for the high jumpers.

In addition, the Games were spread out over five months. It was feared that, after this dismal show, the rest of the world would take the Olympics to be nothing more than a joke. It is amazing that they survived what was then the darkest period of the Games.

Worst Finish for a Marathon.   Although the finishers are always exhausted to the point of collapsing, no one has ever suffered as Dorando Pietri of Italy did during the 1908 Games held in London. Pietri staggered into the stadium well in front of the rest of the field, but as he neared the track something snapped and he started jogging the wrong way! He had to be turned in the right direction, but still he was unable to go on.

As fans exhorted him to finish, others implored doctors to help the man, who looked as though he might die on the track. Finally, he sagged to the track and several attendants rushed out to help him—illegally—across the finish line. Of course since he received help in crossing the line he was disqualified and the race went to John Hayes of the United States.

"The man was practically delirious," wrote a reporter.

"He staggered along the cinder path like a man in a dream, his gait being neither a walk nor a run, but simply a flounder, with arms shaking and legs wobbly."

Although it was obvious that he never could have finished without help, an outcry came from the Italian team upon hearing the decision. Pietri himself was startled.

"I was all right until I entered the stadium," he contended. "When I heard the people cheering and I knew I had nearly won, a thrill passed through me and I felt my strength going. I fell down but tried to struggle to the tape, but fell again. I never lost consciousness of what was going on, and if the doctor had not ordered the attendants to pick me up I believe I could have finished unaided."

The entire incident was a disaster for the Olympics and the cause of Marathon racing. Public opinion in Britain wanted the race banned. "It is a question," said an editorial in the *Times* of London, "whether public opinion ever will support another Marathon race here. Dorando [Pietri]'s condition when he finished, and the condition of many of the contestants, lead people to think that the sport is worse than . . . bullfighting."

Worst International Relations. By far the most deep-seated hatred for a host country—which led to all sorts of incidents—was for the British during the 1908 Games held in London. For several reasons, not the least of which was the Irish revolt (there were quite a few Irish on the American team) the American team and the British hosts were constantly at odds.

In the opening ceremony, for example, the Americans refused to dip the flag to the king, which was customary at the time. However, United States delegation heads scoffed at the idea. "America dips its flag to no monarch!" an angry team member declared. In fact, no American flag has ever been dipped to any head of state in an Olympic parade.

But there were other incidents. Since the Irish team wanted to pull out because of the trouble with the British, many Americans wanted to pull out in sympathy. Perhaps in retaliation, the British "forgot" to place an American
216

flag at the closing ceremonies. The Swedes and Finns, two other countries which also protested British policy in Ireland, also marched without flags. Apparently the British were very forgetful in 1908.

This was different from the fiasco of 1976, when several black African countries pulled out of the Games over the exclusion of Taiwan. There were differences of opinion as to how that incident was handled, but the 1908 affair was the first—and hopefully the last—where a host country publicly snubbed nations who were still competing in the Games.

Worst Overrated Competitor. It was 1968, in Innsbruck, Austria, and skier Jean-Claude Killy of France received much publicity for winning gold medals in three events—the downhill, slalom, and giant slalom. As a result, he became an instant celebrity, for his good looks as much as for his skiing prowess.

However, a more careful examination reveals that Killy's feats—which supposedly equaled those of Toni Sailer of Austria, who also accomplished the triple play, in 1956—were slightly tainted. He won the slalom and giant slalom only by a scant tenth of a second; Sailer had won by more than four seconds!

For all the publicity and notoriety, Killy—a descendant of an Irish mercenary who fought in the Napoleonic wars ("Killy" being a corruption of the Irish name "Kelly")—never put on skis again in Olympic competition, preferring instead to become one of the "beautiful people."

Worst Overshadowed Champion. Because Hannes Kolehmainen of Finland had the misfortune to run in the 1912 Olympics—along with an athlete named Jim Thorpe —his feats have gone unnoticed.

All the young Finn did that year was win the 5,000 meters, setting the then world's record of 14:36.6 and the 10,000 meters, with a world's mark of 31:20.08.

"If Thorpe hadn't been so magnificent in those Games," writes Dick Schaap, "instead of Thorpe's Olympics it would have been known as Kolehmainen's Olympics."

Hannes' championships began a long line of Finnish domination in the long-distance events, which included the incomparable Paavo Nurmi and 1976's Lasse Viren.

Worst Disappointment by an American Team. Although the 1976 American track team won only three gold medals, it was not considered that much of a disappointment. After all, the rest of the world—and especially the East Germans—had finally caught up with us.

But that could not be said about the dismal showing of the 1928 team. The United States team, pampered on the voyage to the Games in Amsterdam, fell out of shape and won only eight gold medals, a mere two of them in track events.

Whythe Williams, who covered those Olympics for *The New York Times,* wrote: "Many explanations and suggestions were offered, but the one heard most frequently was that the team, puffed up with conceit, hadn't trained seriously enough since its arrival in Amsterdam."

They were fed lavishly, for example, often consuming as many as two hundred steaks a night. And the umpteen quarts of ice cream—which were supposed to last them all through the Games—were totally consumed during the voyage.

In addition, the U.S. Olympic Committee, headed at that time by Major General Douglas MacArthur, was in complete disarray. The committee was so fragmented that athletes didn't know whose orders to take. As a result, there was no concrete strategy for training, and, coupled with the overconfidence that characterized so many American Olympic teams, these factors combined to produce a sorry showing indeed.

Worst Heartbroken Athlete. Canada's Myrtle Cook, one of the fastest women in that country, was entered in the 100 meters and was given quite a good chance at the gold medal. But something happened that denied her the chance at glory.

As the contestants lined up, Myrtle's tension and anticipation caused her to jump the gun. Shaken, she tried to ignore the pounding of her heart, but could not. As the contestants lined up again, she jumped the gun for a second time and, under Olympic rules, was disqualified.

Utterly dismayed, she pleaded with the officials, but to no avail. Her lifelong dream of a gold medal shattered, she broke down and wept uncontrollably on the cinder track. The officials stood around, embarrassed, not knowing what to do. Finally, one of them gently took her aside and requested that if she must cry, do it on a pile of cushions in the infield.

Myrtle Cook did, in front of thousands of people, for a solid half hour.

Worst Conduct by a Head of State. Although Adolf Hitler was lambasted for refusing to recognize the accomplishments of Jesse Owens, even this infamous man must take a back seat to the person who, by his conduct, effectively disrupted the Games for almost two thousand years.

The Roman emperor Nero, in A.D. 67, as conqueror of ancient Greece, decided that, as such, he was entitled to enter the Games; after all they now belonged to him, as did everything else in Greece. It did not matter that he supposedly weighed 360 pounds and was as athletic as a beached whale; they were *his* games and he was going to enter. Naturally, no one stopped him.

He then proceeded to make a farce out of the Games. He invented several events on the spot—and, of course, won them all. He also won events that he did not invent, like the chariot race. He accomplished this feat even though he fell from the chariot and had to be assisted back up! Of course the other contestants, respectful of authority, and fearful of their heads, stopped their own horses until the emperor could regain his chariot!

This was only one of the reasons that the Games faded away under the Romans, not to be revived until 1896 by Baron Pierre de Coubertin of France.

Worst Sporting Incident. Hungary vs. the Soviet Union, 1956 water polo semifinal. The 1956 Olympics were clouded by tension, mainly because of Russia's rape of its unfortunate satellite state. The Russian athletes were soundly booed at every turn by the partisan crowd in Melbourne, Australia. However, although tensions simmered, nothing had boiled over, until this particular day.

Although water polo can be a rough sport, the semifinal match between Hungary and the Soviet Union was looked at as the Battle of Budapest all over again! Hungary put in four goals early, however, and they had a comfortable 4–0 lead as time started to run out in the game.

Then, with two minutes to go, Russia's Valentin Prokopov suddenly swam toward Ervin Zador of Hungary and viciously butted him in the head. Zador started bleeding profusely from a cut in the right temple. Because the blood mixed with water, it appeared that the Hungarian was seriously hurt, but actually this was not true. However, the Russians decided that they needed no retaliation on the part of the Hungarians and forfeited the game.

"It looked to me," said Wally Wolf, a veteran American water polo player, "like the Russian was justified. The Hungarians had been pushing him around all game. It really wasn't much of a cut, but with the water dripping down it looked like he was bleeding to death.

"After the incident the Hungarians caucused at one end of the pool, probably trying to decide whom they would hit to get even. The Russians, at the other end, decided to leave the pool and forfeit the match. They were lucky to get out of the stadium alive."

Hungary went on to win the gold medal in water polo, beating Yugoslavia, 2–1, in the finals.

Worst Disappointment for a Small Country. Surinam, a tiny country on the northern coast of South America, between the Atlantic Ocean and Brazil, decided to enter the 1960 Olympics in Rome. They dispatched exactly one athlete—Wim Essajas, a track man, who entered the 800 meters.

Even if he had competed and lost, it would have been a victory for such a miniscule nation. But they were denied even that moral victory, for poor Wim slept through the trials for the event, and thus was prevented from competing at all!

Poor Wim was crestfallen. "What are the folks back home going to say?" he wondered.

The world never knew, and Surinam still awaits its first Olympic champion.

Worst Weather for a Winter Olympics. Innsbruck, Austria, 1964. This town, nestled in the Alps, never lacked for snow—until the winter of 1964, when the Olympics were to be held. In the six weeks preceding the Games, no snow fell and the ski slopes were as bare as the Sahara. Finally, Austrian soldiers had to import snow—more than 20,000 cubic meters of it—from Switzerland!

As soon as they had done this, however, Innsbruck received a 14-inch snowfall, supposedly alleviating the problem. But it didn't! For the day after the snow fell, there was a thaw, and then a freeze. The result was that the slopes were icy and more skiers fell in that Olympics than ever before or since.

Worst Embarrassment for Royalty. No member of the British royal family had ever competed in an Olympics before 1976, so all eyes were on Princess Anne as she went through her paces in the equestrian events.

The equestrian sport consists of three phases: dressage, or showing off the horse in various gaits; jumping; and cross country. The princess was riding her favorite mount, Goodwill, in the cross-country event, when the animal betrayed his name.

He unceremoniously tossed the princess to the ground at the nineteenth obstacle of the thirty-six-obstacle course. Princess Anne lost four minutes in the competition, and was not a serious contender in the three-day event, won by Tad Coffin of the United States.

The princess suffered a slight concussion and a bruised right arm and cheek in the fall, which wasn't her first off the normally contrite steed. Goodwill had thrown her in the 1973 European championships too!

Worst Hammer Toss. No one kept a statistic on this errant throw, but witnesses say it was a near-deadly toss; in fact, they said, it was lucky it didn't kill anyone!

In the semifinals of the event in the 1976 Montreal Games, one contestant—whose name was lost—wound up for a throw in the classic style. Unfortunately, the hammer did not come close to the target.

It landed far to the left—on the running track where runners were warming up for the 5,000-meter event! Fortunately, no one was nailed on the head by this wandering hammer.

Worst Attempt at Diplomacy. Henry Kissinger could not have been too happy with the conduct of high jumper Dwight Stones in the 1976 Montreal Games. Stones, dismayed at the conditions of the Olympic stadium, told a Montreal reporter: "I'm very upset with the French Canadians. The stadium is just not finished and that's just plain rude."

The following day, plastered on the front page of the French-language *Montreal Matin* was the headline: STONES—I HATE THE FRENCH CANADIANS. Naturally, although the quote had been taken out of context, this did not endear him to the French Canadian fans, and they booed him unmercifully. This started counterbooing by the many American fans, which, in turn, led to a few fist fights.

How did Stones take all this?

"These people don't know what they're doing for me," he laughed. "They have psyched me so far out of my mind. The boos have just the opposite effect of bothering me."

Whether that's true or not we will never know, but the Montreal fans got their revenge on Stones when he succumbed to the weather and finished a disappointing fourth.

Worst Olympic Flame. An impromptu imposter was added to the flame which burned high above the Olympic Stadium in Montreal in 1976, when two Englishmen, disgusted at their fourteenth-place finish in the yachting competition, took it out on their boat.

They burned it to the waterline and it sank; Alan Warren and David Hunt swam back to shore vowing never to enter the blankety-blank event again.

Worst Brushoff. Montreal long has been known as a town for athletes on the make, so one Middle Eastern competitor was nonplussed at the response he got from a pretty tour guide, who was waiting for a bus near the Olympic Village.

After the briefest of introductions, the athlete went into his appeal:

"We go out," he implored. "We eat. We make love. Yes?"

"No," the young woman responded.

"Don't you want to make love to an athlete?" the astonished young man asked.

"No," she responded adamantly. "My Olympic fire is out!"

Most Unusual Training Methods. Hurdler Tom Curtis, who won the 110-meter hurdles in the first "modern" Olympics in 1896, was talking one day to a Frenchman who, surprisingly, was entered in both the 100-meter dash and the Marathon!

These two races were decidedly different, one requiring raw speed and the other requiring strong legs and the endurance of an ox. How, Curtis asked the Frenchman, did he manage to train for two such diverse events?

"One day," replied the Frenchman laconically, "I run a leetle way, very quick. The next day I run a long way, very slow."

He did not win a medal in either event.

Most Unusual Olympic Funding. Although several countries fund their Olympic team, others depend on a public grant. But no athlete ever went to the people for help like Felix Carvajal, a Cuban Marathoner who wanted dearly to race in the 1904 Olympics at St. Louis.

The only problem was that Carvajal had no money and Cuba had no official Olympic team. So Carvajal took his case right to the people. He stood in the middle of the public square in Havana and asked for donations! The crowd anted up.

Unfortunately, Carvajal violated the public trust. Once he started running in the Marathon, he built up a huge lead, and stopped to rest in an apple orchard along the route. Deciding he had enough time to momentarily break training, he picked an apple, which was decidedly green, and proceeded to eat it.

However, the apple was too green. Carvajal's stomach did not agree with *yanqui* fruit and he was forced to retire from competition.

Most Unusual Prank in the Marathon. Fred Lorz of the United States was competing in the 1904 Games at St. Louis when, unable to keep up the pace, he decided to drop out.

Since the Marathon course was not too well policed in those days—automobiles and milk wagons joined with the athletes—there was ample transportation available, and Lorz decided to hitch a ride. He hopped on the running board of a passing car and rode five miles through the course, as other runners stared, mouths agape.

When he was a few meters from the Olympic stadium, Lorz thanked the motorist and hopped off the car. Then he resumed running.

As he entered the stadium, the crowd, quite naturally, presumed Lorz to be the winner. They started cheering him, and Lorz, unable to resist the temptation, trotted toward the finish line!

The officials were prepared to drape the gold medal around his neck when his sense of morality prevailed, and Lorz admitted the prank.

Most Unusual Field. The 1904 Olympics, held in St. Louis, were the first to be held in the United States (the first two having been held in Athens, Greece, and Paris, France, respectively). However, although more than twenty countries were invited to compete, more than 80 percent of the athletes were American!

The reason was that St. Louis was, at that time, not the most accessible spot in the world. Nor the cheapest to reach. As a result, Americans dominated the competition, winning the vast majority of medals. Americans won twenty-two gold medals, twenty-two silver, and twenty bronze!

Most Unusual Olympic Year. 1906. Impossible, you say, since the Olympics are held every four years? No, because these Olympics, which were officially designated as such, were the first and last so-called off-year Olympics.

Held in Athens, those Olympics were a concession to people who wanted the Games held only in Athens. This request came from those who said that another session like the 1904 St. Louis Games—where hardly anyone showed up—could ruin the Olympic ideal. The plan, therefore, was to rotate the regular four-year Olympics among cities of the world, and hold interim Games in Athens.

Artistically these Games were a success, especially for the American team, which won its share of events and which sported uniforms for the first time. In addition, Athenians, who had turned out in impressive numbers for the 1896 Games, crowded the stadium again. But financially, it was too great a cost for most countries to send athletes abroad every two years instead of four, and no more interim games were held in Athens.

Most Unusual Diver. In the 1932 Games at Los Angeles, swimmers were preparing for the 100-meter event when, to their—and everyone else's—surprise, a well-dressed man, whose name, unfortunately, is lost to history, executed a perfect belly-flop into the water from the side of the pool.

It turned out that the well-dressed gentleman was a German sportswriter. He had accepted a bet of $100 that he would not dive into the pool! Although he emerged sodden, he had soaked the skeptic who proffered the money.

Most Unusual Weightlifter. When most people think of Olympic-class weightlifters, they think of men like 345-pound superheavyweight Vasily Alexeyev, who set the Olympic record of 970 total pounds in the 1976 Games in Montreal.

But one of the greatest weightlifters ever was one Thomas Kono of the United States, who stood only five feet, eight inches and whose weight varied between 148 and 184 pounds!

This amazing Japanese-American, who spent part of World War II with his family in a relocation camp, lifted a total of 798 pounds in 1952 to win the lightweight championship; he then duplicated his feat in 1956 in the light-heavyweight competition, lifting a total of 986 pounds. Then, in 1960 at Rome, he had slimmed back down to the middleweight class and won the silver medal.

"Successful weightlifting," he said, "is not in the body. It's in the mind. You can lift as much as you think you can."

Most Unusual Rendition of a National Anthem. It is customary to play the national anthem of the winning gold medalist at the conclusion of each event. However, in 1964, the Americans so dominated the track and field events that it seemed "The Star Spangled Banner" was the background music for the crowd! Because it is a rather long anthem, the Japanese solved the problem of redundancy by playing a shortened version of the anthem.

This angered one Van Rasey, a lead horn in the M.G.M. studio orchestra and a track fanatic who had come to Tokyo to see the Americans win. He was so incensed that the anthem was being shortened that he obtained a horn, and, after the aborted anthem, proceeded to play the entire number for his own satisfaction!

Most Unusual Swimming Event. In the 1900 Paris Games, one of the swimming events was an underwater competition, divided into two parts; the first part was scored on the basis of distance, and the second was scored on how long the contestant stayed underwater! Two points were given for each meter swum and one point for each second submerged.

Charles de Vanderville of France won, swimming 60 meters while staying underwater for one minute, 8.4 seconds.

Most Unusual Boxing Foul. In 1924 at Paris, Harry Mallin of Great Britain, who had won the middleweight class gold medal four years earlier, complained to the referee that his opponent, a Mr. Bourisse of France, had bitten him! However, before the complainant could make the official understand, that worthy soul had awarded the bout to Bourisse on points.

After the match, though, a Swedish official launched an investigation and anatomical evidence proved that Mallin, had, in fact, been bitten. Bourisse was disqualified, and Mallin went on to capture his second Olympic gold medal, beating fellow countryman John Elliott in the final.

The Fans

Best Streak of World Series Attendance. Edwin A. Lowenthal, Evansville, Indiana.

Lowenthal, a retired industrialist from Evansville, Indiana, saw his first World Series game in 1916, but he didn't become a serious World Series fan until 1934. From that year until 1966 he saw all but five World Series games played; from 1947 through 1966, he didn't miss one. His explanation for traveling thousands of miles to see the fall classic was simple enough: "Some people want to be millionaires, but I always wanted to see World Series games."

Best Brooklyn Dodgers Fan. Hilda Chester, "The First Lady of Flatbush." Ebbets Field was truly a neighborhood ball park, and "Dem Bums" were a neighborhood team. The Dodgers' pennant-winning parade, in 1941, drew over a million people. A local haberdasher, who made his name with an advertising sign in Ebbets Field's outfield that challenged the Dodgers, "Hit Sign, Win Suit," was elected borough president. And the ball park's an-

228

nouncer, Tex Rickard, would come out with gems like this: " 'Tension, puhleeze. A child has been found lost."

"On any given night," recalled Tommy Holmes, who covered the Dodgers for many years for the Brooklyn *Eagle,* which has long since vanished along with many other newspapers of that era, "half of the thirty or thirty-two thousand fans there could get home in fifteen minutes. It was the hub of several neighborhoods. It had two subways, three or four different streetcar lines. I'll bet there were days when ten thousand of the fifteen thousand there could walk to and from the park. It was in a residential area. All around, for a couple of miles, there was nothing but homes."

And there was Hilda Chester, "The First Lady of Flatbush." From the bleachers of Ebbets Field she cheered on her beloved "Bums" by beating frying pans, ringing brass bells, and, the ploy that won her fame in the forties, ringing a cowbell.

"You know me," she'd say, relishing the recognition. "Hilda wit' th' bell. Ain't it trillin'. Home wuz never like dis, Mac."

Finally, local newspapers began interviewing her, and she made the front pages several times. Her inimitable Brooklyn howl and her cowbell became staples of every Dodgers rally, and a character based on Hilda was featured in Hollywood's *Jackie Robinson Story*.

Some say Hilda took her fame a bit too seriously, and her fame diminished appreciably when she followed Leo Durocher from Ebbets Field to the Polo Grounds in the late forties. Hilda's allegiance finally switched over to the New York Rangers' hockey team, as a result of her friendship with organist Gladys Goodding who played both at Ebbets Field and Madison Square Garden.

Hilda Chester, Dem Bums, and the Giants all became part of New York's folklore when the Giants and Dodgers deserted New York for California in 1957. Years later, a reporter found Hilda Chester in a nursing home in Rockaway Park, New York, and tried to get her to reminisce.

"I never even think of it. The old days, I never give it

a thought," said Hilda. "No. I don't want to talk about it. . . . It's all over, that's it. That's all I can say. I'm sorry."

Brooklyn is as sorry as Hilda Chester that the Dodgers' era is over, but for many of them, the memories of Dem Bums and "The First Lady of Flatbush" linger.

Best Extravagant Kentucky Derby Outing. Harvey Hester, a restaurateur and horseplayer from Smyrna, Georgia, enjoyed the Kentucky Derby so much that he missed just one in a twenty-year period. One year, he decided to do the Derby in style, so he hired a club car and invited a dozen friends. Hester and his friends spent three days living in the club car when they weren't watching the Derby from a glass-enclosed dining room at Churchill Downs.

Best Eloquent Fan. Eddie Andelman, Boston, Massachusetts. Andelman, a millionaire Boston real-estate man, saw many things in the world of sports that he didn't like. Unlike most fans, he went out and did something about it. With two friends, Jim McCarthy and Mark Witkin, he started a radio show called "Sports Huddle," which the three first sponsored themselves by buying time on a local station. The show finally became self-sufficient and was recognized by journals as prominent as *Newsweek* magazine, which called it "the most outrageously innovative sports show in the nation." Andelman later wrote a book, *Sports Fans of the World, Unite!* which made him almost as many enemies in the world of sports as did the radio show, when he took shots at fellow journalists, fat-cat athletes, and insensitive management alike.

Worst Punishing Promotion by a Baseball Team. Bernie Brewer and the Milwaukee Brewers, 1971. Charlie Finley and Bill Veeck notwithstanding, the Milwaukee Brewers' brainstorm in 1971 ranks as one of the most physically and psychologically demanding ever on a promotion man.

230

They hired a man whom they christened as Bernie Brewer, and planned to have him live on a small self-sufficient platform above their stadium until the Brewers' attendance hit the 40,000 mark for a single game.

However, the Brewers' answer to flagpole-sitting soon was replaced by a gimmick christened as "The World's Largest Beer Barrel." It was connected to a chalet and designed so that other, ersatz Bernie Brewers could slide from the barrel into a man-sized beer stein to commemorate each Brewers home run and victory, accompanied by sirens and balloons.

Worst Heckler in Baseball. "Leather Lung" Pete Adelis, Philadelphia.

"Leather Lung" Pete Adelis earned his reputation as baseball's worst heckler by, among other things, on occasion being hired by teams, getting banned for life from Ebbets Field, and actually having his life threatened by a player. Adelis, also known as "The Leather Lung of Shibe Park," was six feet tall, 260 pounds, a size 52, and had the lungs to match. He considered himself a "scientific heckler" and was so good—or bad, if you will—that the Philadelphia Athletics took him on the road to harangue their opponents. The New York Yankees even imported him once to intimidate the Cleveland Indians at Yankee Stadium.

Adelis' most infamous and tasteless bit of heckling took place at Ebbets Field, when he was harassing the Dodgers' Billy Herman. Herman's good baseball buddy, Arkie Vaughn, had just drowned and Adelis yelled, "Herman, the wrong guy drowned." It is said that Herman tried to kill Adelis; Herman managed to get Adelis banned for life from Ebbets Field.

Worst Fan Violence at a Sporting Event in North America. Montreal Forum, March 1955. In that month, National Hockey League president Clarence Campbell suspended Montreal Canadiens star Maurice "Rocket" Richard for the final three games of the regular season, and the Stanley Cup playoffs as well. This was hard enough for

Montreal fans to take, but Campbell rubbed salt in their wounds by having the bad judgment to show up at a Detroit Red Wings–Canadiens game at the Montreal Forum. When the fans spotted Campbell, they began to pelt him with programs and whatever else they could get their hands on, and he escaped amid a flying wedge of police. But the incident didn't end there; the fans rioted both inside and outside the Forum, forcing the suspension of the game, looting stores, breaking windows, and battling Montreal police in a cloud of tear gas. When the smoke cleared, more than forty people had been arrested, the Canadiens had forfeited the game, and $100,000 worth of property had been damaged.

Worst Behavior by Fans at a Baseball Playoff Game. Shea Stadium, New York, 1973. Shea Stadium fans nearly forced the New York Mets to forfeit the third game of the 1973 National League championship series to the Cincinnati Reds. Pete Rose slid into second base, and got into a scrap with Mets shortstop Bud Harrelson. The fans fueled the fire by throwing beer cans and bottles at Rose, and only the intervention of a group of Mets players, who begged the fans to stop, prevented the game from being forfeited.

Worst Stunt by a Football Fan.   Donald Ellis, of Rochester, New York, Baltimore, December 1971.

It started innocently enough, but it almost cost Donald Ellis his life and resulted in a quarter-million-dollar lawsuit. The Miami Dolphins were playing the Baltimore Colts, and all was right with the world—until the third period of the game, when something got into Donald Ellis. He vaulted the fence, ran up to the line of scrimmage and grabbed the football.

"My friends didn't think I would do it," said Ellis. "I didn't know I would do it either. But suddenly I was out there."

Fine and dandy. The Colts and Dolphins ignored Ellis, with the exception of Colts linebacker Mike Curtis. Unfortunately for Ellis, Curtis did what he was being paid to do. He chased Ellis, caught up to him and gave him a vicious forearm smash, at which point Mr. Ellis became unconscious.

Instead of being thankful for remaining alive, Ellis, when he came to, turned around and sued the Colts for $250,000, claiming he was attacked "without provocation."

Curtis did not agree. His explanation was logical enough. "I believe in law and order. That fellow had no right on the field. I felt it was in line to make him aware of his wrongdoing. And I couldn't take the idea of people getting in my way when I was doing my job."

Most Unusual Olympic Fan. Passersby outside the Montreal Olympic Stadium were surprised to see a gentleman named Elzear Duquette, standing alongside a coffin which Duquette claimed was his. It seemed that the gentleman, who hailed from Montreal, traveled around the world, billing himself as "King of the Walk."

Duquette apparently went to important functions, or wherever there was news. He told reporters he had been to more than eighteen countries and had traversed more than 140,000 miles.

"I can't sleep anywhere but my coffin," he said, matter-of-factly. "I hate hotels, and I love cemeteries. Anytime I find a cemetery I jump at the chance of sleeping there. I've seen it all, met all the dignitaries . . . Nixon, Trudeau, Haile Selassie. It's a free, interesting life."

As long as the moon is full . . .

Most Unusual Method of Rooting. Detroit's Pete Cusimano and his octopi. The Cusimanos' octopi were a family tradition that may or may not have had something to do with the success of Gordie Howe and the Detroit Red Wings in the fifties and sixties. It all started in the 1952 Stanley Cup playoffs, when Pete and Jerry Cusimano wanted to do something to extend the Red Wings' streak of seven straight playoff game victories.

"My dad was in the fish and poultry business," Pete recalled, "and my brother and I helped him. We'd often go to Red Wings games straight from work, so before the eighth game, Jerry suggested, 'Why don't we throw an octopus on the ice for good luck? It's got eight legs and that might be a good omen for eight straight wins.'"

So, on April 15, 1952, Jerry Cusimano heaved a three-pound crimson, partially boiled octopus onto the ice of the Detroit Olympia. Pete and Jerry's good-luck gesture was such a smashing success that the Red Wings went on to win the Stanley Cup that spring, so for the next fifteen years the Cusimanos threw an octopus at least once in every Detroit playoff series. Everyone loved it, apparently, but the referees.

"You ever smelt a half-boiled octopus?" asked Pete. "It ain't exactly Chanel No. 5, y' know. And it's not exactly cherry custard, either. You should see how the referees jump when the octopus hits the ice!"

Most Unusual Cheering Section.   Valdis Slakans, Galveston, Texas. Slakans' problem was that he was in the wrong city at the wrong time. The Galveston, Texas, factory worker was a Detroit Lions fan whose local team was, unfortunately, the Houston Oilers. Undaunted, Slakans would sit in the stands at Oilers games in his Lions windbreaker, carrying a Lions banner. With any luck, his shortwave radio would pull in the Lions game. Sitting under a sign proclaiming him "V. J. Slakans, World's Greatest DEE-troit Lion Fan," Slakans explained that he'd rather be at the Oilers game, watching a contest whose outcome mattered not, than in his living room, "because I like the atmosphere."

Miscellany

Best (Most Comfortable) Arena or Ball Park. The Houston Astrodome. Billed as "the Eighth Wonder of the World" when it opened for business in 1965, the ball park featured theater-type seats—the first ball park in the United States to do so; super-luxurious sky boxes, another innovation; and, most important, a constant, rain-free, 72-degree environment.

This was an immediate improvement over the outdoor, unshielded surroundings of Colt Stadium, where the Astros (formerly the Colt 45's) had played for the first three years of their existence. Not only was the new stadium comfortable for the players, with huge locker-room areas and training rooms, but the fans, who previously had to suffer through mosquito attacks seemingly every second, rejoiced. They actually could sit back in comfortable seats and enjoy the ballgame! In addition, the ball park was in the middle of the city, so there was no need to take long drives into the Texas countryside.

Some of the newer indoor stadia—like the Louisiana Superdome or the Seattle Kingdome—may be more extravagant. But it was the Astrodome which revolutionized outdoor spectator sports.

Best Unknown Sports Book. *Left Wing and a Prayer*, the story of the aborted Ottawa franchise of the World Hockey Association, written by Doug Michel and Bob Mellor.

Michel was one of the original partners of the Ottawa Nationals of the WHA, which lasted for one year and then moved to Toronto (and then Birmingham, Alabama). He relates how he, an owner of an Ottawa electrical company, plunged into the world of major league hockey, against all odds.

"Somewhere deep in every Canadian hockey fan's mind," Michel explains, "there lurks a subconscious conviction that he could be a greater strategist than Punch Imlach, a keener hockey mind than Emile Francis, and a manipulator of talent to surpass even the inimitable Sam Pollock of Montreal."

Michel started by sponsoring a kids' hockey team, and then, when the WHA came along, decided to get involved with that. "The whole idea was pretty intangible, but the mere idea of someone attempting to begin a new major league had us just intrigued enough to follow it up," he said.

The story unfolds of how the club, unable to attract fandom, slowly sank until it was necessary to sell to wealthy Toronto playboy John Bassett.

It is an unusual tale—the inside story of a franchise, and this is an area which never has been dealt with before.

Unfortunately, the book has been published only in Canada (by Excalibur Sports Publications, 234 Argyle Street, Ottawa, Ontario, Canada) and, to our knowledge, remains unknown in the United States. Perhaps it should be required reading for those get-rich-quick types who like the prestige of owning a major league franchise.

Best Crowd at a Funeral. An estimated 150,000 Argentines came out to Luna Park in Buenos Aires in May

1976 to pay their last respects to heavyweight boxer Oscar Bonavena, who had been shot to death outside a brothel in Mustang, Nevada, that month.

Bonavena's body lay in state all day, and people lined the park's lanes to see their national hero. The newspapers said the city hadn't seen so many mourners since the funeral of Carlos Gardel, the tango singer, who had died in 1935.

Best Money Winner in Sports History. Sonja Henie, the figure skater who delighted Olympic fans and later went into ice shows and motion pictures, is estimated to have received $47,500,000 during her career.

According to Dick Schaap, who wrote a history of the Olympics, in which Sonja gained her fame, "the plots of her movies mostly were simple and just vehicles to get her to do her stuff." But that suited her fans just fine, who couldn't get enough of her on skates. She popularized the sport of figure skating to the point where ice shows and other exhibitions earn millions of dollars a year (see *Best Olympic Figure Skater*).

Best Single Purse in One Sporting Event. The $25,000 or so given to each winning member of a Super Bowl pales by comparison to the moolah received by Muhammad Ali for winning the heavyweight championship in the "Thrilla in Manila" on October 1, 1975.

Ali was handed an estimated *$6 million* for his efforts. Frazier was no slouch either, walking away with an estimated $1.5 million for losing. The total gross, before taxes, was a reported $9 million.

Best Female Money Winner in One Year. Olympic figure skater Janet Lynn, who left amateur ranks in 1973, earned an estimated $750,000 in her first year as a pro, and signed a $1.5 million contract for 1975. Her earnings in 1976, including ice shows and payment for her work as a color commentator in various events and television specials, amounted to well over a million.

237

Best Longevity for a Champion. How do you assess a champion? Do you count Joe Louis' twelve-year reign as heavyweight champ the best? Or how about Gene Sarazen's long term as golf's number one man?

A lot of candidates may claim the title, but we doubt anyone has ever monopolized a title like Pierre Etchbasterm, a Basque tennis champion, born in France. Etchbasterm, a world amateur champ, held the title for twenty-seven years, from 1928 to 1955, and finally retired undefeated.

Best Crowd for Any Sporting Event (Not on TV). Not the 100,000 or so who annually view in person the Indianapolis 500 or the Kentucky Derby, but the more than *one million* spectators who each year line the streets of São Paulo, Brazil, to view the San Sylvestre Road Race.

Best Multisport Broadcaster. The consensus seems to be Curt Gowdy of NBC, for the diverse work he does in baseball, football, and basketball. What distinguishes Gowdy is his extreme sense of professionalism; he has seen so many games of every type that he displays no rooting interest on the air. In addition, the amount of preparation he does for each game minimizes his mistakes. There never has been a broadcaster who had been able to handle so many sports as Gowdy does, as well.

Best TV-promoted Sport. Never has TV made—then broken—and then made again—a sport as it did roller derby.

The game, which started out as a gimmick developed by one Leo Seltzer during the early forties, was on the verge of extinction, until Seltzer paid to have one of his matches televised by a Chicago TV station. Crowds which had been thinner than tissue paper before the sport hit the tube, were riveted to the home screen. Almost overnight large crowds came out to see the skaters bash, crash, and even skate around the banked wooden track.

The game, as a result, sold itself overnight. "Thousands of Americans," wrote an observer, "hunkered down happily in their living rooms to watch as the Derby captured prime-time evening showings in New York three nights a week and were [shown] throughout the country on a national TV hookup. . . . By [1949] the Derby was topping TV popularity ratings and had become what *The New York Times* television columnist Jack Gould called 'an accepted way of life in pub and parlor.

" 'The Derby's disruptive effect on the household is virtually absolute,' he wrote. 'Never before has roller-skating meant so much.' "

In time, however, television "overexposed" roller derby and interest waned. It became a barnstorming venture, with two teams—the San Francisco Bay Bombers, led by their stars Charlie O'Connell and Joanie Weston; and another group, variously called the Midwest Pioneers, All-Stars, and what-have-you—carrying their banked track with them in station wagons, from town to town.

However, Jerry Seltzer, Leo's son, rediscovered television. He videotaped the Bombers' games and syndicated the tapes, so that they could be shown in market areas throughout the country. In addition to the taped games, the telecasts always were accompanied by a message telling viewers when roller derby would be in their area.

Buoyed by the tapes—which made the Bay Bombers the "home" team of millions of derby fans—attendance soared again. One Palm Sunday match in 1970 attracted a record 15,000-plus to Madison Square Garden in New York.

By the mid-seventies attendance declined again.

Best Scoreboard. The huge piece of equipment developed for the Olympic Stadium in Montreal is capable of showing instant replays—with astonishing clarity—as well as tapping into a computer bank which instantly updates statistics, notes, etc.

It was good enough to keep the fans at the Olympics accurately informed as to the progress of all Olympic events—not only the ones taking place at the stadium. And the timing devices were at least as accurate as the timing devices used in the TV coverage.

239

The scoreboards—one is at each end of the 75,000-seat stadium—measure approximately 200 feet across, or about the length of an ice hockey rink. In addition, they are situated in such a manner that there are no blind spots—that is, they are visible from every seat in the stadium.

Best TV Coverage of a Sporting Event. The 1976 Olympic Games, covered by ABC. For their efforts, they gave the viewing public excellent camera shots of each event, particularly the skiing and bobsledding competition —two fast sports which are difficult to carry. In addition, they provided mobile coverage of the Marathon, complete with overhead helicopter shots and trucks with cameras mounted atop them which followed the runners through the streets of Montreal.

They were able to keep the viewer informed as to the timing of the events via the computer system which was then used to time the events themselves. In fact, the more accurate timing was made necessary by television, which was able to provide instant replays and stop action, thus putting more pressure on the judges.

And finally, their "Up Close and Personal" series, vignettes with the athletes themselves—was a warm human interest touch. And, they did it all without the commercialism that usually permeates such coverage. It will be a huge order for NBC, which has the 1980 Games in Moscow, to top them.

Best Public Address Announcer. Bob Sheppard, Yankee Stadium. Sheppard, an English teacher at a Long Island school, has become the most recognized voice in any ball park.

His voice, a deep, melodious baritone, is both attention-getting and calm all at once. "Your attention please, ladies and gentlemen," he intoned during one particularly hairy time at the Stadium, when fighting in the stands threatened to spill over to the field, "we heartily request that you cease the actions in the stands because of the possible effects on the outcome of the game. We know that passions run high, but we ask that you conduct yourselves in a responsible manner. Thank you."

This calm plea had a soothing effect on the fans and the fighting soon abated.

Best Behaved Fans. Those who attend the matches at center court in Wimbledon must have the highest boiling point of any fans in sport. They sit patiently, anticipating the play and taking it all in, then issue a respectable—but energetic—round of applause for the winners.

Tennis fans are so restrained, in fact, that when the then New York Sets (now Apples) of World Team Tennis were playing their first match in the Nassau Coliseum on Long Island, the players were upset that nothing was coming out of the stands, and management encouraged fans to root harder. Unfortunately, this brought about a storm of protest from the traditionalists.

"These are rowdies," Ilie Nastase of Rumania screamed. "You cannot concentrate on the games in this snake pit."

The fans settled down, as they always have done, especially at Wimbledon.

Best Baseball Brawl of the Seventies. Yankee Stadium, New York City, May 20, 1976. It seems as though the Yankees and Boston Red Sox stage at least one battle royal in each decade. But the punch-out to end all punch-outs was staged at the refurbished Bronx ball yard in the Bicentennial year.

The first-place Yankees had led the defending American League champs by six games as the two clubs began a four-game series. In the bottom half of the sixth inning, New York was threatening to add to their precarious 1–0 lead with Lou Piniella on second base and Graig Nettles on first. The batter, Otto Velez, lined a Bill Lee fastball into right field.

As the medium-fast Piniella chugged around third base with the green light from coach Dick Howser, the charging Dwight Evans scooped up the ball in right field, reared back and fired an accurate one-hop throw to Boston catcher Carlton Fisk.

The Sox's talented backstop received the skidding throw on the first-base side of the plate, turned on his knees to meet the sliding Yankee runner and tagged him out. But it didn't end there.

Piniella thought the ball had been jarred loose by the collision and tried desperately to kick it away so that umpire Terry Cooney would see it. Instead of the ball, Piniella inadvertently kicked Fisk.

"I was down on my knees with the ball," Fisk said, "and the next thing I know, his knees are at my head. We went down and he's rolling and kicking all over the place. It was his kicking that started the whole thing. He was being malicious."

Having suffered several painful groin injuries on previous plays like this one, Fisk took exception to Piniella's actions. He tagged him with the ball a second time—only harder—in the jaw. Lou grabbed the catcher's chest protector to get out from under him and Fisk rapped him again on the chin; this time with the ball in his bare right hand. Then the donnybrook began.

At that moment, Boston first baseman Carl Yastrzemski and Yankee on-deck hitter Sandy Alomar raced to home plate, acting as peacemakers. The rest of the players figured Yastrzemski and Alomar were going to fight, too, so they stormed the diamond with fists cocked.

Bill Lee was the next "outsider" to join the fracas, followed by the Yankees' Velez and Nettles, who put both his arms around the Boston pitcher to try and drag him off the pile-up of players. Meanwhile, New York outfielder Mickey Rivers, who also had charged out of the dugout to lend physical support, jumped Lee from behind, dragged him to the ground with a hammerlock and uncorked a number of vicious hammerlike punches in a windmilling manner.

With Boston's ace lefthander now lying on the turf in pain, Nettles tried to explain to a few of Lee's teammates that he only wanted to get him off the pile. Suddenly, Lee got up, walked over to Nettles and delivered a barrage of invectives that made the Yankee third baseman sorry he

242

even attempted to make peace. At one point, Lee told Nettles, "If you ever hurt my shoulder again, I'll kill you." That was all the usually mild-mannered Nettles had to hear.

Nettles then connected with a right cross to the eye which decked Lee. They finished their private war on the ground. By now the pain in Lee's shoulder was excruciating. Red Sox trainer Charley Moss rushed to the aid of the fallen pitcher and escorted him to the dressing room. It turned out to be Lee's last appearance in uniform for about six weeks.

The rest of the casualty list read like a typical weekly National Football League injury report. Carl Yastrzemski suffered a bruised thigh, Mickey Rivers injured his foot, Lou Piniella hurt his hand, but, miraculously, the injury-prone Carlton Fisk escaped unscathed.

"It was the worst fight I've ever seen," Yankee first base coach Elston Howard commented after the fist-swinging subsided.

Funny, the New York baseball fans thought it was the *best* they'd ever seen.

Best Performance by a Basketball Slugger in a Continuing Series. Ricky Sobers, Phoenix Suns, 1976 National Basketball Association playoffs. Sobers, a freshman guard, established himself as the George Foreman of the basketball court when he engaged in three fights—one in each playoff round.

First, the six-foot-three-inch Sobers slugged it out with seven-foot-two-and-a-half-inch center Tom Burleson of the Seattle Supersonics in the quarterfinals and demolished Golden State Warriors forward Rick Barry with a sledge-hammer shot in the mouth in the first half of the seventh and deciding game of the Suns' Western Conference final playoff. The rookie's decision over the six-foot-seven-inch veteran superstar sparked his teammates, who turned from toads to tigers and outplayed the Warriors the rest of the evening.

"I don't think of myself as leading the league in fights,"
243

Sobers explains. "I like to think of myself as leading the league in gaining respect."

Sobers' most one-sided victory came in the championship finals against Kevin Stacom, a six-foot-three-inch guard with the Boston Celtics. Finally, he had picked on someone his own size.

"Sobers is not afraid of anyone," said Boston *Globe* columnist Bob Ryan after the Celtics took the Suns in six games for the NBA championship. "He'll start a fight regardless of race, creed, color, size, national origin, or amount of facial hair. He could start a fight at a tea party."

Best Arena in the Worst Location.   The Richfield (Ohio) Coliseum, which seats more than 19,500 for basketball and over 18,000 for hockey, features perfect sightlines, comfortable seats, and excellent facilities for those who can afford them. In many ways it is the best indoor arena to watch a hockey or basketball game.

But the Coliseum is located in a backwoods, dismal, out-of-the-way place that is so isolated that Stanley would have trouble finding Livingston there. According to one NHL broadcaster, the place is so far from the madding crowd that "the cab fare out to the place from downtown Cleveland costs more than the airfare from New York to Cleveland!"

Although the Cavaliers are one of the best teams in the National Basketball Association, they always have had trouble drawing people to the place. And the hockey Barons drew so few people that the empty seats far outnumbered the humans.

Best TV Coverage of a Single Team.   The Chicago Cubs televise *all* of their games, home and away. And this does not subtract from the gate. The Cubs consistently fill Wrigley Field with a million or more spectators each year. On the other hand, the Oakland A's, who hardly ever televise their games in the hopes of drawing more fans to their ball park, barely draw 500,000 each year.

244

Best Sportswriter. In the golden age of sport, during the late twenties, there were a few writers considered to be the class of the profession. But none of them ever topped—and we believe none of them ever will top—the great Grantland Rice.

Rice, who started out as a correspondent for the Atlanta *Journal,* in 1902, had tremendous responsibility for a twenty-two-year old: he put out the entire sports page! He was paid $12.50 a week. From Atlanta he went to the Cleveland *News* as sports editor, and finally the New York *Evening Mail,* where his career blossomed.

He authored the single most famous story in sports history, a report of a Notre Dame football win over Army which began: "Outlined against a blue-gray October sky, the Four Horsemen rode again. . . ." In addition, Rice authored countless poems—to friends, to ideas, and to sports in general, much of which appeared in his syndicated column, "The Sportlight."

Rice died on July 13, 1954, at the age of seventy-three, while writing his column in his home. Bruce Barton, a longtime friend of Rice, said, in his eulogy to the great journalist:

"He was the evangelist of fun, the bringer of good news about games. . . . He made the playing fields respectable, never by preaching or propaganda, but by the sheer contagion of his joy in living, he made us want to play . . .

"Gainsborough, the artist, cried exultantly, 'We are all going to heaven, and Vandyke is of the company.'

"We are all going to heaven, and Grant is there already—telling his stories, talking his wisdom, cracking his jokes, and, we may be sure, encouraging play. Already they have learned to love him. . . ."

His immortal words did much to shape not only the literature of sport, but literature in general. Who has not read or heard of the following words:

When the One Great Scorer comes
To mark against your name,

He writes—not that you won or lost—
But how you played the game.

There never will be another Grantland Rice.

Best Accessible Arena or Stadium. Madison Square Garden, New York. With suburban ballparks and arenas, such as the Cleveland Coliseum in Richfield, Ohio, or Giants Stadium in the New Jersey Meadowlands, becoming the order of the day, it is a pleasure to go to the Garden, which is easily accessible from all areas of New York City, and its suburbs.

Eleven subway lines, bus lines, the Long Island Railroad, and Conrail commuter trains stop at Pennsylvania Station, which was rebuilt in 1967 and now is below the Garden. In addition, located in midtown Manhattan (Thirty-fourth Street between Seventh and Eighth avenues) it is almost directly at the heart of the city.

The Garden is a throwback to the old, inner-city arenas, which include Boston Garden, the Montreal Forum, and others. Unfortunately, they are being replaced by newer, gaudy showplaces in the sticks, which cater more to the motoring population than the mass transit user.

Best Sports Movie. *Pride of the Yankees,* starring the immortal Gary Cooper. Besides the marvelous acting of Coop and Theresa Wright in the leading roles, the picture also featured several cameo appearances by the New York Yankees themselves, including Hall of Famers Bill Dickey and Babe Ruth.

The story itself, one of the most heartrending in sports, is another reason why this picture is the best. Any viewer, sports fan or not, can readily identify with Coop as he stands before the Yankee Stadium crowd and announces, "Today I consider myself the luckiest man on the face of the earth." We challenge anyone to sit through this film dry-eyed.

Worst Disaster. Far greater than any soccer riot, or other man-made disaster, it occurred in Hong Kong on February 26, 1916, when the grandstands of the Hong Kong Jockey Club, a local racetrack, collapsed, killing 606 spectators and injuring hundreds more.

Worst Mistake by a Broadcaster. Broadcasting mistakes are not treated as seriously now, with the advent of television, because fans can immediately notice when the announcer calls the wrong man scoring a touchdown, running with the ball, etc. But it was not so in the days of radio, which made Clem McCarthy's face even redder when he called the wrong winner of the Preakness Stakes race on May 10, 1947.

"The horses actually disappeared on me for a moment on the far turn," he said, years later, "and I actually lost the field." Here is the actual transcript of the final stages of that race, where McCarthy just blew it, and sent countless fans to their bookies, and countless others screaming, realizing they had torn up winning tickets:

"This is going to be an awful tough horse race down here. . . . but In Trust is still there. Jet Pilot is coming on him, like a game horse. Jet Pilot has got him . . . Jet Pilot a neck . . . Jet Pilot a half length. In Trust second by three. Phalanx is third and in fourth place . . ."

Then, realizing his mistake: "What am I talking about? Ladies and gentlemen, I've made a terrible mistake; I've mixed my horses and I've given you the winner as Jet Pilot, and it is Faultless. Just at what point I was looking at Phalanx and Jet Pilot disappeared on me, I don't know. The winner of the race is Faultless. All right, we missed, we struck out. Well, Babe Ruth struck out once, so I just might as well get in famous company."

Most Unusual Soccer Brawl. Catanzaro, Italy. Referee Vittorio Benedetti, who hailed from Rome, was designated to officiate at a match in Catanzaro. The Catanzaro team was playing host to a club from Palermo in a match that subsequently caused the general metabolism to flow faster than usual. With the score tied, 1–1, a dispute arose over alleged fouls committed by Palermo. According to sports-fan–historian Neil Offen, the Catanzaro fans—which included the entire population of the town—insisted that their team deserved two penalty kicks. "Almost the entire town wanted to tell referee Benedetti about the kicks," said Offen.

However, Benedetti disagreed with the local burghers and the game resumed without Catanzaro getting their kicks. But they obviously didn't forget. As soon as the game ended, a riot erupted. Benedetti was pursued like a hare being chased by so many greyhounds. The fleet referee sprinted across town and found sanctuary in a private house. "They tried to storm the house," said Offen, "to huff and puff and blow it down. They all gathered round, and so did the local police. The police encircled the house and tried to keep the mob away."

The mob ignored the police, demanding Benedetti's scalp. In no time at all, eight policemen and one fan were injured in what developed into a chain reaction of incidents. But the police held fast; reinforcements arrived with gas grenades and the phalanx of irate fans finally was sent into disorderly retreat. With the brief respite, the police dashed into the house, rescued the referee, and rushed the traumatized Benedetti all the way to Rome.

Most Unusual Footrace. The "Bunion Derby," which was the sobriquet for an amazing and improbable cross-country race, held in the United States in 1928.

Promoted by an entrepreneur named C. C. Pyle—some said the C. C. stood for "cash and carry"—the race offered a total of $48,500 in prize money, with $25,000 to go to the winner.

It was billed as "the titanic struggle between the greatest long-distance runners in the entire world"; 199 runners and pseudorunners of all sizes, shapes, and ages kicked in $100 apiece to enter. Most of them were not Olympic-class athletes, but rather, as Bill Severn put it in his book *A Carnival of Sports:* "They were homegrown unknowns of all kinds, ages and conditions. Attired in a colorful assortment of track suits, determined old men jogged alongside youngsters in their teens, all hopeful of finishing in the big money."

The race began on the morning of March 4, 1928, at Ascot Speedway in Los Angeles; the destination, Madison Square Garden in New York City! The route would carry the supermarathoners through many towns, all of which had arranged to pay Pyle for the privilege of having them jog through.

A snag developed almost immediately; seventy-six runners quit before they reached Puente, California, only 16 miles away! But the rest who hung on tried for 40 miles a day. By the halfway mark in the long, long distance run, the second month, only seventy runners were left.

By this time, interest in the event had dwindled almost as much as the field. City councils reneged on their deals to permit runners to come through their towns, and, as a result, Pyle took a financial beating. Only four thousand people paid their way into Madison Square Garden to see the remaining runners circle a wooden track and officially finish the race.

The winner was one Andy Payne, an Oklahoman, who said he had entered so he could use the money to pay off the mortgage on his family's farm in Oklahoma. He covered the 3,422 miles in 573 hours, 4 minutes, 34 seconds.

Pyle was the loser—of an estimated $150,000. "There has been a lot of talk about how these boys suffered," he told reporters, "but there is not one of them who suffered more than I did. My arms were sore all the time from digging down into my pockets and shelling out cash."

Most Unusual Cross Country Run. Anatole "Yanny" Levkoff. A sports reporter for the Brooklyn College *Kingsman* (newspaper) in the late fifties, Levkoff also was a member of the track and field team. Once, he entered a cross country race at Van Cortlandt Park in the Bronx. Levkoff, never known for his geographic prowess, got lost midway through the race and, as darkness fell on

New York City, found himself without compass and without any knowledge of an exit to the park. "At about midnight," Levkoff recalls, "I finally stumbled out of the woods and made my way to the IRT subway station. The experience taught me a valuable lesson; when in doubt, stick to the typewriter and leave running to the runners!"

Fawcett Books is also the publisher of Felton and Fowler's *The Best, Worst & Most Unusual* and Felton and Fowler's *More Best, Worst & Most Unusual* by Bruce Felton and Mark Fowler with the Editors and Staff of Information House Books, Inc.

Felton & Fowler's

BEST, WORST AND MOST UNUSUAL

23020-1 $1.95

AND

Felton & Fowler's

MORE BEST, WORST AND MOST UNUSUAL

23485-1 $1.95

Astounding facts and curious lore about Fine Arts, Literature and Language, The Performing Arts, Pop Culture, Government, Sports, The Law, The Military, Religion, Health and Death, Behavior, Nature and Science, Plants and Animals, Business and Finance, Food, Life-Styles, Fashion and Grooming, Places and Architecture.

John D. MacDonald

"The king of the adventure novel" John D. MacDonald is
one of the world's most popular authors of mystery and
suspense. Here he is at his bestselling best.

☐ CONDOMINIUM	23525-4	$2.25
☐ ALL THESE CONDEMNED	13950-6	$1.50
☐ APRIL EVIL	14128-4	$1.75
☐ AREA OF SUSPICION	14008-3	$1.75
☐ BALLROOM OF THE SKIES	13852-6	$1.50
☐ THE BEACH GIRLS	14081-4	$1.75
☐ BORDER TOWN GIRL	13714-7	$1.50
☐ THE BRASS CUPCAKE	13807-0	$1.50
☐ A BULLET FOR CINDERELLA	14106-3	$1.75
☐ CANCEL ALL OUR VOWS	13764-3	$1.75
☐ CLEMMIE	14015-6	$1.75
☐ CONTRARY PLEASURE	14104-7	$1.75
☐ THE CROSSROADS	14033-4	$1.75
☐ CRY HARD, CRY FAST	13969-7	$1.50
☐ DEAD LOW TIDE	13901-8	$1.50
☐ DEADLY WELCOME	13682-5	$1.50
☐ DEATH TRAP	13557-8	$1.50
☐ THE DECEIVERS	14016-4	$1.75
☐ THE DROWNERS	13582-9	$1.50
☐ THE EMPTY TRAP	13911-5	$1.50
☐ THE END OF THE NIGHT	13731-7	$1.50
☐ A FLASH OF GREEN	13938-7	$1.75
☐ THE GIRL, THE GOLD WATCH & EVERYTHING	13745-7	$1.50
☐ THE LAST ONE LEFT	13958-1	$1.95
☐ A MAN OF AFFAIRS	14051-2	$1.75

Buy them at your local bookstores or use this handy coupon for ordering:

FAWCETT BOOKS GROUP
P.O. Box C730, 524 Myrtle Ave., Pratt Station, Brooklyn, N.Y. 11205

Please send me the books I have checked above. Orders for less than 5
books must include 75¢ for the first book and 25¢ for each additional
book to cover mailing and handling. I enclose $_____ in check or
money order.

Name_____
Address_____
City_____ State/Zip_____
Please allow 4 to 5 weeks for delivery.

*Bestselling Excitement from
the International Master of
Action and Suspense.*

Alistair MacLean

☐ THE BLACK SHRIKE	13903-4	$1.75
☐ FEAR IS THE KEY	14011-3	$1.95
☐ THE GUNS OF NAVARONE	X3537	$1.75
☐ H.M.S. ULYSSES	14083-0	$1.95
☐ NIGHT WITHOUT END	14129-2	$1.95
☐ THE SATAN BUG	14009-1	$1.75
☐ THE SECRET WAYS	14010-5	$1.95
☐ SOUTH BY JAVA HEAD	14023-7	$1.95
☐ BEAR ISLAND	23560-2	$1.95
☐ BREAKHEART PASS	22731-6	$1.75
☐ CARAVAN TO VACCARES	23361-8	$1.75
☐ CIRCUS	22875-4	$1.95
☐ FORCE 10 FROM NAVARONE	23949-9	$2.25
☐ THE GOLDEN GATE	23177-1	$1.95
☐ THE GOLDEN RENDEZVOUS	23624-2	$1.95
☐ ICE STATION ZEBRA	23234-4	$1.75
☐ PUPPET ON A CHAIN	23318-8	$1.75
☐ THE WAY TO DUSTY DEATH	23571-8	$1.95
☐ WHEN EIGHT BELLS TOLL	23893-8	$1.95